D0122201

eugenics laws by allowing the involuntary sterilization of Carrie Buck on the basis that 'three generations of imbeciles is enough!' Believing that some humans had greater value than others darkly inspired German academics Karl Binding and Alfred Hoche to claim some humans are 'life unworthy of life'—this long before Hitler was a dark cloud on the political horizon. It's not just bad times past. In our own day, we again see advocacy that explicitly rejects the unique dignity and equal moral value of human life, opening the door to the possibility of suffering similarly catastrophic consequences. People for the Ethical Treatment of Animals (PETA) explicitly equated the owning of a leather couch with the lampshades made from human skin during the Holocaust—thereby equating the worst evil in human history with animal husbandry. But if animals are equal to people, it also means we are no better than animals—which is precisely how we will act. Meanwhile, Belgium's law allowing euthanasia has led to doctors harvesting the mentally ill and physically disabled by conjoining medicalized killing with organ procurement. Readers may find the many historical and contemporary facts adduced by Weikart in an unremitting and systematic recounting to be disturbing. Indeed, it is an alarming sign of the times that some are sanguine about these developments. Weikart's compassionate Christianity might cut against the grain of the contemporary mindset, but whether one is religious or secular, we ignore Weikart's prophetic warnings at the very great risk to our own—and more particularly, our posterity's—liberty and flourishing."

—Wesley J. Smith, Senior Fellow at the Discovery Institute's Center on Human Exceptionalism and Author of *Culture of Death: The Age of "Do Harm" Medicine*

"Richard Weikart's work effectively draws out the clear implications of humans abandoning the biblical God, who is the very basis of their dignity and rights. This is no mere theoretical discussion, however; Weikart's meticulous historical research shows—in this book as in previous ones—the devastating results of God-defying ideologies that predictably turn into dehumanizing ones as well. Highly recommended!"

—Paul Copan, Professor and Pledger Family Chair of Philosophy and Ethics, Palm Beach Atlantic University, and Co-author of *An Introduction to Biblical Ethics*

"Richard Weikart's book *The Death of Humanity* is a very well-written, cogently argued work that makes an important contribution to contemporary discussions about bioethics and the value of humans. I endorse it wholeheartedly."

—Jennifer Lahl, President of the Center for Bioethics and Culture and Producer of the documentaries *Eggsploitation* and *Breeders: A Subclass of Women?*

"With the receding tide of Christianity in the West, a wave of neo-paganism, atheism, and materialism is washing over our civilization. The rapidity and complexity of this transformation make it difficult for us to understand what is happening to us. In this deeply insightful book, Dr. Richard Weikart brings together trends in bioethics, environmentalism, artificial intelligence, evolutionary biology, and population control and weaves a coherent story: Christian ethics and the Christian understanding of man is being replaced by Nietzschean will to power and by the reduction of man to a meat machine. Dr. Weikart deftly draws together the loose ends of our cultural collapse and shows that it is our loss of the Christian worldview that is at the root of our fall. *The Death of Humanity* is a masterful exegesis of the atheist and materialist transformation that is rending our civilization. Dr. Weikart's remedy—the return to Christ—is a call to trace back our steps to the Christian humanism that, in our hubris, we have left behind."

—Michael Egnor, Professor and Vice-Chairman of the Department of Neurosurgery at the State University of New York at Stony Brook

"Richard Weikart's book, which develops insightful themes by artfully weaving together references from a variety of significant figures across the intellectual landscape, is an ideal text for any integrative humanities class wishing to track the assault on human dignity that has occurred in the world of ideas over the last 150 years. It will also help students gain a deeper understanding of and appreciation for the essential issues underlying the current academic and cultural debates over what it means to be human."
  —Paul Nesselroade, Professor of Psychology,
    Asbury University

"For centuries the cornerstone of Western Civilization has been the intrinsic value of all human beings, an idea founded upon the Judeo-Christian ethic. However, Darwinists, postmodern relativists, secular humanists, and a menagerie of so-called 'freethinkers' and self-styled 'experts' have assailed this fundamental principle and have lodged themselves in the academy and in our culture as the new 'wisdom' of the age. Richard Weikart exposes these poseurs and their destructive influences on all aspects of human rights and dignity. Thoroughly researched and persuasively argued, this is truly a book for our times. It calls upon the reader to look squarely and honestly at those who would seek to transform humanity from the image of God into automatons no better than beasts and perhaps even worse. Weikart declares the timeless Truths that have established the moral and ethical foundations of our traditional social order with boldness and clarity and charts the sad and dangerous course of its destruction. A must read!"
  —Michael A. Flannery, Professor and Associate Director
    for Historical Collections, University of Alabama at
    Birmingham

"Timely, clear, informed, and engaging, *The Death of Humanity* actually breathes new life into age-old debates about the value of individual human lives in our cosmos. Fortunately, our participation in such debates—in states and churches, in bedrooms and classrooms—is *not* doomed to repeat history, *if* we can learn from it. Weikart helps us learn, by showing how historical changes of ideas—of what we think we *know*—can govern historical changes of practices concerning human life and death like eugenics, suicide/euthanasia, and infanticide/abortion. No matter what your view is on how these implicate our humanity, you can now think about them better—and in less of a historical and philosophical vacuum—thanks to this book."

—Russell DiSilvestro, Associate Professor of Philosophy and Director of the Center for Practical and Professional Ethics, Sacramento State University, and Author of *Human Capacities and Moral Status*

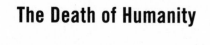

The Death of Humanity

The Death of Humanity

and the case for life

Richard Weikart

REGNERY
FAITH

Regnery Faith™ is a trademark of Salem Communications Holding Corporation; Regnery® is a registered trademark of Salem Communications Holding Corporation

Cataloging-in-Publication data on file with the Library of Congress

ISBN 978-1-62157-489-7

Published in the United States by
Regnery Faith
An imprint of Regnery Publishing
A Division of Salem Media Group
300 New Jersey Ave NW
Washington, DC 20001
www.RegneryFaith.com

Manufactured in the United States of America

10 9 8 7 6 5 4 3 2 1

Books are available in quantity for promotional or premium use. For information on discounts and terms, please visit our website: www.Regnery.com.

Distributed to the trade by
Perseus Distribution
250 West 57th Street
New York, NY 10107

CONTENTS

Preface

Are humans intrinsically valuable, or are they simply a cosmic accident with no real meaning or purpose? Since the Enlightenment this debate has raged in Western culture, profoundly influencing our understanding of bioethics and informing the debate over abortion, infanticide, euthanasia, genetic engineering, etc. The title of this book, *The Death of Humanity*, refers not only to the demise of the concept that humans are intrinsically valuable, but also to the resultant killing of actual human lives.

This book explains first why the Judeo-Christian sanctity-of-life ethic has declined historically since the Enlightenment. Second, it depicts the deleterious consequences this has had on contemporary society. Third, it demonstrates the poverty of many secular alternatives to the Christian vision of humanity, such as materialism, positivism, utilitarianism, Marxism, Darwinism, eugenics, behaviorist psychology, existentialism, sociobiology, postmodernism, and others. Finally, it defends the sanctity of human life on a variety of fronts—abortion, euthanasia, infanticide, suicide, eugenics, and transhumanism, among others.

Introduction

A scientist, a priest, and a teenager were flying in a small plane, taking in the sights. All of a sudden, the pilot announced that the engines had failed, and they would need to bail out. Then, he sheepishly offered this grim news: they only had three parachutes for the four of them, so they had a difficult decision to make: Who gets one? The scientist immediately seized the initiative: "I am a genius, and science contributes immensely to humanity by advancing knowledge. This priest, on the other hand, peddles fables. I clearly have claim to one of these parachutes, so I'm taking one and diving out. See two of you on the ground." So, he bailed out. The priest looked at the other two and exclaimed, "What do we do now?" The teenager calmly replied, "Not to worry, we have parachutes for all of us." The priest quizzically asked, "But I thought the pilot said we only have three?" "We do only have three," the teenager explained, "but the genius grabbed my backpack."

This somewhat macabre joke illustrates three main points I want to make in this book:

1. Scientists and intellectuals, even ones who are geniuses, can make incredibly naïve mistakes.
2. Not all scientists and intellectuals, even if they are geniuses, place a premium on the value of human life, except perhaps their own.
3. Justice can come, sometimes in unusual ways, to those who relegate others to inferior status. As the proverb goes, "Whoever digs a pit will fall into it, and he who rolls a stone will have it roll back on him."[1]

The parachute joke is eerily reminiscent of a popular imaginative exercise my teachers in the 1970s conducted in their junior high and high school classes—but the exercise was not a joke. We were instructed to imagine we were in a scenario in which a wrenching choice needed to be made: who lives and who dies in a situation of scarcity. In one scenario, a space capsule contained a dozen or so people. We were told their ages, marital status, and occupations. The spaceship experienced a malfunction and only had enough oxygen for half the people on board to arrive at their destination. If everyone continued breathing the air, they would run out and all would die. We teenagers were asked to vote for who should live and who should die. In essence, we were trying to decide whom we should murder in order to save the rest. I am embarrassed to admit that I played along with this "game," as did everyone else in my class. We vigorously debated which people's lives had greater value and which had lesser value.

Only several years later did it dawn on me that by playing along, we were agreeing with two dangerous presuppositions:

1. that some people's lives have greater value than other people's
2. that it is permissible to kill some people to benefit others

Education wonks touting the merits of this enterprise that turned us into imagined murderers called it "Values Clarification," but it might be more accurate to call it "Values Assassination." Implicitly we were denying that "all men are created equal, that they are endowed by their Creator with certain unalienable Rights, that among these are Life, Liberty and the pursuit of Happiness."[2]

Perhaps you think I am overreacting to this seemingly harmless exercise in "Values Clarification." But I have come to recognize that the two flawed presuppositions are also lurking behind many of the dehumanizing tendencies in modern thought and culture. And there are many examples of the deadly consequences that can flow from worldviews that do not value all humans, which I will discuss shortly, Nazi Germany being one of them.

In the course of my research, one particular scientist stands out to me as the epitome of this devaluing of human life. A biologist and professor at a major research university, he received a prestigious prize for being an outstanding scientist. While accepting the award, he gave a shocking speech in which he suggested it would be beneficial if 90 percent of the world's human population was wiped out by ebola. Indeed, he told the audience he hoped this would occur. He also suggested that humans were no better than bacteria. When he completed his lecture, he received a standing ovation.

Shockingly, this biologist was not a German scientist during the Nazi period, as you might suppose. The speech took place in 2006, and the biologist in question is an evolutionary ecologist at the University of Texas named Eric Pianka. He was addressing the Texas Academy of Science, so it was Americans honoring and applauding him. When reports about Pianka's speech began circulating, it created a minor media uproar. Confronted with the public outcry, Pianka tried to backpedal, insisting he had been misunderstood. However, before he had time to do damage control, I went to his website and discovered that the student evaluations posted there confirmed the reports of his detractors. One student reported, "Though I agree that convervation [sic] biology is of utmost importance to the world, I do not think that preaching that 90% of the human population should die of ebola is the most effective means of encouraging conservation awareness."[3] The student's statement is so

Poster displayed at Earth Day 1998, "Save the Planet, Kill Yourself."
Church of Euthanasia website

shocking that one wonders why Pianka allowed it to be posted—perhaps
it simply slipped through the cracks.

From various statements on his website both by him and his students,
it is clear that Pianka is zealously campaigning against what he calls
anthropocentrism, i.e., the idea that humans are unique, special, and
have greater value than other organisms. When Pianka told a neighbor
that he specialized in lizards, the neighbor innocently asked him, "What
good are lizards?", to which he responded, "What good are you?"[4]
Pianka's desire for 90 percent of humanity to die is radical, but unfortunately his attack on anthropocentrism is becoming mainstream in our
"culture of death."

As Pianka's story makes clear, we can no longer take for granted that
our colleagues and neighbors regard human life as valuable and sacred.
One of the most prominent bioethicists today, Peter Singer, urges us in
his book, *Unsanctifying Human Life*, to throw out the notion that
human life is unique and special. He popularized the term "speciesist"
to denigrate anyone who dares to insist that humans are unique and
deserving of a special status above other animals. He hopes that in the
future those who consider human life more valuable than other animals
will be held in the same contempt as racists are today, because he is

convinced they are committing the same fallacy. Singer, who holds an endowed chair in bioethics at Princeton University's Center for Human Values, ironically does not believe that human life has intrinsic value, so he is a leading advocate for abortion, infanticide, and euthanasia. His philosophical justifications for killing people with disabilities have aroused considerable controversy, leading disabled rights proponents in Germany to demonstrate against his lecture tour there in 1989. They even called Singer a Nazi, despite the fact that three of his grandparents perished in the Holocaust because of their Jewish ancestry.

The devaluing of human life has even wormed its way into Holocaust studies. In 2009 I attended a Holocaust conference, where a prominent Holocaust historian gave an after-dinner talk to the participants. He enjoined us to always study the Holocaust in the context of human history, and proceeded to sketch out current thinking about the evolution of the cosmos and humanity. He explained that the universe is about fifteen billion years old, and our planet about four billion years old, but human history only reaches back about 150,000 years. He then informed us that sometime in the future the human race would be extinct. I was not quite sure what the punch line would be to this rather bleak and hope-deprived vision of history, which seemed to minimize the significance and value of human life. Given this context, his closing remark was jarring. He stated: "We [as Holocaust historians] need to make sure that this human extinction happens later rather than sooner." I was completely dumbfounded by this non-sequitur. According to the purposeless vision of history that he had just enunciated, why would it make any difference? If extinction is our only destiny, what is the point in delaying it? Why should we care?

Don't get me wrong. I am delighted that he cares. I applaud his words encouraging us to do everything we can to help preserve human life. Deep down this historian understands that humans are special, have value, and have a right to live. However, unfortunately he has somehow come to embrace a worldview that undermines the value and dignity of human life. I much prefer his inconsistency, however, to those who embrace a similar worldview as his, but are more ruthlessly consistent.

I am referring here to those who draw the logical conclusion that if we are simply the product of chance events happening over eons of time, then humans are not special and have no intrinsic value. In this view human rights, including the right to life, are a chimera.

Bill Nye the Science Guy was also confronted with the question of the meaninglessness of life while discussing the end of the universe in an interview. Someone tweeted the interviewer a comment for Nye: "This is why nobody should care about the future. If everything will cease to exist anyway, then nothing really matters." Nye's response was blood-curdling, at least to me:

> Well, why get up in the morning? Apparently we are driven to live. Everybody works pretty hard for the last breath. If this person is not just being flip and off-handed and has this nihilistic approach, I say donate your car, if you own one, to charity, donate all your stuff to charity, and take the black capsule. And let the rest of us get on with it.[5]

Get on with what? Apparently with a life devoid of purpose we are nonetheless "driven to live." Those who do not share that drive to stay alive can step aside, and—in Nye's view—good riddance. But somehow, thankfully, Nye does not really believe what his worldview implies—that human life has no value, meaning, or purpose. He smuggles meaning back into the universe, because he thinks that charity toward our fellow humans has value. If the universe really had no meaning, any nihilist committing suicide might as well shoot up a bunch of people before departing from this world, rather than making donations to charity. Neither action would have any meaning in the final analysis.

As we've seen with the individuals discussed so far, many people with dehumanizing worldviews do not physically end up harming their fellow humans. But sadly, some follow their views to their logical conclusions. Animal rights extremists calling themselves the Animal Liberation Brigade and Animal Liberation Front targeted UCLA pediatric ophthalmologist Arthur Rosenbaum from 2006 until his death in 2010, because he conducted animal experiments. He and his wife faced a barrage of threats, and in 2007 the animal rights activists even firebombed his car.[6]

A more extreme example is the serial killer and cannibal Jeffrey Dahmer—arrested in 1991 for brutal sex crimes. He explained in a TV interview how his actions didn't occur randomly, but were influenced by his worldview. He had always believed that "the theory of evolution is truth, that we all just came from the slime, and when we died...that was it, there was nothing—so the whole theory cheapens life." With this vision, he saw no reason not to kill and eat other men. As he confessed, "If a person doesn't think there is a God to be accountable to, then what's the point in trying to modify your behavior to keep it in acceptable ranges?"[7]

While Dahmer did not perform his diabolical deeds in the name of ideology, some mass murderers have been inspired more directly by dehumanizing ideologies. Eric Harris, the co-conspirator behind the Columbine High School massacre in 1999, confided to his journal just a few months before his rampage, "I just love Hobbes and Nietzche [sic]." On the day of the shooting he wore a T-shirt that proclaimed "Natural Selection," and in his journal he stated that he loved natural selection and thought we should return to a state of nature where everyone had to fend for themselves. He wanted the weak and sick to die; his solution was to "kill him, put him out of his misery." He also expressed utter contempt for humanity and dreamed of exterminating the entire human population. Although Harris had personal reasons for his hatred of humanity—he felt belittled and left out socially—he had also absorbed ideas prominent in our society today. It seems clear from his musings that Harris thought life was meaningless and death was natural, so why worry about it? On the same day that he wrote in his journal, "I say, 'KILL MANKIND' no one should survive," he also remarked, "theres no such thing as True Good or True Evil, its all relative to the observer. its just all nature, chemistry, and math. deal with it." Earlier he had written, "just because your mommy and daddy told you blood and violence is bad, you think its a law of nature? wrong, only science and math are true, everything, and I mean everything else is man made."[8]

Another self-styled intellectual who perpetrated mass murder justified his act of terror in a manifesto reflecting similar beliefs. Pekka-Eric Auvinen, who nicknamed himself "Natural Selector," murdered eight students at a high school in Finland in 2007. In a YouTube video made shortly before the atrocity he wore a T-shirt emblazoned with the words "HUMANITY IS OVERRATED" and pointed a pistol at the camera. In his manifesto he listed what he hated: human rights, equality, "religious fanatics," and the "moral majority." He also listed what he loved: existentialism, freedom, truth, evolutionary biology, and eugenics. He explained why he thought humans had no special value:

> Humans are just a species among other animals and world does not exist only for humans. Death and killing is not a tragedy, it happens in nature all the time between all species. Not all human lives are important or worth saving. Only superior (intelligent, self-aware, strong-minded) individuals should survive while inferior (stupid, retarded, weak-minded masses) should perish.

However, elsewhere in his manifesto he said he favored a "final solution": the "death of the entire human race," not just the "stupid."[9]

Auvinen's desire to kill the rest of humanity made perfect sense in light of his worldview, where life is meaningless and every individual can freely make choices without being bound by religion, morality, or social conventions. He explained,

> Life is just a meaningless coincidence...result of long process of evolution and many several factors, causes and effects. However, life is also something that an individual wants and determines it to be. And I'm the dictator and god of my own life. And me, I have chosen my way. I am prepared to fight and die for my cause. I, as a natural selector, will eliminate all who I see unfit, disgraces of human race and failures of natural selection.

He closed the manifesto with a similar thought: "HUMANITY IS OVERRATED! It's time to put NATURAL SELECTION & SURVIVAL OF THE FITTEST back on tracks!"[10]

Why should we be shocked when young people like Auvinen take the arguments of prominent intellectuals seriously, who assure us that we humans are not special, that human life has no intrinsic value, and that morality is illusory or even oppressive? And why wouldn't those who seem perfectly normal and well adjusted wonder about the status of their own lives? Believing that one is merely a cosmic accident does not seem to provide any foundation for considering one's own life valuable and meaningful.

Indeed the software engineer and musician Gil Dodgen exemplifies this problem. His father was a brilliant professor of physical chemistry at Washington State University and worked on the Manhattan Project. His father and most of his father's colleagues were atheists, so almost as a matter of course he embraced atheism, too. According to Dodgen, from his youth "[I] believed that I was just a complex piece of biochemistry that came about by chance." He still remembers the place he was standing at age seven when he came to the stark realization that his own life had no meaning or purpose. For the next thirty-six years he often contemplated suicide. After all, what difference would it make if he were dead rather than alive? Even though he never tried to kill himself, by his own account he was "cynical about life." All this changed for him in 1994 when at age forty-three he converted to Christ. From that time forward he was filled with joy, recognizing that he was created for a purpose and his life had meaning. Never since that time has he contemplated suicide. Now he knows that his life—and the lives of others—is valuable.[11]

Remarkably, many people today insist that they value human life, and they may even call themselves humanists, when in reality they are reducing humanity to insignificance by insisting that humans, including their minds, are nothing more than chance combinations of chemicals. As in Peter Singer's case, they often only value certain traits that some humans have rather than valuing humans qua humans. (Usually these intellectuals value reason and intellect, since this puts them on the top of the pile.) Once we admit that some humans are more valuable than others, we have entered perilous territory. Some call this the slippery slope.

Some philosophers have doubts about the validity of the slippery slope argument. They point out that support for abortion does not logically entail support for infanticide or euthanasia; and favoring voluntary euthanasia does not necessarily translate into favoring involuntary euthanasia. However, though I agree that the slippery slope argument is not tight logically, it does have truth to it. This is because once someone has moved away from valuing all human life, any stopping point is arbitrary and based on constantly-shifting priorities of whoever happens to be in the driver's seat of society. Thankfully, some people recoil from the harsh consequences that flow from their presuppositions, so not everyone glides all the way to the bottom of the slippery slope. However, embracing the wrong presuppositions about the value of human life provides little resistance to downward motion, leading sooner or later to inhumanity permeating the whole culture.[12]

The slippery slope argument is not just theoretical, either. Valuing some humans above others—and disdaining the rest—brings us to the mindset that led Germany into the abyss under the Nazi regime. As I have shown in considerable detail in my book *Hitler's Ethic* (2009), Hitler and his minions were not amoral beasts who desired power purely for the sake of power. They truly believed that the detestable acts they were committing would benefit humanity by improving the human species. Soon after coming to power in 1933, they began sterilizing hundreds of thousands of disabled Germans they identified as "inferior," "defective," or "unfit." Then they proceeded in 1939 to mass killing of the disabled, murdering about two hundred thousand in Germany in five years (and untold thousands more in occupied territories). Finally, in 1941 they began their program of racial extermination that targeted primarily Jews and Gypsies. Hitler, Himmler, Goebbels, the SS, and their accomplices did all of this out of love for their fellow Germans (but only *healthy* Germans—the disabled need not apply). In 1943 Himmler stated,

"One principle must be absolute for the SS man: we must be honest, decent, loyal and comradely to members of our own blood and to no one else.... Whether the other peoples live in comfort or perish of hunger interests me only in so far as we need them as slaves for our culture: apart from that it does not interest me."[13]

One reason the Nazis were able to carry out their programs of mass murder of the disabled and members of what they called inferior races was that they found many ready accomplices. Shockingly, many of the worst mass murderers were physicians, men and women who were supposed to be dedicated to bringing healing and life. For decades before the Nazi period, many German physicians, psychiatrists, and medical professors had insisted that some people are "lives unworthy of life." In 1912 a German medical professor, Hugo Ribbert, stated a position that tragically became rather common among physicians (and not just in Germany): "The care for individuals who from birth onwards are useless alike mentally and physically, who for themselves and for their fellow-creatures are a burden merely, persons of negative value, is a function altogether useless to humanity, and indeed positively injurious."[14] Ribbert's comments reflect contempt for any individuals who do not measure up to his own standards. Over a decade before the Nazis came to power, a prominent German law professor Karl Binding and a leading psychiatrist Alfred Hoche co-authored a book *Permitting the Destruction of Lives Unworthy of Life* arguing that some people, such as the mentally disabled, are "lives not worthy of life," and therefore it is permissible to kill such people to benefit the rest of society. Attitudes such as these smoothed the way for Nazi atrocities. Historically the slope was slippery indeed.

Viktor Frankl, a Holocaust survivor who endured the horrors presided over by Himmler's SS at Auschwitz, astutely commented on the way that modern European thought had helped prepare the way for Nazi atrocities (and his own misery). He stated,

> If we present a man with a concept of man which is not true, we may well corrupt him. When we present man as an automaton of reflexes, as a mind-machine, as a bundle of instincts,

as a pawn of drives and reactions, as a mere product of instinct, heredity and environment, we feed the nihilism to which modern man is, in any case, prone. I became acquainted with the last stage of that corruption in my second concentration camp, Auschwitz. The gas chambers of Auschwitz were the ultimate consequence of the theory that man is nothing but the product of heredity and environment—or, as the Nazi liked to say, of "Blood and Soil." I am absolutely convinced that the gas chambers of Auschwitz, Treblinka, and Maidanek were ultimately prepared not in some Ministry or other in Berlin, but rather at the desks and in the lecture halls of nihilistic scientists and philosophers.[15]

Frankl suffered under a regime completely devoted to biological determinism, the view that heredity—today we would say genes—completely determines not only physical and intellectual traits, but also behavior and moral character. According to Nazi ideology, positive traits such as loyalty, honesty, diligence, and thriftiness; or immoral characteristics, such as greed, deception, sexual promiscuity, or laziness, were biologically ingrained. Some races, such as the Aryan or Nordic race (Nazis often used these terms synonymously) were inherently moral and upright, while others, especially the Jews, were predisposed to evil behavior by their heredity. Ironically, then, for the Nazis the only way to get rid of immorality was to extinguish, somehow or other, the bearers of "bad heredity." For Hitler and his associates, one reason to murder the Jews en masse was to bioengineer the human race to improve its moral character.[16]

While the Nazis committed barbaric atrocities in the name of biological determinism, communist regimes in the Soviet Union, China, and elsewhere went on a rampage against humanity in the name of environmental determinism, the view that human behavior is determined by one's upbringing, education, and environment. Following Marx's philosophy, communists believed that human behavior is shaped primarily by the economy. Instead of race warfare, they engaged in class warfare to "exterminate the bourgeoisie as a class," as an early leader of Lenin's secret police put it. Some of their methods were remarkably similar to the Nazis': one-party state, suppression of civil liberties, secret police, and concentration camps. However, their ideology was diametrically opposed to Nazism. Their utopian project aimed at altering the environment, specifically the economic system, to reshape human nature and produce harmony and bliss. However, most people today do not associate Stalin, Mao, or Pol Pot with harmony and bliss. Something apparently went wrong. But what was it? I am convinced that the main problem with communism was not their economic system (as problematic as it undoubtedly was). The corruption ran deeper. Their fundamental flaw was their impoverished view of the nature of humanity—their view that human behavior is determined by the environment. This stripped humanity of its dignity and undermined reverence for human life.

Nazism and communism are two of the most obvious symptoms of the decline of respect for human life in the modern world. However, the erosion of the Judeo-Christian sanctity-of-life ethic in Western culture runs much deeper.

We might congratulate ourselves in the U.S. or UK for having helped overcome the inhumanity of Nazism and Soviet communism, but from the chilling examples I have already mentioned—and many more that I will discuss in the subsequent chapters—it should become clear that Western society is in deep trouble today. Once we identify some segments of humanity as "life unworthy of life" or "sub-human," to use phrases commonly used before and during the Nazi period, we have jettisoned any basis for valuing humans as humans. We have effectively undermined all human rights, because now we can decide which humans have rights and which do not. We decide which human lives are valuable and which are valueless, or even of "negative value," to borrow Ribbert's pathetic terminology. However, the recent progress we have made in fighting racism and in providing assistance to those with disabilities has blinded us to our moral deterioration.

Our society considers itself morally superior to the Nazis since we take great pride in our present rejection of racism, which played such a central role in the Nazi worldview. When the white supremacist James Von Brunn shot and killed a security guard at the United States Holocaust Memorial Museum in June 2009, almost everybody in the U.S. condemned his violence, as they should have. In the manifesto he wrote in 2002 Von Brunn had articulated many of the same points that Hitler had made in *Mein Kampf*. Von Brunn called human equality a liberal, Marxist, Jewish idea designed to trick the white race. Like Hitler, he based his views on a racist view of evolution, claiming that "miscegenation is totally inconsistent with Natural Law: the species are improved through in-breeding, natural selection and mutation. Only the strong survive. Cross-breeding Whites with species lower on the evolutionary scale diminishes the White gene-pool while increasing the number of physiologically, psychologically and behaviorally deprived mongrels."[17] Unfortunately there are some neo-Nazis and white supremacists still around, like Von Brunn, but they are extremists who are marginalized in Western culture. Most Americans consider his ideas ridiculous. For this we can be thankful.

We can also be thankful that our society has sought to improve the lives of many who have been disadvantaged in the past. This includes passing legislation to promote the rights of people with disabilities, such as the Americans with Disabilities Act. Indeed, in some respects we as a society recognize the value and dignity of every individual, no matter how poor, no matter what race, religion, or ethnic group, and no matter what their physical and mental abilities are. In the case of disabilities we now have genetic screening tests that alert parents about their children's disabilities before they are born. In some cases, this can lead to pre-birth surgeries or other life-giving medical interventions. In many other cases, however, we allow multitudes of parents to abort their disabled children because we do not quite believe that these children are as valuable as their non-disabled counterparts. There is a profound tension between the life-affirming currents in our society and the life-denying ones.

Thus, before congratulating ourselves too much for diminishing racism or for our humane attitude towards people with disabilities, we should pause and ask: What was the basis for our society's rejection of racism and the promotion of rights for the disabled? Was it not largely based on a vision of human rights that are inherent in all human beings? The American Civil Rights Movement was founded on the idea that all men and women are created equal and have value and dignity, no matter what kinds of differences there might be among us. Martin Luther King Jr. overtly appealed to the Judeo-Christian understanding of equality and morality to reject unjust laws.

While jailed in Birmingham for non-violently protesting segregation laws, King wrote, "A just law is a man-made code that squares with the moral law or the law of God. An unjust law is a code that is out of harmony with the moral law. To put it in the terms of Saint Thomas Aquinas, an unjust law is a human law that is not rooted in eternal and natural law. Any law that uplifts human personality is just. Any law that degrades human personality is unjust." King believed that human dignity is rooted in the equality of everyone, grounded on unshakable moral laws. He was outraged by segregation, because it "ends up relegating persons to the status of things."[18] Unfortunately, many intellectual trends today run contrary to King's vision of human rights, and once again we have to fight against forces that want to equate people with things. King also showed his respect for human life by commending early Christianity for ending "such ancient evils as infanticide and gladiatorial contest."[19]

Thankfully King's respect for human life and equality won the hearts and minds of many Americans, so racism is officially taboo most places in our society (though it still persists in far too many places, and we still need to continue fighting against it). However, unfortunately, many intellectual trends in modern society are undercutting the very foundation of King's vision for human dignity and equality in arenas other than race relations. We need to confront the dehumanizing tendencies of our culture by combating the false philosophies that have produced and reinforced this "culture of death." We should rightfully be grieved and even horrified by the wanton destruction of human life through abortion, infanticide, and euthanasia today.

We HOLD THESE TRUTHS TO BE SELF-
EVIDENT: THAT ALL MEN ARE CREATED
EQUAL, THAT THEY ARE ENDOWED BY THEIR
CREATOR WITH CERTAIN INALIENABLE
RIGHTS, AMONG THESE ARE LIFE, LIBERTY
AND THE PURSUIT OF HAPPINESS. THAT
TO SECURE THESE RIGHTS GOVERNMENTS
ARE INSTITUTED AMONG MEN. WE ···
SOLEMNLY PUBLISH AND DECLARE, THAT
THESE COLONIES ARE AND OF RIGHT
OUGHT TO BE FREE AND INDEPENDENT
STATES ··· AND FOR THE SUPPORT OF THIS
DECLARATION, WITH A FIRM RELIANCE
ON THE PROTECTION OF DIVINE
PROVIDENCE, WE MUTUALLY PLEDGE
OUR LIVES, OUR FORTUNES AND OUR
SACRED HONOUR.

The Jefferson Memorial. The Declaration of Independence grounds human equality and human rights in a Creator. *Photo by author*

However, we will never overcome such injustice until we can convince our fellow citizens that human life is valuable and indeed sacred. As long as many people in our culture, especially in the academy and media, regard human life as the chance product of impersonal forces having no real purpose or meaning, we will make little or no headway in combating the dehumanizing tendencies rampant in our society. As long as many Western intellectuals keep insisting that not all humans are equal, that only some people are really "persons," then the death of those deemed non-persons will continue apace. Even those who are not killed will be stripped of their human dignity, reduced to mere pleasure-seeking machines.

So where did this malaise come from? Since the time of the Enlightenment in the eighteenth century—and especially in the nineteenth and twentieth centuries—many prominent Western intellectuals have dispensed with the view that humans are created in the image of God and thus have immeasurable value and inalienable rights. To be sure, most mainstream Enlightenment thinkers agreed with Thomas Jefferson's position in the Declaration of Independence, because they still believed in some kind of God who had created humans and had legislated immutable moral laws. The Enlightenment philosopher Immanuel Kant, for instance, insisted that we have reasons to believe in God, free will, and immortality (though he perilously consigned them to a realm inaccessible to "pure reason"). Both the American and the French Revolutions grounded human rights on the conviction that they were based on divinely-ordained natural moral laws.

However, during the Enlightenment some thinkers—often called the Radical Enlightenment—embraced philosophical materialism, an atheistic view denying the existence of anything except matter and energy. Though it was a minority view in the eighteenth century, even among intellectual elites, the Radical Enlightenment would spawn secular philosophies that grew stronger over the course of the next couple centuries. Ironically, many of these secularists called their philosophies humanism, while simultaneously stripping away the philosophical foundations for believing that human life has any intrinsic value or importance. By calling their philosophies humanism, philosophers like Marx and Sartre (and others) hoped to signal that they were recognizing the importance of humanity. They promised to exalt humanity by liberating us from bondage to the tyranny of archaic religions (primarily Christianity, since it was the dominant religion in their societies).

Contrary to the intentions and expectations of the secularizers, rather than elevating humanity their philosophies have contributed to dehumanization. They stripped human life of any significance by insisting that human life is meaningless and purposeless, the product of random events. Humans are merely a cosmic accident, a jumble of chemicals that came together by a stroke of dumb luck (actually, millions of strokes of dumb luck that scientists call mutations). Calling it luck actually puts too nice a construction on it: if secularist accounts of our origins are true, we are the result of millions of genetic copying mistakes. I suppose that makes us a colossal mistake. Most secularists also deny the existence of any fixed morality, undermining all human rights. Many even overtly attack the central tenets of Christian morality. It is no surprise that they deny the highest commandment of Christianity—to love God. Many take it a step further and deny the validity of the second highest commandment: love your neighbor as yourself. They substitute selfish pleasure-seeking for sacrificial love.

Thus, while claiming to exalt humanity, many so-called humanists actually debase humanity. They run afoul of the paradox that Jesus taught: "Whoever exalts himself will be humbled, and he who humbles himself will be exalted."[20] Strangely, many of the dehumanizers accuse Christians and other theists of arrogance for believing that human life is sacred or that God created us for a special purpose. How dare we presume that we are superior to other creatures! Shouldn't we have a little more humility?[21] Let us examine this charge briefly. Christians believe that there is a higher being who is wiser and holier than they are, so they submit to his will and ways. The dehumanizers believe there is no such being to whom they are responsible, so they can make up their own rules. Christians believe that all humans are equal, so they are not superior to any other human being, no matter how small, unintelligent, or weak. Many of the dehumanizing humanists, at least the intellectual types, believe that humans are not equal. They consider rationality one of the key characteristics endowing creatures with value, so those with more rationality are thereby more valuable. Guess where that puts them in the rankings? Thus, the secular intellectuals believe they are the highest (known) beings in the universe, and not only most animals, but most humans are inferior to them. So, who is arrogant?

The "who is more arrogant" question is really beside the point. The real question is: Whose worldview comports better with reality? It seems to me that the Christian worldview makes better sense of the human condition than do secular philosophies. Christianity teaches that humans are intrinsically valuable because they are created in the image and likeness of God. Their lives have purpose and meaning. They have attributes that set them apart from other animals, such as rationality, linguistic ability, creativity, free will, aesthetic sense, and religious yearnings. Their consciences let them know that some behaviors are good and others are evil, that love exceeds hatred, and that there is more to life than just getting as much sensual pleasure as you can.

Though some thorough-going secularists admit that their worldview denies free will, objective morality, purpose, and the intrinsic value of themselves and their fellow humans, many try to evade some of these unsavory implications. Many secularists want to cling to some kind of purpose and meaning in life, even though they have exploded the foundation for it. For instance, the evolutionary biologist George Gaylord Simpson in his book *The Meaning of Evolution* (1950) stated, "Man is the result of a purposeless and materialistic process that did not have him in mind. He was not planned. He is a state of matter, a form of life, a sort of animal, and a species of the Order Primates, akin nearly or remotely to all of life and indeed to all that is material." Earlier in the book he declared, "Man was certainly not the goal of evolution, which evidently had no goal. He was not planned, in an operation wholly planless. He is not the ultimate in a single constant trend toward higher things, in a history of life with innumerable trends, none of them constant, and some toward the lower rather than the higher. Is his place in nature, then, that of a mere accident, without significance?" The answer, of course, in light of his philosophy, should be "yes." However, Simpson still had enough cognizance of his humanity that he could not bring himself to face the obvious consequences of his own theory, so instead he insisted that humans still have significance, because they are the "highest animal." But what can "highest" mean in a worldview that has no ultimate measuring rod?[22]

Simpson and many others who call themselves humanists have stolen commodities from worldviews foreign to their own to blunt the dehumanizing implications of their own perspective. They have retained vestiges of the Judeo-Christian vision of humanity, while annihilating the basis for that vision. These inconsistencies occur for a variety of reasons. Many secular intellectuals received a moral (and sometimes religious) upbringing that continues to influence their thought and behavior, even though they now deny the moral foundation that has shaped their character. Even those who deny that human life has any purpose, value, or meaning, still have a conscience and an innate knowledge that human life really is valuable. They cannot escape their own humanity.

Again, I'm happy that many people are not ruthlessly consistent, because I'd rather interact with kindly humanists who believe in human rights than with ruthless, power-hungry cynics.[23]

I hope that this book will give them pause to reflect on their inconsistencies and consider the claims of Christianity, which provide a valid explanation for the human condition. Unfortunately, within the scope of this book I cannot provide a rigorous argument to prove this position. Nor will I take the opportunity to discuss the many lines of evidence that cause me to believe that Christianity is not only intellectually viable, but uniquely true—many good works on Christian apologetics are already available.[24] However, in the course of my critique of secular ideologies I hope to make enough suggestive comments to indicate some of the reasons I find Christianity the worldview best aligned with what we know about the human condition.

If modern secular philosophies do not adequately explain our humanity, as I will argue, why have they gained so many adherents in the past couple centuries? This is a complex question that would require a multi-volume answer, but let me suggest one contributing factor: those calling themselves Christians have failed to live up to the teachings of the one they claim to follow. Secularists regularly complain about the atrocities that Christians have committed throughout history, sometimes in the name of Christ. We all know the list: the Inquisition, Crusades, witch trials, slavery, various religious wars, and priests blessing weapons (sometimes for both sides of the same war). How can Christians complain about the secularists' devaluing of human life, when Christianity has been notorious for its bloodshed and torture? Good question. One answer is that Christians who have perpetrated these atrocities were acting inconsistently with Jesus' message of love. However, instead of explaining this away, Christians should do some real soul-searching and repentance. They need to become renowned for acts of love toward the weak and sick, for the help they provide for the poor and the downtrodden. Christians need to show the world that every human being is valuable, that their lives are worthwhile.

I am by no means implying that all Christians have been complicit in atrocities that showed little regard for the value of human life. Most Christians today are just as horrified by the Inquisition as the staunchest secularists. Furthermore, many Christians throughout the ages have reflected the sacrificial love of Jesus by establishing hospitals, orphanages, soup kitchens, homeless shelters, schools, and many other charitable organizations devoted to helping the poor, weak, and disadvantaged. Many Christians have been on the forefront of fighting against injustices and oppression. They have led the struggle against slavery and racism. Today Christians are one of the primary bulwarks against the cultural devaluation of human life.

In the final analysis, then, I am suggesting that the solution to the death of humanity is a revival of Christian love and compassion, a renewed sense that human life has meaning and purpose, because we are created in the image and likeness of God. I have hope that such a revival is possible. The somber title of my book is not intended as a proclamation of hopelessness and despair. On the contrary! There would be no point in writing this book if our situation is irreversible. I have complete confidence that the truth will ultimately prevail, and I wrote this book in the hope that we as a society can heed its warning to turn away from the false, but alluring, philosophies of nihilism to embrace the reality of a loving, personal God who cares about each one of us. To be sure, this book will spend more time discussing the problems, rather than the solutions, but hopefully it will rock the complacency of secularists and Christians alike and bring us all into the quest for solutions to our deepest spiritual problems. "Seek and you shall find."[25]

ONE

Man the Machine

It is a dangerous thing when people are treated as things.
—Joni Eareckson Tada[1]

On February 10, 1996, humanity's hierarchy in the world was called into question when a machine defeated the reigning world chess champion. Garry Kasparov was shaken up after losing the first game of a six-game match with the IBM supercomputer Deep Blue. He recovered sufficiently to win the match, putting machines back in their place. But not for long. The following year humanity was defeated when Deep Blue beat Kasparov, who was able to win only one game out of six, while the machine won two (the rest were draws). Many commentators drew the seemingly obvious conclusion: the human mind is nothing more than a complex machine, and now we can make machines capable of doing just about anything that we can do. This assessment, like many underlying dehumanizing trains of thought, is premature.

The machine that beat Kasparov by analyzing millions of chess moves per second was the product of human intelligence, and designed for a purpose. Rather than demoting humanity, it can be seen as the triumph of human ingenuity. It took the collaboration of many people, including computer experts and chess masters—not to mention the millions of innovations preceding it—to design and program Deep Blue. Its ability to play brilliant chess demonstrates the power and creativity of human intelligence.

While feats of technology like Deep Blue are new to the scene, the notion that humans are just sophisticated, complex machines is by no means new. We can trace the basic idea back at least to some ancient Greek philosophers, who believed that everything in the cosmos, including humans, could be understood in completely material terms. In modern times, especially since the eighteenth-century Enlightenment, the philosophy of materialism, i.e., the notion that humans—and everything else—are nothing but chance combinations of matter and energy, has gained in intellectual respectability. While materialism is inherently atheistic, some leading intellectuals in the nineteenth century and thereafter opted for an agnostic approach to reality, which they called positivism. Pioneered by Auguste Comte, positivism shared the materialist veneration of reason and science, but refused to take a position on the existence or non-existence of a divine being. In the end, however, positivism also demoted humanity to machines, because it insisted that humans are completely subject to scientific laws.

The intellectual drift toward materialism and positivism received considerable impetus from two seventeenth-century philosophers: René Descartes and his avid follower Baruch Spinoza. Neither embraced a full-fledged materialist position, but they both stressed the power of reason and logic in gaining knowledge about reality. Descartes provided a mechanistic explanation for all physical phenomena, including the anatomy and physiology of animals and humans, although he remained staunchly committed to body-soul dualism and refused to apply this mechanistic view to the human mind. Not all of his followers were so restrained. Indeed, Spinoza, though adopting Descartes' rationalistic method of gaining knowledge, abandoned body-soul dualism, insisting on the unity of the physical and mental. Spinoza rejected the notion that humans have free will, because even the human mind is completely subject to natural causation, meaning humans would not be independent agents making real decisions. Rather, human behavior is determined entirely by the concatenation of events preceding an individual's "decision."

In eighteenth-century France, in the aftermath of Descartes and Spinoza, materialism gained in intellectual respectability, even though most Enlightenment thinkers rejected it and considered it inconsistent with their rationalist philosophy. The most notorious materialist of the French Enlightenment, Julien Offray de La Mettrie, provoked quite a stir among his contemporaries by authoring *Man the Machine* in 1747. Therein he insisted that human nature could only be understood by physicians such as himself, because everything about humanity—including reason, aesthetics, and morality—flows exclusively from our anatomy and physiology.[2] Two years earlier in *The Natural History of the Soul* he had dismissed the existence of the human soul, a point he confirmed in *Man the Machine*, stating, "the soul is but a principle of motion or a material and sensible part of the brain, which can be regarded, without fear of error, as the mainspring of the whole machine."[3] The brain, in turn, was just a cog in a ceaseless chain of cause and effect, lacking any ability to choose moral good or evil. Human behavior was shaped entirely by antecedent causes, including heredity, diet, and education. Of these three, La Mettrie considered heredity the strongest influence on our moral character, asserting that there are "a thousand hereditary vices and virtues which are transmitted from parents to children."[4]

However, La Mettrie also argued that diet has a profound impact on moral character and behavior. His proof? It may be hard to believe that he actually wrote this, but here is this arch-rationalist's strange and misguided line of "reasoning":

Raw meat makes animals fierce, and it would have the same effect on man. This is so true that the English who eat meat red and bloody, and not as well done as ours, seem to share more or less in the savagery due to this kind of food, and to other causes which can be rendered ineffective by education only. This savagery creates in the soul, pride, hatred, scorn of other nations, indocility and other sentiments which degrade the character, just as heavy food makes a dull and heavy mind whose usual traits are laziness and indolence.[5]

Aside from the absurdity of blaming the pride and hatred of the English on their habit of eating bloody meat, there are some logical problems with La Mettrie's position. If the English are just machines, then why moralize about it? What could it possibly mean that these English man-machines have a "degraded" character? The only way a machine could be degraded would be if it is not performing the function for which it was devised. However, if humans operate like machines, but were not created for any particular purpose, and especially if they have no fixed moral norms to guide their behavior, the term "degraded" is meaningless. They are what they are. Period. Move on. La Mettrie also forgot to ask himself what caused the English to eat bloody food, or what caused the French to cook their meat more thoroughly. According to his own philosophy, it would seem that these dietary behaviors sprang from previous causes over which they had no control. So why frown on their "savagery"?

In light of his thoughts about the influence of diet, we might be tempted to ask: What about La Mettrie's diet? As it turns out, La Mettrie had a reputation for gluttony, so what impact did his diet have on his behavior? Wait a minute. Gluttony *is* a behavior. Again, we are caught in an infinite regress of causes and effects. La Mettrie was just a machine obeying the laws of physics when he engaged in gluttony, so no matter how his diet affected him, it was an inescapable fate. You cannot really change your diet, because there is no "you" capable of doing anything. There is no human person to make choices about behavior, just a machine. In any case, La Mettrie's gluttony eventually put an end to all of his behavior, because in 1751 he died at age forty-one from eating tainted delicacies. In his case, diet did influence behavior, but not in the way he expected. (Remember the proverb I quoted in the Introduction about the person who digs a pit or rolls a stone?)

La Mettrie recognized that if humans are machines, they cannot be blamed for their behavior. He claimed this made it easier to live with others, because

> lack of confidence in a friend and lack of faithfulness in a wife or a mistress are only slight defects in humanity, and even theft, seen with the same eyes, is a bad habit rather than a crime. Do you know why I still have some respect for men? Because I seriously believe them to be machines. If I believed the opposite hypothesis, I know few of them with whom I would wish to associate. Materialism is the antidote to misanthropy.[6]

As La Mettrie suggested in this passage, if humans are machines, then it would be silly to blame them for their behavior or to feel guilty for one's own behavior. Indeed I suspect that his man-as-machine philosophy salved his conscience, rescuing him from having to reflect on his own hedonistic and immoral lifestyle.

However, the implications of La Mettrie's reductionism, the penchant to reduce human mental and moral qualities to the physical, were much more far-reaching than his own behavior. If his worldview rescues humanity from the taint of sin and moral shame, it also eliminates any sense of moral goodness, respect, dignity, or love. One would hardly praise a machine for operating according to the laws of physics, and it seems grotesque to suggest that we might genuinely love a machine. Ultimately he thought all human depravity and evil was the result of mindless natural laws that have no intrinsic purpose or meaning. The ogres of history, such as Genghis Khan, or the vilest criminals, are not a blot on humanity, because they were not autonomous moral agents. Rather they were marionettes dancing along the stage of history without any ability to control their destiny. La Mettrie interpreted this to mean that human evil is illusory, and this—he thought—makes it bearable to live among fellow humans who do not always act as we wish they might.

By explaining away human immorality, it might seem that this would elevate humanity. La Mettrie seemed to think so, claiming his view of humans as machines is "the antidote for misanthropy." However, in reality La Mettrie's view contributes to dehumanization, because it also reduces anything noble about the human spirit to mere atoms crashing against each other. Mother Teresa's self-sacrificial love, Rembrandt's and Bach's masterpieces, and Newton's intellectual achievements, are all reduced to the mindless functioning of physical laws. They are all machines. Beauty, truth, and moral goodness evaporate, losing all objective meaning.

Further, La Mettrie was unwilling to grant human status to all members of the human species, not that he thought humans were much better than animals. He claimed our ability to harness education to shape human culture is the only human feature that raises us above the animal state, and thought in many respects humans are inferior to many animals—in strength and agility, for instance. Regarding individual members of the human species, he asked,

> But shall we grant this same distinction to the deaf and to the blind, to imbeciles, madmen, or savages, or to those who have been brought up in the woods with animals; to those who have lost their imagination through melancholia, or in short to all those animals in human form who give evidence of only the rudest instinct? No, all these men of body but not of mind, do not deserve to be classed by themselves.[7]

La Mettrie had utter disdain for any of his fellow humans who were uneducated, whether because of mental disability or lack of opportunity. In his view they were no better than animals. He told his readers, "Only open wide your eyes... [and] you will be persuaded that the imbecile and the fool are animals with human faces."[8] Expressing contempt for some categories of people in a book that reduces all humans to machines is rather ironic, I think. Apparently all humans are machines, but somehow some are more valuable than animals, while others are not. La Mettrie never explained how any human could be "higher" than animals in a universe devoid of God, morality, and purpose.

Though society at large was not receptive to La Mettrie's outspoken materialist philosophy—he was forced to seek refuge in Frederick the Great's palace—other prominent French thinkers continued promoting materialism in Paris. In the 1750s and thereafter the materialist Baron Paul Henri Thiry d'Holbach gathered a coterie at his house to discuss the latest intellectual trends. Many of the leading personalities of the Enlightenment attended his salon at one time or another. When British philosopher David Hume visited Paris, he made a point to attend. Not all the participants were convinced materialists, but one of the more prominent members of Holbach's circle who did convert to materialism—but surreptitiously—was Denis Diderot, famous for editing the *Encyclopedia*, a compendium of Enlightenment thought and culture. Diderot kept his overtly materialistic writings under wraps until after his death, probably to avoid persecution and censorship. However, he gave a friend (who was a convinced materialist) permission to publish them posthumously.[9]

Another radical French thinker to attend Holbach's salon when he was in Paris was Claude Adrien Helvétius, who spelled out the implications of La Mettrie's man-as-machine philosophy. In his *Treatise on Man* (1773), Helvétius upheld a completely mechanistic view of human behavior, stating, "Man is a machine, that being put in motion by corporeal sensibility, ought to perform all that it executes." In the opening pages of the book he compared humans to puppets: "Mankind are, but too often, unknown to him that governs them; yet to guide the motions of the human puppet, it is necessary to know the wires by which he is moved."[10] It is unclear to me how those in government can "guide the motions of the human puppet" in any meaningful sense, since government leaders would also be mere human puppets, would they not? While agreeing with La Mettrie that human behavior is completely determined, Helvétius disagreed with La Mettrie about the primary influences on human behavior. As we shall see in greater depth in chapter four, Helvétius believed that the influence of human heredity was negligible. Instead he embraced environmental determinism, stressing the power of education in shaping human character and behavior.

The historian Lester Crocker summarized it well, saying that Holbach, Diderot, and Helvétius, as well as many other Enlightenment thinkers, not only situated humans entirely within nature, but thereby made humans cosmically unimportant.[11]

In the early nineteenth century, French materialism was eclipsed not only by emotionally-charged Romanticism but also by Auguste Comte's positivism, a system that makes intellectual progress and understanding of reality totally dependent on physical data and observation. Comte cuts a quirky figure across the stage of European history. He spent some time in an insane asylum, and many people today consider him mentally imbalanced. In some ways he was intellectually brilliant, but his interpersonal relationships were largely a disaster. His inflated ego convinced him that he was being unfairly treated when he did not receive a teaching position. He thought patrons owed him a living and complained bitterly when they refused to support him any longer. After years of enthusiastic correspondence with Comte, John Stuart Mill, one of his most influential disciples, finally broke off his relationship with Comte. He tired of Comte using him to drum up patronage and, according to historian Mary Pickering in her three-volume biography of Comte, Mill came to recognize that Comte was "closed-minded, ungrateful, and egotistical."[12]

While preaching universal altruism—a word he coined to describe benevolent feelings he considered innate—he could not manage to get along with his parents, siblings, wife, or most other people. His wife finally left him in 1842, the same year he completed his massive six-volume work, *Course of Positive Philosophy*. She departed, according to Pickering, "after years of feeling neglected by a man obsessed with his work for humanity."[13] Even his disciples had to do damage control when Comte introduced his "Religion of Humanity" in the 1850s, which included bizarre ceremonies and rites, such as praying to some worthy female "saint." Comte, of course, styled himself the high priest of this new religion and even signed his letters with that lofty title.

Despite his problems with egotism and maintaining human relationships, Comte was a prolific writer and lecturer. His ideas—especially in his earlier writings—resonated with many contemporary intellectuals. Comte's positivism was different from materialism because he rejected all metaphysical claims, including materialism. The only valid road to knowledge, he maintained, was through scientific investigation, which would supplant not only religion but all kinds of metaphysical speculation. Since science could not tell us anything about God, religion, or metaphysics, they were outside the purview of human knowledge.

Though he rejected materialism, his positivist philosophy did not regard humans all that differently from materialism. Comte believed that all phenomena, including human psychology and sociology—another term he coined—could come under the microscope of scientific investigation. Everything came under the sway of natural causation. Thus, his vision of human history was largely deterministic. Human free will was severely constrained, though he did think that humans had a little wiggle room to speed up or slow down historical developments. Interestingly, however, despite his insistence that no knowledge, not even scientific knowledge, is absolute and unchanging, he was a staunch moralist. Different from the later Logical Positivists, who, like many other intellectuals, appropriated his positivist epistemology, but without the moral and religious trappings, Comte believed that a science of morality was possible. He was convinced that humans were innately altruistic, and he hoped that his philosophy would promote the betterment of humanity—indeed the worship of Humanity (in 1848 Comte began capitalizing Humanity in his writings).

Unfortunately, however, while trying to foster altruism and exalt Humanity, Comte's philosophy ended up reinforcing the dehumanizing tendencies besetting materialism. He rejected natural rights philosophy, human rights, and human equality as metaphysical phantoms. In *Course of Positive Philosophy* he acknowledged that his rejection of God undermined the notion that humans are somehow special. He stated,

> These fantastic hopes, these exaggerated ideas of the importance of man in the universe, which originate in theological philosophy and which wither away at the first breath of positive philosophy, are an initial stimulant without which it would be inconceivable that the human mind could address itself in the primitive state to painful toil.[14]

Thus his philosophy dealt a blow to the view that humans have importance, meaning, or real significance in the universe. Pickering explains that Comte placed humans and animals on the same level, and he regarded "theologians' and metaphysicians' worries about degrading human nature a barrier to scientific progress."[15]

Perhaps this is why Comte was never able to get along with real people: he was more concerned with Humanity as a collective entity than he was with specific individuals. In 1848 he wrote, "Man properly speaking exists only in the excessively abstract brain of the metaphysicians. There is basically nothing real except Humanity."[16] By worshiping Humanity as an abstract entity, however, Comte was subjecting the individual to a Religion of Humanity and a social system that most of his contemporaries derided as despotic—and bizarre. Ironically, the more Comte stressed universal love and altruism in his Religion of Humanity, the more isolated he became from his society and friends.[17]

Worse yet, Comte was caught in a contradictory position in relation to morality. His scientific approach to reality—together with his rejection of belief in God—gave him no reason to suppose that any kind of objective morality existed in the cosmos. He admitted this in his works. Once he wrote that "speaking in an absolute sense, there is nothing good, there is nothing bad; the only absolute is that everything is relative."[18] He rejected human rights, equality, and popular sovereignty as doctrines belonging to the outmoded metaphysical age.[19] On the other hand, Comte was a staunch moralist, arguing for the primacy of altruism in human behavior and promising that positivism could lay the basis for a scientific morality.[20] A technocratic elite would govern society and enforce this scientific morality. Most positivists after Comte—especially the Logical Positivists—resolved this tension in his thought by jettisoning morality as an illusion and subjecting human behavior and society fully to scientific explanations. They despaired of discovering a scientific morality, so they pretended that morality was purely subjective. "Thou shalt not kill" was a personal opinion, they claimed, equivalent to "I don't like broccoli." Comte's vision of humanity and morality thus had devastating implications, ironically contributing to an intellectual climate where altruism disappeared from the realm of reality. Positivists could no longer provide cogent reasons why we should treat each other decently and lovingly.

Though positivism seemed to eclipse materialism in the number of adherents and intellectual influence during the nineteenth century, materialism also experienced an upsurge. In the 1850s scientific materialism exploded onto the popular stage in Germany, especially through the writings of the scientist Karl Vogt and the physician Ludwig Büchner. Vogt, a professor of biology at the University of Geneva, once affirmed that "man as well as the animal is only a machine," since thoughts are purely the product of material processes. He strenuously denied that humans have free will or moral responsibility, because: "In no moment are we masters over ourselves, over our reason, over our mental powers, any more than we are masters over whether our kidneys excrete or not. The organism cannot control itself, but the law of its material composition controls it."[21]

Vogt seems to have been quite taken with the materialist philosopher Ludwig Feuerbach's famous aphorism: "Man is what he eats." (It sounds much jazzier in the original German: "Der Mensch ist, was er isst.") Vogt once stated, "Tell me what you eat, and I will tell you who you are."[22] In an 1851 book, he claimed that nourishment determines not only the production of muscle fiber and the secretion of urine, but also determines the "secretion" of our mind, i.e., our thoughts. It is a law of nature, he insisted, that those imbibing the same nourishment would have the same thoughts and instincts. As a political radical promoting anarchism, Vogt hoped to be able to harness this "scientific" insight about diet to engineer humanity. By controlling people's diet, Vogt optimistically believed that humans could fulfill their longing for freedom and successfully introduce a cooperative society that needs no government. He argued: "Only the alteration of the material conditions, the successive improvement of diet, the final implementation of balance in the brain secretions [Vogt's term for "thoughts"] through appropriate arranging of food makes the anarchistic condition possible."[23]

Despite Vogt's claims about promoting human freedom, his materialistic vision of humanity did not provide him a moral fulcrum for treating humans as equal, nor did he believe that humans have any inherent rights, including the right to life. In a major two-volume work on anthropology, he overtly denied that any absolute moral values exist. Good and evil, he stated, differ from one society to the next. Some societies even justify murder in some circumstances, he explained: "Even though in the civilized world it is a capital offense to kill one's old paralyzed father, there are Indian tribes in which this is reckoned as an entirely praiseworthy deed for a son."[24] While Vogt did not explicitly say that he favored killing the old and infirm, he clearly argued that it is not objectively evil. Thus he opened the door for discussions about the propriety of this formerly taboo practice. This is particularly ominous, because elsewhere Vogt stripped the mentally disabled of their human status, arguing that they were no more than apes.[25] While glorying in human freedom, he was unwilling to extend that freedom to all humans.

Büchner's writings on scientific materialism reached an even larger audience than Vogt's, though it also torpedoed his academic career. In his 1855 book, *Force and Matter*, which was a publishing sensation, he emphasized that since only matter and energy exist, humans are no different from any other part of the cosmos. He stated, "The human is a product of nature, both in its physical, as well as its mental, state. Thus not only what he is, but also what he does, desires, feels, and thinks rests on the same natural necessity as the entire structure of the world." He denied that humans have any free will, since they are completely determined by natural causes (he quoted Spinoza on this score). He claimed that external conditions not only determine historical development of societies, but "the individual human is no less a product, a sum of external and internal natural effects, not only in his entire physical and moral essence, but even in every single moment of his action."[26]

Büchner recognized that if humans are nothing more than a combination of chemicals brought together by the laws of physics, as he thought they were, then their actions must be determined by some combination of heredity and the environment. In *Force and Matter* he seemed to think that the environment was more decisive. For example, he stated, "The lack of understanding, poverty and lack of education are the three factors spawning crime."[27] However, later he changed his tune. In 1882 he wrote an entire book on *The Power of Heredity and Its Influence on the Moral and Mental Progress of Humanity*. This entire work promoted the idea that heredity was more important than education or the environment in shaping human character and behavior. Vice and crime, as well as virtue, are primarily hereditary, he thought, and primitive peoples have little or no hereditary disposition to compassion, love of the truth, honesty, or thankfulness. He also claimed that Jews have inherited the biological disposition to become merchants.[28]

After Darwin published his theory of evolution in 1859—which we will look at in detail in chapter two—Büchner became one of his leading German apostles. Büchner had enunciated a non-Darwinian theory of evolution already in *Force and Matter*, before he knew anything about Darwin's theory. In many of his writings he taught that humans are not the special creation of God, but rather "a natural product like every other creature," arising purely from natural processes. He dismissed the "anthropocentric" view that humans are special, calling it a myth with the same status as geo-centrism.[29] He also demoted the individual human being, whose importance was minimal in the overarching scheme of the cosmos. According to Büchner, "But what does the concept of time mean in the eternal course of nature and history? The individual is in relation to this course [of nature] nothing, the human race is everything; and like nature, history marks every one of its steps forward, even the smallest, with innumerable piles of corpses."[30] Büchner's worldview left little or no room for significance for individual people. On the contrary, he considered their deaths both necessary and beneficial to bring about evolutionary progress.

�֍

Throughout the nineteenth century and into the twentieth, *The Secularization of the European Mind*, as Owen Chadwick explained, continued apace. The growth of secular philosophies and worldviews among European and American intellectuals contributed to undermining the view that humans were created in the image of God and therefore have value and significance. This eroded the Judeo-Christian sanctity-of-life ethic.

One of the leading British intellectuals of the twentieth century, the philosopher Bertrand Russell, exemplified this trend of devaluing human life. He, like many other secular intellectuals, rejected all religious beliefs, including the idea that humans were created for a divine purpose. Rather he regarded humans as nothing more than the chance combination of chemicals. In 1903 he stated this rather baldly:

> That Man is the product of causes which had no prevision of the end they were achieving; that his origin, his growth, his hopes and fears, his loves and his beliefs, are but the outcome of accidental collocations of atoms; that no fire, no heroism, no intensity of thought and feeling, can preserve an individual life beyond the grave; that all the labors of the ages, all the devotion, all the inspiration, all the noonday brightness of

human genius, are destined to extinction in the vast death of the solar system, and that the whole temple of Man's achievement must inevitably be buried beneath the debris of a universe in ruins—all these things, if not quite beyond dispute, are yet so nearly certain, that no philosophy which rejects them can hope to stand.[31]

One can almost envision the preacher of Ecclesiastes whispering in Russell's ear: "Vanity of vanities, all is vanity."

However, one wonders how seriously Russell took his own philosophy of ultimate meaninglessness and purposelessness. Did he really believe that all of "his [own] loves and his [own] beliefs" are nothing but "the outcome of accidental collocations of atoms"? If so, why would he expect us to take his beliefs seriously, as though they might have some objective truth value? Why should the "accidental collocations of atoms" in my brain care what the "accidental collocations of atoms" in his brain believes? Also, since Russell rejected free will, why should he care if anyone agrees with his randomly-produced beliefs, since neither he nor his critics have any choice in the matter. Further, if love is also merely an accidental by-product of nature, as he claimed, then why did Russell in a later essay maintain, *"The good life is one inspired by love and guided by knowledge"*?[32] What is it that would give love (or knowledge for that matter) value in a world where it is the product of random events?

Russell admitted that his worldview makes human life insignificant. In a 1925 essay on "What I Believe" he repeated his belief that humans, including "our desires, our hopes and fears," are natural products that physicists can investigate. He then continued, "The philosophy of nature must not be unduly terrestrial; for it, the earth is merely one of the smaller planets of one of the smaller stars of the Milky Way. It would be ridiculous to warp the philosophy of nature in order to bring out results that are pleasing to the tiny parasites of this insignificant planet."[33] While Hitler and his minions repeatedly used the trope of "parasites" or "bacillus" to dehumanize their racial rivals, especially the Jews, Russell ended up reducing all of humanity to "tiny parasites" on an "insignificant planet." I wonder again how this vision of humanity could possibly inspire us to love others. I am happy that Russell retained enough vestiges of humanity to enjoin us to love others, but it doesn't seem consistent with his own perspective. Could anyone really love "tiny parasites" who are merely the "accidental collocations of atoms"?

Given his perspective toward humanity in general, perhaps it is unsurprising that Russell imbibed the dehumanizing attitudes of the eugenics movement, which sought to improve human heredity by controlling reproduction. Russell, like most eugenicists, believed that some humans were more valuable and some were less valuable than others. After explaining his position that the differences in people's mental abilities are (at least partly) congenital, he added, "I shall assume also, what is perhaps more dubious, that clever people are preferable to their opposite." (Of course it is no accident that this places intellectuals, such as Russell, at the apex of humanity.) Russell admitted that his vision of humanity is inegalitarian, and he favored policies that would encourage "desirable" parents to reproduce, while penalizing "undesirable" parents from procreating. Not only did he condemn "undesirable" parents to second-class status, but he patronizingly called children of mentally disabled ("feeble-minded") women "wholly worthless to the community."[34] Not only do I find Russell's dismissive attitude toward people with disabilities morally troubling, but I wonder why he thinks that the "accidental collocations of atoms" that comprise intellectuals is any more valuable than the "accidental collocations of atoms" of people with mental disabilities.

In addition to eugenics, Russell was an early proponent of euthanasia, which he called "positively useful" to society. Indeed Russell argued that the proper criterion for judging behavior was whether it "is the most likely to promote the general good," and apparently he thought euthanasia would promote the good of society. But what about the individual? Indeed Russell dismissed any appeal to individual rights, claiming that "the 'objectively right' act is that which best serves the interest of the group that is regarded as ethically dominant." Clearly the individual is given short shrift here, but to what group is the individual supposed to be sacrificed? Russell threw up his hands, candidly admitting that it could be the family, the community, or the nation, and there is no basis for preferring one group above another.[35]

A few pages later he undermined the idea that there is anything "objectively right" at all, claiming that "when I say that an act is 'objectively right' I am really expressing an emotion, though grammatically I seem to be making an assertion." Thus moral statements have no real objectivity and do not correspond to any external reality, but are nothing more than an emotional response.[36] Elsewhere he stated his view of moral subjectivity this way: "Outside human desires there is no moral standard."[37] By taking this position, Russell relegated his own statement—*"The good life is one inspired by love and guided by knowledge"*—to the status of an emotional non-assertion. What he calls the "good life" might make us feel warm and fuzzy inside, but it has no claim to objectivity or truth. Russell thus undermined his own proposition, so why should we take any of his moral statements seriously? Ironically, Russell did expect his contemporaries to take his moral and political pronouncements seriously—he even spent time in jail for his pacifist convictions. He was extremely politically and socially engaged, and he harshly criticized those who did not share his moral views. I guess his emotions got the best of him.

Russell's daughter, Katharine Tait, noticed these tensions in her father's character. In her memoir about her life with her father, she called him a "passionate moralist" who would have made a good saint in a more religious age. She admitted that despite his philosophical position to the contrary, "he was always an absolutist; things that involved his emotions were either good or bad." Further, she noted that if he were asked about free will when writing philosophically, he would give a resounding "no." However, "he acted 'yes' and wrote 'yes' when his moral passions were engaged." Russell could intellectually deny free will and morality, but he could not seem to bring his own life into line with these insights.[38]

Tait also understood the problems plaguing her father's vision of humanity. She pointed out that in his writings, he mocked Christians "for imagining that man is important in the vast scheme of the universe, even the high point of all creation—and yet my father thought man and his preservation the most important thing in the world, and he lived in hopes of a better life to come." Tait disagreed with her father's insistence that the preservation of humanity was essential and an "absolute good." She wrote, "I have never regarded the mere existence of humanity as good in itself [as her father did], and I can contemplate without panic a world devoid of human beings. (Unwittingly, my father was responsible for this callous point of view, having taught us that mankind was no more than an accident of evolution.)" She explained that her father loved humanity in general, but had little affection for individual people. At one point she quoted her father, who wrote, "The sea, the stars, the night wind in waste places, mean more to me than even the human beings I love best, and I am conscious that human affection is to me at bottom an attempt to escape from the vain search for God." Tait then wistfully lamented, "We who loved him were secondary to the sea and stars and the absent God; we were not loved for ourselves, but as bridges out of loneliness." Despite his intense concern for his daughter, Russell never really met his daughter's need for love and acceptance. Tait only found that love and acceptance later in life when she embraced Christianity.[39]

Russell had to live with the tensions inherent in his philosophy. On the one hand, he had a yearning for the well-being of humanity. He staunchly opposed economic oppression and militarism, because as a human being himself, he recognized that humans do have some value. In his tract promoting a one-world government to avert a nuclear holocaust, Russell specifically claimed that humans do have value, because "it is within human power to create a world of shining beauty and transcendent glory."[40] But how can "accidental collocations of atoms" possibly attain transcendence? Russell wrestled with this question intensely, as is evident in some of his private correspondence. In 1916 he confided to his love, Constance Mellon:

> I am strangely unhappy because the pattern of my life is complicated, because my nature is hopelessly complicated; a mass

of contradictory impulses; and out of all this, to my intense sorrow, pain to you must grow. The centre of me is always and eternally a terrible pain—a curious wild pain—a searching for something beyond what the world contains, something transfigured and infinite—the beatific vision—God—I do not find it, I do not think it is to be found—but the love of it is my life—it's like passionate love for a ghost. At times it fills me with rage, at times with wild despair, it is the source of gentleness and cruelty and work, it fills every passion that I have—it is the actual spring of life within me.

I can't explain it or make it seem anything but foolishness—but whether foolish or not, it is the source of whatever is any good in me.... At most times, now, I am not conscious of it, only when I am strongly stirred, either happily or unhappily. I seek escape from it, though I don't believe I ought to.[41]

Russell later claimed in his *Autobiography* that his whole life was animated by three passions: love, knowledge, and pity for human suffering.[42]

However, he was never able to square his search for God and transcendence, together with his love of compassion, with his intellectual dismissal of God and the concomitant view that humanity is nothing more than a cosmic accident. Here is how Russell described this tension in his *Autobiography*: "What Spinoza calls 'the intellectual love of God' has seemed to me the best thing to live by, but I have not had even the somewhat abstract God that Spinoza allowed himself to whom to attach my intellectual love. I have loved a ghost, and in loving a ghost my inmost self has itself become spectral."[43] Russell was conflicted, because he loved God, but did not believe in his existence; he loved humanity, but believed humans were accidents "destined to extinction." Deep in his inner self he seems to have sensed that humans were not merely a cosmic mistake; they were somehow more than just "accidental collocations of atoms." But, blinded by his atheistic worldview, he could not quite bring himself to admit it.

❋

The Nobel Prize–winning co-discoverer of the double-helix model of DNA, Francis Crick, has probably done as much as anyone to promote the idea that humans can be reduced to their material basis. In his 1966 book *Of Molecules and Men*, Crick presented humans as nothing more than matter in motion. He hoped that "scientific values" would supplant traditional cultural values derived from Christianity and would allow us to answer questions of vital importance to humanity, such as "'What are we?' 'Why are we here?' etc. It is remarkable to me," Crick continued, "that there is not more urgency to answer questions of this kind." He believed that the scientific method was the sole path leading to answers to our deepest philosophical questions, so he had great faith that science could transform our vision of humanity. Crick insisted that "science in general, and natural selection in particular, should become the basis on which we are to build the new culture."[44] What he was really calling for was the reign of materialism over human affairs.

In his later book, *The Astonishing Hypothesis* (1994), Crick explained his view of humanity in the opening paragraph of his book: "The Astonishing Hypothesis is that 'You,' your joys and your sorrows, your memories and your ambitions, your sense of personal identity and free will, are in fact no more than the behavior of a vast assembly of nerve cells and their associated molecules. As Lewis Carroll's Alice might have phrased it: 'You're nothing but a pack of neurons.'"[45] Notice that he reduces every individual's significance by putting scare quotes around "You," indicating that "You" are not a real entity, much less a morally significant person. Given his diminishing of the human person to nothing more than an accidental assemblage of matter, perhaps it is unsurprising that Crick promoted infanticide for babies that did not pass muster genetically. He once stated, "No newborn infant should be declared human until it has passed certain tests regarding its genetic endowment and that if it fails these tests it forfeits the right to life."[46] Why not just eliminate any "pack of neurons" that we judge inferior or even inconvenient?

❉

Another atheistic scientist today who denies the significance of humanity is Lawrence Krauss, an eminent cosmologist who elegantly (but ultimately unconvincingly) argues that the universe came into existence from nothing (but not really, because for Krauss nothing is not really nothing). In his book *The Universe from Nothing* he makes clear that his naturalistic vision of cosmology rids the universe of any underlying purpose or meaning. He deflects criticism of this view by telling us more than once that we simply need to get over it and take the universe as it is, not how we want it to be. It does not matter if the universe is bleak or comforting—just accept the facts as they are. However, in the epilogue he seems to revel in his own worldview in a way that makes one wonder if he is really just hewing to the bald facts. There he states, "A universe without purpose or guidance may seem, for some, to make life itself meaningless. For others, including me, such a universe is invigorating. It makes the fact of our existence even more amazing, and it motivates us to draw meaning from our own actions and to make the most of our brief existence in the sun, simply because we are here, blessed with consciousness and with the opportunity to do so."[47] Krauss, like many other secularists, wants to have his cake, but eat it, too. He demolishes meaning, but still wants to have meaning; he denies purpose, but still wants to have purpose; he rejects objective morality, but still uses the language of moral judgment ("make the most of"). However, as he admits, the meaning and purpose that he is left with are simply his own creations. When it comes to meaning and purpose, Krauss is no longer the hard-nosed empiricist who accepts the world as it is, but he is creating a world of illusion to cushion him from his own bleak worldview. Why doesn't he simply accept the cosmos as it is, instead of inventing fictitious meanings and purposes for his life?

Krauss, who believes that the only kind of real knowledge is empirical, insists that everything about humans, including morality, is (at least in principle) subject to scientific investigation. Free will, he thinks, is illusory and naïve, so neuroscience and evolutionary biology will one day provide cogent explanations for human behavior. Indeed, Krauss even demotes love to "the firing of neurons and biochemical reactions." What else could love possibly be, if humans are just products of physical and chemical forces? Krauss also crosses the is-ought divide by claiming that our understanding of biology should influence our morality. He stated, for instance, "I think that science can either modify or determine our moral convictions. The fact that infidelity, for example, is a fact of biology must, for any thinking person, modify any 'absolute' condemnation of it."[48] Really? Must the biological fact that humans commit genocide or rape or environmental devastation or oppression of workers or slavery or racism make "any thinking person" back off from condemning these? I do not know how Krauss would respond to this question, but given his claim that human behavior is explicable in purely naturalistic terms, it is hard to see how he could condemn any behavior. Just as he told us about the universe: People's behavior is what it is. Get over it.

Indeed Krauss seems to understand the implications of his worldview for the importance and value of human life—or should I say, for the non-importance and lack of value of human life. Once he explained, "We're just a bit of pollution. If you got rid of us, and all the stars and all the galaxies and all the planets and all the aliens and everybody, then the universe would be largely the same. We're completely irrelevant."[49] By calling humans a bit of pollution, Krauss shows his contempt for humanity. Indeed this pronouncement moves a step beyond his frequent claims that human life is purposeless, because pollution is normally something we try to eradicate. If humanity is really just pollution, then annihilating the entire human race would seem to be a praiseworthy deed.

❧

Another cosmologist who rejects the idea that humans have any significance in the universe is the Harvard physicist Steven Weinberg.

Most of his 1977 book, *The First Three Minutes*, explains big bang cosmology. However, at the close of his book, he looks forward to the future and waxes philosophical. Humans, he tells us, are not special, but are insignificant, accidental products of an impersonal cosmos. He states,

> It is almost irresistible for humans to believe that we have some special relation to the universe, that human life is not just a more or less farcical outcome of a chain of accidents reaching back to the first three minutes, but that we were somehow built in from the beginning.... It is very hard to realize that this is all just a tiny part of an overwhelmingly hostile universe. It is even harder to realize that this present universe has evolved from an unspeakably unfamiliar early condition, and faces a future extinction of endless cold or intolerable heat. The more the universe seems comprehensible, the more it also seems pointless.[50]

In Weinberg's worldview the entire cosmos is the product of accidental, impersonal events. He recognizes the implications of this: Human existence is "farcical" and everything is "pointless." However, he then tries to escape the bleak consequences by claiming in his closing paragraph that "there is at least some consolation in [scientific] research itself.... The effort to understand the universe is one of the very few things that lifts human life a little above the level of farce, and gives it some of the grace of tragedy."[51] Weinberg apparently does not understand that both "farce" and "tragedy" are meaningless if life has no ultimate purpose. Also, while it is understandable why as a scientist he would find scientific research consoling and ennobling, he never explains how this could happen, if our pursuit of scientific research is just as much the product of impersonal cosmic forces as every other human endeavor (including religion). Weinberg's understanding that scientific research is not farcical should cause him to question his vision of humanity as a cosmic accident.

✤

Those scientists and other intellectuals who zealously endeavor to explain all of reality using the scientific method err. They are presupposing that humans, including their mind and consciousness, are nothing more than conglomerations of physical particles in motion. This, as we saw earlier with La Mettrie, is reductionism, because it reduces a human being to the sum total of his or her physical parts. We must be clear here that reductionism is an assumption, not an empirically verifiable fact. This is important, because many scientists and other intellectuals want to claim that they will only accept empirical evidence, and since no one can provide scientifically verifiable proof of any kind of immaterial beings, they cannot accept the existence of such an entity. However, the philosophy underlying their reductionist form of science suffers from the same problem: reductionism itself is not empirically verifiable. It is a presupposition that guides their research, but also limits the possible answers. It forecloses on solutions that are outside the reach of science.

Not only that, but reductionism flies in the face of many empirical observations. Scientists have not yet been able to explain the enigma of consciousness, for instance, and some empirical studies of the human mind provide fodder for anti-reductionist views of consciousness. However, even when faced with seemingly intractable problems, such as explaining consciousness, reductionists usually promise that the problem can be resolved by scientific advances in the future. But what gives them such confidence (faith, I would say) that their post-dated checks will clear the bank? To shift analogies, why are they shouting victory before the game is over, and even before they have scored a single point? Human consciousness and behavior must be scientifically explicable, in their view, simply because they do not want to accept any other alternative, not because the other alternatives have been empirically disproven.

Harvard biologist Richard Lewontin candidly admits the philosophical nature of his commitment to the omnipotence of scientific explanation. In a 1997 article he states,

We take the side of science *in spite* of the patent absurdity of some of its constructs, *in spite* of its failure to fulfill many of its extravagant promises of health and life, *in spite* of the tolerance of the scientific community for unsubstantiated just-so stories, because we have a prior commitment, a commitment to materialism. It is not that the methods and institutions of science somehow compel us to accept a material explanation of the phenomenal world, but, on the contrary, that we are forced by our *a priori* adherence to material causes to create an apparatus of investigation and a set of concepts that produce material explanations, no matter how counterintuitive, no matter how mystifying to the uninitiated. Moreover, that materialism is absolute, for we cannot allow a Divine Foot in the door.[52]

Even though Lewontin opposes some of the more flagrant examples of scientism—this impulse to believe the scientific method can be applied to everything—around today, such as sociobiology and evolutionary psychology, his commitment to materialism still implies that all human behavior can be explained by material causation. He may not embrace the just-so stories of the evolutionary psychologists, but he substitutes for them faith that science will solve all problems later. At least he is honest enough to admit that this faith is based on materialist philosophy rather than scientific evidence. Interestingly, he divulges one of the most powerful motivations behind his materialism: it keeps God out of his life.

Materialism is not just a passionless, disinterested embrace of cool logic and scientific rationality, despite its public pose. It provides a way to escape from the authority of God and to deny the existence of moral laws, thus excusing one's immoral behavior. A few years ago I was at a conference at Oxford University where I was conversing with a prominent philosopher of science who had been raised in a Christian family. He told me that from an early age he and God had never really got along. Then he stated, "I don't want anyone telling me what to do in this life, and I sure don't want anyone telling me what to do in the next one." Materialism and positivism are ways to keep God and his moral law out of our way, so we can tell our consciences to get lost. At the same time, however, materialism and positivism strip us of our humanity by explaining away love, kindness, truth, and beauty as illusions accidentally spewed forth by a mindless, impersonal universe where human life is insignificant. While construing humans as machines, materialists have indeed reduced humans to less than a machine. A machine, after all, is built for a purpose, but in the materialist worldview, humans are accidental products with no purpose at all.

TWO

Created from Animals

Humans Going Ape

Man in his arrogance thinks himself a great work. worthy the interposition of a deity, more humble & I believe true to consider him created from animals.
—Charles Darwin[1]

I n February 2003 People for the Ethical Treatment of Animals (PETA) announced a publicity campaign, Holocaust on Your Plate. They set up a poster display at universities and elsewhere that juxtaposed pictures of Nazi concentration and death camps with photos of farm animals in cages. They equated American farms with Auschwitz and implied that farmers are the moral equivalent of the Nazi SS. Just a month earlier PETA had initiated a boycott against Kentucky Fried Chicken (KFC) to protest their suppliers' factory-farming methods of raising chickens. Apparently, Colonel Sanders's smile masked the grim reality that he was as diabolical as Hitler (and PETA actually placed on their boycott website a caricature of Colonel Sanders with devilish horns). PETA's campaign to smear KFC might have been even more effective if they had reminded Americans that before Heinrich Himmler became the "Architect of Genocide," as historian Richard Breitman has called him, he was—gasp—a chicken farmer. Apparently it is just a small step to go from killing chickens to massacring people.

When confronted by PETA's advertising blitz, most Americans were shocked and horrified—but not in the way that PETA intended. Instead of feeling revulsion toward KFC and chicken farmers, most were outraged at PETA for insulting the victims of the Holocaust by equating them with chickens. Abraham Foxman, director of the Jewish Anti-Defamation League, called the campaign outrageous and cogently explained why: "Abusive treatment of animals should be opposed, but cannot and must not be compared to the Holocaust. The uniqueness of human life is the moral underpinning for those who resisted the hatred of Nazis and others ready to commit genocide even today."[2] In 2009 the German Supreme Court banned the "Holocaust on Your Plate" display in Germany, since they considered it beyond the pale of acceptable discourse, even in a free society.

Despite PETA's horror at killing chickens, ironically both the Nazi perpetrators of the Holocaust and PETA shared the same mistake: they assumed that humans and animals are basically the same. PETA's error is encapsulated in the 1986 statement of its leader, Ingrid Newkirk: "A rat is a pig is a dog is a boy. They are all mammals."[3] Hitler also wanted to erase the distinction between humans and animals.[4] The eminent historian Gerhard Weinberg noted that a "significant facet of [Hitler's] racialist doctrine was its rejection of the biblical distinction between man and other creatures."[5] Out of concern for the welfare of animals, Hitler was a vegetarian, Himmler opposed vivisection, and the Nazis passed conservation legislation. However, while protecting animals in some cases, the Nazis also believed that if humans and animals are just about the same, they could treat humans like animals. PETA, on the other hand, applied the equation the opposite direction by wanting to treat animals like humans.

The Nazi Holocaust and PETA's Holocaust on Your Plate campaign are, to be sure, extreme examples of blurring the distinction between humans and animals. Fortunately, most people still recognize the great gulf between humans and other animals, so PETA's campaign found relatively little traction among the general public. Nonetheless, Western culture is becoming increasingly confused about the status of humanity. We live in a topsy-turvy world today, where humans are being put on display in zoos, but apes and other animals are being granted "human rights."

In August 2005 the London Zoo opened a special primate display— a four-day exhibit of *Homo sapiens*. Visitors gawked at eight humans wearing bathing suits with fig leaves pinned on. In some sense, this was a publicity stunt, but it also had a serious purpose. A zoo spokesperson explained, "Seeing people in a different environment, among other animals, teaches members of the public that the human is just another primate."[6] One of the people on display, a twenty-six-year-old chemist, reflected on the take-away message of the exhibit: "A lot of people think humans are above other animals. When they see humans as animals, here, it kind of reminds us that we're not that special."[7] Worse yet, the zoo issued a communiqué that explained the intent of the exhibit was "to highlight the spread of man as a plague species."[8] I doubt many zoo visitors saw these eight scantily-clad Brits as particularly threatening, but it is clear that the zoo was trying to get people to see humans as nothing more than another animal. Perhaps you had to read the accompanying placards to understand why humans are a "plague species."

This is not the only time zoos put humans on display to try to convince their visitors that humans are just animals. Nine years before the London Zoo's human exhibit the Copenhagen Zoo put humans on display for a couple of weeks. Unlike the London display, in Copenhagen the Danish couple was fully clothed and surrounded by the latest human technology and cultural comforts. A spokesman for the zoo explained that the two people on exhibit "are monkeys in a way, but some people find that hard to accept. This is a way to maybe help people realize that."[9] Inspired by the London exhibit, officials at Adelaide Zoo in Australia decided to sponsor a month-long display of humans at their zoo in 2007. They hoped "to encourage people of all ages to re-think their place in the animal world."[10] One of the humans on display at Adelaide explained,

Ota Benga, an African pygmy on display among primates in the Bronx Zoo in 1906. *Public domain*

"This will put a few of us in our place by reminding us we really are great apes we [sic] are part of the animal kingdom, just like our zoo neighbours the chimpanzees and gorillas."[11] These exhibits gave new meaning to the expression "going ape."

Unlike these more recent displays, Ota Benga, a black African pygmy, actually shared a cage with primates in the Bronx Zoo in 1906. Many people at the time—including many biologists and anthropologists—considered black Africans far lower on the evolutionary scale than those of European descent and thus little more than apes. One newspaper reported that Benga played with the orangutan as if he were one of them, and that he chattered to them in "his own guttural tongue, which they seem to understand." When African American pastors in New York protested the incarceration and display of Benga, the zoo director responded that the protest was ridiculous, because Benga was well cared for and had "one of the best rooms in the primate house." By forcing Benga to "go ape," the zoo reinforced the prevalent view that some humans are no different from primates.[12]

Working in the opposite direction, some secularists today are campaigning for the release of all apes from zoos, since this allegedly violates their rights. Spearheaded by Peter Singer and supported by many other prominent intellectuals, including biologist Richard Dawkins, bestselling author Jared Diamond, and chimp expert Jane Goodall, the Great Ape Project aims at extending the moral circle beyond humans to include apes. The declaration they issued in 1993 demands that apes be included in the "community of equals," which should be comprised of humans, chimpanzees, gorillas, and orang-utans. According to their declaration, these great apes should all be granted certain moral rights, including the right to life, the right to individual liberty, and freedom from torture. These sound like noble goals, but the devil is in the details. Singer and his colleagues do not really mean to grant the right to life to everyone belonging to these four species, despite the high-minded rhetoric about a "community of equals." No, as in George Orwell's *Animal Farm*, some animals are more equal than others. Singer and his compatriots base moral rights on the "capacities" of these animals, so unborn humans and mentally disabled humans are not included in the moral community. Rights are granted on a sliding scale rather than being inalienable.[13] Thus, while insisting that their goal is greater equality across species, the result is greater inequality within the human species, because not all humans have the same "capacities."

The notion that humans are not intrinsically more valuable than other creatures did not arise for the first time with Charles Darwin in the nineteenth century. Various theories of biological evolution had emerged the century before Darwin's theory took the world by storm, and as we saw in the preceding chapter, some materialists had already reduced humans to the level of machines. However, Darwinian evolutionary theory was one of the most influential intellectual factors that convinced people that the distance between humans and other animals was not all that great. Many concluded from evolutionary theory that humans were not any more important than other animals. Several features of Darwinian theory lent themselves to devaluing human life:

1. the animal ancestry of humans
2. the denial of purpose in life
3. the undermining of morality and human rights
4. its stress on human inequality
5. its view of death as the engine of progress

Let us look at each of these in greater depth.[14]

When Darwin published *The Origin of Species* in 1859, he studiously avoided the topic of human evolution, except for an oblique reference at the close of the book. In his private research notes, he did not show the same reticence, discussing human evolution extensively. He kept those ruminations about human evolution under wraps in 1859, because he rightly recognized that this was the most explosive and controversial part of his theory. However, after others had broached the subject in the 1860s, Darwin published *The Descent of Man* in 1871, confirming what everybody already knew: he did believe that humans had evolved from other organisms.

In order to convince his contemporaries that humans had evolved from primates, Darwin tried to show that humans are only quantitatively, not qualitatively, different from other animals. Sure, we have a little more rationality, a little more social instinct or morality, and a little more aesthetic sense, Darwin admitted, but other animals have these in some measure, too. He tried to explain (away) every human trait that most people considered uniquely human by arguing that other animals have the same or similar traits. Darwin denied that any species— including humans—had any essence to it, as they are connected historically by gradual steps. There is thus no perceptible moment when a species actually begins. Determining when the "first human" appeared is entirely arbitrary. Any individual one might select as the "first human" would have a father and mother who were barely different.

By blurring the distinction between humans and other animals in *The Descent of Man*, Darwin implicitly rejected the existence of the human soul. In his notebooks he explicitly denied that humans had souls. Though he remained agnostic about philosophical materialism (the view that only matter and energy exist), he nonetheless embraced a fully materialistic view of mind. In his notebooks he even used the word materialism to describe his view of the mind. He stated that "thought, however unintelligible it may be, seems as much function of organ, as bile of liver."[15]

❋

Many of Darwin's contemporaries understood his views undermined the Christian view that humans have souls setting them apart from the rest of creation. The theologian David Friedrich Strauss, who created a sensation in 1835 with his book *The Life of Jesus*, abandoned Christianity altogether in his later work, *The Old Faith and the New*, published in 1872, one year after Darwin published *Descent of Man*. For Strauss, the new religion was scientific materialism, and Darwinism played a prominent role in this worldview. Strauss argued that humans were not distinct from animals and that the human soul was simply a manifestation of the physical brain.[16]

Darwinism was not, of course, the only intellectual movement stimulating a rejection of the Christian doctrine of the human soul, but it was nonetheless a significant factor. For example, August Forel, who later became professor of psychiatry at the University of Zurich, described his first encounter with Darwin's theory in 1865 as almost a religious conversion experience: "But when I read *The Origin of Species* it was as though scales fell from my eyes, while the light of a new and higher knowledge began to dawn upon them." What was this new knowledge? It was that psychology, including human psychology (and this was based on his reading of Darwin's *Origin*, which did not discuss human evolution!), was based entirely on physiology. Later in his memoirs Forel stated that he considered evolutionary theory the greatest achievement of the nineteenth century, which he called "the century of Lamarck and Darwin, in which the doctrine of evolution gave birth to the germ of the discovery of the identity of the human soul with the brain, and therewith dealt the deathstroke to the dualism of body and soul."[17] Forel, along with Darwin and Strauss and many other contemporaries, believed that evolutionary theory effectively erased any significant distinctions between humans and other animals.

Based on this view of humans as animals, Forel did not think that humans had an inalienable right to life. Thus he believed that some humans' lives had more value than others', and he approved of infanticide and euthanasia for those deemed unfit or inferior. As a leading figure in the early eugenics movement, he continually warned against the reproduction of the "inferior." In *The Sexual Question* (1905) he implied that he supported infanticide for babies with mental disabilities, whom he called "little apes."[18] He opened a 1908 published lecture on "Life and Death" with the question, "Is life worth living?" Not always, he replied, since those who are mentally abnormal or hereditary criminals, whose existence is "a plague for society," may not consider their lives worth living. Though he refrained from overtly passing judgment on them, Forel implied that he did not consider their lives worth living.[19] Two years later he explicitly advocated killing the physically and mentally disabled. He asked, "Is it really a duty of conscience to help with the birth and even the conception of every cripple, who descends from thoroughly degenerate parents? Is it really a duty to keep alive every idiot (even every blind idiot), every most wretched cripple with three-fourths of the brain damaged?" He answered with a resounding no. The irrational idea that we should keep such people alive derives from outmoded other-worldly ethics, according to Forel.[20] Apparently, by sweeping aside other-worldly (especially Christian) ethics, Darwinism opened the door for this-worldly killing.

�֍

The understanding that Darwinism demolished the divide between humans and other animals still has a profound influence on Western thought and culture. Peter Singer admits that Darwinism informs his own position that humans are not special or uniquely valuable. He claims that Darwin "undermined the foundations of the entire Western way of thinking on the place of our species in the universe." According to Singer, it stripped humanity of the special status that Judeo-Christian thought had conferred upon it. He complains that even though Darwin "gave what ought to have been its final blow" to the "human-centred view of the universe," the view that humans are special and sacred has not yet vanished. Singer is now hoping and laboring to provide the deathblow to the sanctity-of-life ethic.[21] Indeed Singer argues forcefully that human life has no meaning and purpose, because biological life began "in a chance combination of gasses; it then evolved through random mutation and natural selection. All this just happened; it did not happen to any overall purpose."[22] According to Singer's worldview, human life is just a cosmic accident without any real significance.

One of Singer's book titles divulges poignantly what he is aiming at: *Unsanctifying Human Life.* In a 2004 interview, Singer claimed that there is nothing special about humans, and then stated, "All we are doing is catching up with Darwin. He showed in the nineteenth century that we are simply animals. Humans had imagined we were a separate part of Creation, that there was some magical line between Us and Them. Darwin's theory undermined the foundations of that entire Western way of thinking about the place of our species in the universe."[23] Unfortunately, Singer is so consistent in rejecting human dignity and placing humans on par with animals that he even thinks bestiality is perfectly fine. Surely he knows better (if he has any conscience at all), but if so, he will not admit it.

Singer's friend and colleague James Rachels agreed wholeheartedly with Singer about the impact of Darwinism on the value of human life. He devoted an entire book, *Created from Animals: The Moral Implications of Darwinism* (1990), to discussing this issue. Rachels's thesis is that Darwinism—which he avidly upheld—undermines the Judeo-Christian sanctity-of-life ethic: "I shall argue that Darwin's theory does undermine traditional values. In particular, it undermines the traditional idea that human life has a special, unique worth." He considered this a positive development and vigorously applauded Darwinism for discrediting the outmoded "idea of human dignity." Rachels stated, "I shall argue, however, that discrediting 'human dignity' is one of the most important implications of Darwinism, and that it has consequences that people have barely begun to appreciate." In his view, "humans and non-humans are, in a sense, moral equals." Like Singer, Rachels uses this philosophy of human-animal equality to support his pro-abortion, pro-euthanasia, and animal rights agenda.[24]

Some twenty-first century Darwinian biologists also are trying to blur the distinction between humans and other animals. In 2001 Richard Dawkins, probably the most famous Darwinian biologist in the world today, made an impassioned plea for genetically engineering an *Australopithecine*, which is allegedly an evolutionary ancestor of *Homo sapiens*. Producing such a "missing link" half-way between apes and humans would, according to Dawkins, provide "positive ethical benefits," since it would demolish the "double standard" of those guilty of "speciesism." Dawkins specifically claims that producing such an organism would demonstrate the poverty of the pro-life position, because it would show that humans are not different from animals. In the midst of this acerbic attack on the sanctity of human life, Dawkins expressed the hope that he will be euthanized if he is ever "past it" (whatever that means).[25] In his zeal to demolish the pro-life position, Dawkins has stated (repeating a position taken earlier by Singer) that "any fetus is less human than an adult pig."[26] In August 2014 Dawkins stirred up controversy when he tweeted that it would be immoral not to abort a fetus that had Down syndrome.[27] Dawkins, like Singer and Rachels, believes that Darwinism undermines the sanctity of human life, and instead of recoiling, these scholars exult in this.

On New Year's Day in 2009 Edge.org asked some of the world's leading intellectuals to answer the question: "What will change everything?" In his answer Dawkins criticized the pro-life position, whose "deeply un-evolutionary" view that human life is sacred leads them to oppose abortion and euthanasia. He proposed four discoveries or scientific developments that would destroy the pro-life movement by conclusively demonstrating that humans are not distinct from other animals:

1. the not-likely discovery of hominids thought to be extinct
2. the successful hybridization of humans and chimpanzees
3. the creation of a chimera with half human and half chimpanzee cells;
4. the reconstruction of a common ancestor of humans and chimpanzees, such as *Australopithecus*[28]

Dawkins fully approves of scientific experimentation to produce half-human, half-ape hybrids, hoping that the production of these monstrosities will finally convince us humans that we are not all that special, that we are merely insignificant matter in motion.

Dawkins may have been the first to suggest genetically engineering *Australophecines*, but he was not the first to suggest hybridizing humans and primates. In 1905–1906 a Dutch teacher, Bernelot Moens, approached the biologist Ernst Haeckel, the most famous Darwinist in Germany, with an idea for a scientific experiment to bolster the theory of human evolution. He wanted to use artificial insemination to cross a human with a primate. He planned to procure sperm from a "Negro" and inseminate an ape with it. Haeckel believed this experiment could succeed, because he thought the lower human races were very close to apes anyway, so he encouraged Moens to proceed. However, Haeckel told Moens not to mention his name publicly as supporting this experiment. Apparently he knew this would shock the moral sensibilities of most Europeans (as it should!). Another researcher approached Haeckel in 1916 with a similar proposal, and Haeckel suggested using Negro sperm to inseminate a chimpanzee.[29]

The idea that Darwinism has demolished the Judeo-Christian sanctity-of-life ethic has become so widespread among scientists that many regard as unthinkable the claim that humans are made in the image of God. One of the leading science journals, *Nature*, published an editorial in 2007 blasting U.S. Senator Sam Brownback for daring to question evolution.

Brownback, at that time a Republican contender for the presidency, argued in a *New York Times* editorial, "Man was not an accident and reflects an image and likeness unique in the created order. Those aspects of evolutionary theory compatible with this truth are a welcome addition to human knowledge. Aspects of these theories that undermine this truth, however, should be firmly rejected as atheistic theology posing as science."

The scientists at *Nature* took umbrage, claiming that the evolution of the human mind and even morality was "not atheistic theology. It is unassailable fact." They also retorted: "With all deference to the sensibilities of religious people [which being translated means: I am now going to trounce your religious sensibilities], the idea that man was created in the image of God can surely be put aside." The scientists writing this editorial explained that it "seems a priori unlikely" that a mind creating the universe could have a mind similar to "an upright ape adapted to living in small, intensely social peer-groups on the African savannah." In case you did not catch it, the upright ape means us.[30] This article reflects the view widespread among scientists that evolutionary theory has completely demolished the allegedly benighted dogma that humans are created in the image of God, so we are nothing but an "upright ape."

By blurring the distinction between humans and other animals, Darwinism has fostered the view that there is greater equality among creatures, thus giving impetus to the animal rights movement. However, ironically, at the same time Darwinism has contributed to or reinforced philosophies of human inequality, undermining human rights. Darwinism, after all, stresses variation within each species, including humans. Evolution cannot get off the ground without significant variations arising within populations. As individuals differ, those best adapted (the fittest) produce new varieties that continue evolving gradually until they eventually become new sub-species and later give rise to new species, new genera, and new classes.

This emphasis on human variation has led many Darwinists from the nineteenth century to the present to argue that humans are inherently unequal. Many even forthrightly rejected human equality as misguided and unscientific. Darwin, good Victorian liberal that he was, expressed ambivalence about human inequality. In *Descent of Man* he insisted on the unity of the human species, and he was a staunch foe of slavery. However, he also argued—as he had to, if he wanted to convince his contemporaries that humans had evolved—that humans varied considerably. He suggested that different races could be classified biologically as sub-species, and he also called some human races higher than others. He not only believed that some races had higher mental capacities, but he also thought some were more advanced morally than the "savage" races. In both cases, of course, Darwin believed that white Europeans were the highest race.

Many Darwinian biologists and anthropologists in the late nineteenth and early twentieth centuries embraced scientific racism, which they saw both as evidence for Darwinism (it showed variation within the human species) and as a logical corollary of Darwinism (because Darwinism required variation). Some argued that racial inequalities provided evidence to help prove Darwinism (this was Darwin's position), while others claimed that Darwinism proved that races are unequal. Either way, by 1900 racism had become an integral part of the Darwinian explanation for human evolution.

Haeckel was one of the most radical to apply Darwinism to inegalitarianism. He not only propagated an intensely racist brand of evolutionary theory, but he also applied inegalitarian principles to domestic politics. He wrote extensively about human evolution, constantly depicting racial inequalities as powerful evidence for Darwin's theory. In order to stress the supposedly vast difference between human races, he not only divided human races into ten separate species, but he also split these ten "species" into four distinct genera! He remarked that the mental distinction between the highest human and the lowest human was greater than the difference between the lowest human and other animals, such as primates or even dogs.

Haeckel believed these biological inequalities had moral implications. In a 1904 book, *The Wonders of Life*, he discussed racial inequalities in a chapter entitled "The Value of Life." The primary point of that chapter is that not all humans have the same value of life. He stated, "The value

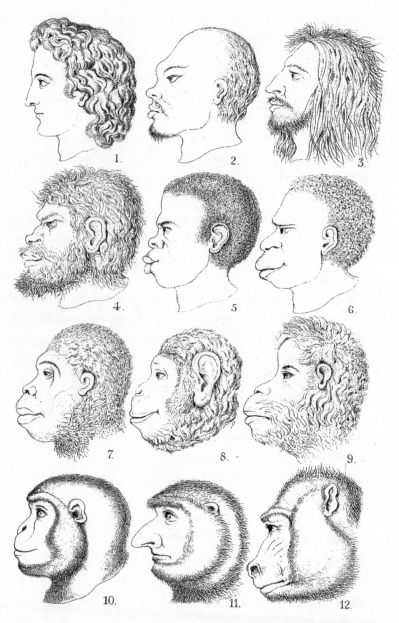

The famous German Darwinist Ernst Haeckel's hierarchy of human races and primates, from his popular 1868 book on evolution, purporting to show that the lowest human races are very close to the highest primates.
Ernst Haeckel, Natürliche Schöpfungsgeschichte

of life of these lower wild peoples is equal to that of the anthropoid apes or stands only slightly above them."[31] Haeckel also appealed to his belief in Darwinism to bolster his anti-socialist political philosophy. In 1878 he vociferously opposed a famous biologist who had warned in a lecture that Darwinism promoted socialism. On the contrary, Haeckel countered, Darwinism proves that humans are biologically unequal, thus rendering socialist egalitarianism completely unscientific. Haeckel supported a meritocracy, where the political, social, and economic structure would encourage competition among unequal rivals. This would allow the "fit" to flourish, while the "unfit" would perish. However, Haeckel also thought that the "fit" should be allowed to help the "unfit" perish in some circumstances. Sometimes, he believed, "Thou shalt not kill" did not apply. Specifically, he did not believe that the lives of people with disabilities had value, so he favored their elimination. In 1870 Haeckel became the first German to publicly endorse infanticide for people with disabilities, and in 1904 he advocated involuntary euthanasia for disabled adults.[32]

Haeckel's views may have been more radical than most, but nonetheless many other Darwinists in the late nineteenth century shared his belief that inegalitarianism flowed from Darwinism. The Yale sociologist William Graham Sumner, who always kept Darwin's picture at his desk, claimed Darwinian grounds for rejecting human equality. He stated, "Let it be understood that we cannot get outside this alternative: liberty, inequality, survival of the fittest; non-liberty, equality, survival of the unfittest. The former carries society forward and favors all its best members; the latter carries society downwards and favors all its worst members." He favored human competition to rid society of the "unfit" and specifically denied that humans have any inherent rights, including the right to life. In nature, he stated, a human has "no more right to life than a rattlesnake; he has no more right to liberty than any wild beast; his right to the pursuit of happiness is nothing but a license to maintain the struggle for existence if he can find within himself the power with which to do it."[33] Sumner thus dismissed human rights, including the right to life, because humans are biologically unequal and need to fight for their place in the world. For him humans were no different than beasts.

As we have already seen with Haeckel, Darwinian inegalitarianism often targeted people with disabilities, labeling them the "unfit." In the 1860s the biologist and anthropologist Karl Vogt argued that mental disabilities provided evidence supporting evolutionary theory. He considered disabled people atavistic, i.e., throwbacks reverting to more primitive evolutionary ancestors. Microcephalic individuals, he thought, were "missing links" whose brains are the size of an ape's. Even more bizarre, he claimed that they have excellent tree-climbing skills, allegedly demonstrating their affinity with monkeys. Vogt's prejudices against people with disabilities are so outrageous that one wonders why they were not considered ridiculous by his contemporaries. However, they were not; even Darwin expressed general approval of his position.[34]

Darwinian-inspired inegalitarianism flourished in the late nineteenth and early twentieth centuries. Just about all the early leaders in the eugenics movement, whether in Britain, Germany, the United States, or elsewhere, saw their movement to improve human heredity as applied Darwinism. Inegalitarian rhetoric permeates eugenics discourse, implying or often explicitly stating that the lives of people with disabilities were less valuable than the lives of other humans. One of the leading figures in the German eugenics movement, the physician Wilhelm Schallmayer, dismissed egalitarianism with scorn. "Making the unequal equal," he wrote in an influential book on eugenics, "can only be an ideal of the weak."[35]

Eugenicists all over the world regularly referred to the disabled as "inferior," "having lesser value," "unfit," "lower," "useless," "burdens to society," "degenerate," "defective," and even "worthless." For instance, Ignaz Kaup, a professor of social hygiene at the University of Munich in the early twentieth century, wrote an article on "What Do the Inferior Elements Cost the State and Society?" In the article, he warned against false compassion for the "inferior," since "our healthy offspring have the right to be protected from decay through those who are genetically pestilent (*Keimschädlinge*), and every progressive nation has the duty to reduce the ballast of the costs of inferiority."[36] The term I have translated as "pestilent" (*Schädlinge*) often means pests, parasites or vermin. Though sometimes it is also used to describe people, it usually refers to evil people who exert noxious influences on others. Using this term—as well as "ballast"—to describe people with disabilities shows the utter contempt toward disabled people that reigned in eugenics circles. Some eugenicists referred to people with disabilities as weeds needing eradication, while others called them parasites, which became a favorite trope of the Nazis to describe those they deemed hereditarily inferior.

Nowhere did belief in biological inequality have more sinister consequences than in Nazi Germany. We all know that Hitler killed millions in his quest to rid the world of inferior races to clear away "living space" for the so-called "master race." In *Mein Kampf* Hitler argued that the Aryan race was the only culture-creating race, which made them

> the real founders of everything we include in the word *human-ity*.... The human culture, the results of art, science and invention which we see before us are almost exclusively the creative product of an Aryan. But this very fact permits the not unfounded deduction that he alone was the creator of a higher human life, and thus is the prototype of what we today mean by the word *man*.[37]

This implies that other races are not included in humanity. Much Nazi propaganda underlined this point by continually dehumanizing non-Nordic races, including even other European races, the Slavs being one of them, whom they called "subhuman." The Nazi regime also persecuted fellow Germans they deemed biologically inferior, such as those with congenital disabilities. Nazi functionaries and cooperating physicians and nurses murdered about two hundred thousand disabled Germans in less than six years (and this does not include the thousands of disabled people they killed in occupied territories, too).

But what significance does any of this have today? Haven't Darwinists abandoned inegalitarianism and embraced racial equality? Yes indeed, and for this we can be thankful. Haven't they, like most of Western society, become more sensitive to people with disabilities? After all, we now have the Americans with Disabilities Act and other legislation to ensure that the disabled can lead a dignified life and participate in society. No one would think of publicly calling people with disabilities "ballast," "weeds," or "parasites" in the Western media today. Despite all these positive developments, Western culture is schizophrenic in its treatment of people with disabilities. While laudably providing more humane treatment and many new opportunities for them, our society nevertheless kills multitudes of disabled people before they are born (or sometimes even soon after they are born or in the final stages of their life). If companies offering pre-natal diagnostic tests fail to detect genetic abnormalities, parents can sue for "wrongful birth," as an Oregon couple did in March 2012 when their child was born with Down syndrome (the jury shamefully concurred that the child should never have been born and awarded the couple almost $3 million). The ideology many bioethicists use today to justify these "selective abortions" of disabled infants is that not all humans are equal. Singer, for instance, supports selective abortions and even infanticide based on the idea that babies are not equal to adult humans. He states, "It's a simple fact that a three-year-old human has pretty much the same self-awareness, rationality and capacity to feel pain as an adult ape. So they should be given equal moral consideration."[38] The corollary to this, which Singer spells out in detail in many of his writings, is that an infant—and even a mentally disabled adult—should not be given equal moral consideration with a "normal" adult.

In addition to challenging human equality, Darwinism has also contributed to devaluing human life by undermining teleology, the notion that organisms, including humans, were created for a purpose. Darwin was convinced that his evolutionary theory refuted William Paley's natural theology. Paley's book, *Natural Theology* (1802), was required reading at the University of Cambridge when Darwin attended, because it reflected the prevailing philosophy of nature in early nineteenth-century England. Paley described the intricate design in nature, which indicated that all organisms must have been designed by a Supreme Being. Darwin disagreed. Instead, he believed that organisms had evolved without any plan or purpose. Even though he did not know the source of biological variation (since scientists knew very little about heredity at the time), he insisted that it must be random. Evolution proceeded without any guiding hand behind it. Darwin's theory also explained why organisms—such as mammalian species in cold climates having long hair—look like they are designed to fit their environments. Darwin denied that organisms had adaptations because a Creator designed them that way. Rather, the individuals with variations that were better adapted survived and reproduced, while those less well adapted perished. Darwin's explanation for adaptations provided a powerful challenge to those believing in design in nature.

After Darwin published his theory, some religious scientists thought that biological evolution could be squared with purpose and providence. Asa Gray, a botanist at Harvard University and a devout Presbyterian, tried to convince Darwin that natural selection was not contrary to design or purpose in nature. Darwin did not budge, telling Gray in July 1860 that he did not believe there is any design in nature.[39] Later Darwin repeatedly dismissed the idea that nature was designed. Why did Darwin reject design and insist on randomness in the evolutionary process? It was not because he had any scientific evidence for it, because he admitted that he did not understand the causes of biological variation. Rather, it seems clear that religious and philosophical considerations drove him to reject teleology. Darwin confessed that the problem of evil in nature hindered him from accepting the design argument: "I cannot persuade myself that a beneficent and omnipotent God would have designedly created the Ichneumonidae with the express intention of their feeding within the living bodies of caterpillars."[40] Darwin also had other more personal reasons for rejecting the Christian Creator God. He admitted in his autobiography that he could not bear to think that "my Father, Brother and almost all my best friends, will be everlastingly punished."[41] Thus, for these and other reasons, Darwin abandoned theism and through his theory stripped nature of all purpose and design.

Many of Darwin's contemporaries recognized that his theory annihilated purpose and design in nature, or at least made them superfluous. Thomas Henry Huxley, nicknamed Darwin's bulldog for the vigorous support he gave his friend's theory, stated that reading Darwin's *Origin of Species* convinced him "that teleology, as commonly understood, had received its deathblow at Mr [sic] Darwin's hands."[42] In 1861 Karl Marx wrote to a colleague that with Darwin's theory, "for the first time teleology in the natural sciences is not only dealt a mortal blow, but its rational sense is also empirically explained."[43] Many scientific materialists and positivists in the late nineteenth century likewise exulted that Darwin had explained away design in nature.

Today many scientists still appeal to Darwinism to try to prove that nature, including the human species, has no purpose. In November 2009 I attended an academic conference at San Diego State University on "150 Years of Evolution: Darwin's Impact on the Humanities and the Social Sciences." The keynote address at the conference was by the evolutionary biologist Michael Ghiselin, whose primary point was to adjure biologists to stop using any teleological language. He noted with dismay that many biologists regularly use the "d-word" (i.e., design) in their writing. He argued that design does imply a designer, so we should purge our biological vocabulary of any vestige of design-language, even eschewing terms like the commonly used term "body plan," which implies a designer. Design must be completely banished from our thought-patterns, since Darwinism has completely annihilated teleology. Ghiselin's views did not surprise me in the slightest, as they are textbook orthodoxy in biology.

Richard Dawkins has devoted much of his career to combating teleology. His entire book, *The Blind Watchmaker*, is an attempt to convince us that everything in the universe appears to be designed for a purpose, but is not really. Everything, no matter how intricate, is the product of mindless processes. According to Dawkins, "Natural selection, the blind, unconscious, automatic process which Darwin discovered, and which we now know is the explanation for the existence and apparently purposeful form of all life, has no purpose in mind."[44] In another place he stated, "The universe that we observe has precisely the properties we should expect if there is, at bottom, no design, no purpose, no evil, no good, nothing but pitiless indifference."[45] According to Dawkins, finding purpose in the cosmos or in one's life may be comforting, but it is false comfort based on a delusion.

Evolutionary biology's denial of design and purpose played a key role in converting the Cornell University historian of biology William Provine to atheism. In recounting his own intellectual journey, Provine admitted that when he was growing up, he had a deep sense of design in nature. This feeling ran so deep that he was greatly disturbed by reading Theodosius Dobzhansky's *Genetics and the Origin of Species*, which explained evolution as a random process. He confessed, "I was upset as usual that Dobzhansky had left out the purposive design I could see so obviously in nature." He complained about this to one of his biology professors, who challenged him to find any purpose in the evolutionary process. After studying evolutionary biology more and rereading Dobzhansky several times, he abandoned his belief in teleology. Provine testified that "my belief in purposive design in nature disappeared for good. Evolution exhibited no sign whatever of purpose. Evolution just happens. I can remember that the pain of loss lasted less than a week. As the creationists claim, belief in modern evolution makes atheists of people."[46] Provine followed the logic of his atheistic position relentlessly, persistently asserting that humans are "complex machines" that have no free will. He further insisted that modern "science directly implies that there are no inherent moral or ethical laws, no guiding principles for society."[47]

Another scientist who used Darwinism to promote a vision of history as a random, meaningless sequence of events, was Stephen Jay Gould, a Harvard University paleontologist who wrote many popular books and articles on evolution in the late twentieth century. In *Rocks of Ages: Science and Religion in the Fullness of Life* (1999), Gould argued that

A humorous view of Stephen Jay Gould's Non-Overlapping Magisteria (NOMA). *Courtesy of Brett A. Miller, evidentcreation.com*

science and religion do not conflict, because they are dealing with different phenomena. While science describes biological life, including its origins, religion deals with the purpose and meaning of life. According to this view, which Gould called Non-Overlapping Magisteria (NOMA), science should not make pronouncements about morality or the meaning of life, but religion should refrain from making claims about empirical reality. Gould thereby claimed to set up an impermeable shield between nature, on the one hand, and design or purpose, on the other.

However, despite his best efforts Gould could not always keep these two realms so neatly apart. They are far more permeable than he allowed. Indeed, it seems obvious that his own view of evolutionary history as an undesigned, chance process influenced his own beliefs about religion and morality. In the closing paragraph of *Rocks of Ages* he comments on the insignificance of human existence, the lack of purpose in our lives, and the freedom we have to choose our own morality. He stated,

> *Homo sapiens* also ranks as a "thing so small" in a vast universe, a wildly improbably evolutionary event, and not the nub of universal purpose. Make of such a conclusion what you will. Some people find the prospect depressing. I have always regarded such a view of life as exhilarating—a source of both freedom and consequent moral responsibility. We are

the offspring of history, and must establish our own paths in this most diverse and interesting of conceivable universes— one indifferent to our suffering, and therefore offering us maximal freedom to thrive, or to fail, in our own chosen way.[48]

Inexplicably Gould apparently did not understand that these closing comments violated his NOMA principle, since they are loaded with religious and moral significance.

The interpenetration of Gould's science and his moral vision are even more obvious in his earlier book, *Wonderful Life: The Burgess Shale and the Nature of History* (1989). Aside from the rich descriptions of the explosion of fossilized life forms in the Burgess Shale, *Wonderful Life* carries an overt philosophical message. Gould continually stressed the contingency of history, the accidental character of events that led to the extinction of so many species. This was not just a peripheral point, for in the introduction he explained that his book is "a statement about the nature of history and the awesome improbability of human evolution." Gould also informed us that scientific advances have resulted in the "psychological cost of progressive dethronement [of humans] from the center of things, and increasing marginality in an uncaring universe. Thus, physics and astronomy relegated our world to a corner of the cosmos, and biology shifted our status from a simulacrum of God to a naked, upright ape."[49]

Gould then declared that his own discipline, geology, has taken matters even further by proving that we humans have only existed during "the last geological millimicrosecond" of earth history. Then Gould continued: "We cannot bear the central implication of this brave new world. If humanity arose just yesterday as a small twig on one branch of a flourishing tree, then life may not, in any genuine sense, exist for us or because of us. Perhaps we are only an afterthought, a kind of cosmic accident, just one bauble on the Christmas tree of evolution." Indeed, as Gould makes clear throughout this book, he did indeed consider humanity a mere accident. He surmised that if we replayed the tape of life

(Gould was writing to an audience familiar with cassette tapes), humans would not likely exist. They are the chance product of contingent events.[50]

The entire book, *Wonderful Life*, has religious and moral implications, so it continually violates Gould's NOMA paradigm. The closing words of the book, for instance, are saturated with religious and moral significance:

> And so, if you wish to ask the question of the ages—why do humans exist?—a major part of the answer, touching those aspects of the issue that science can treat at all, must be: because *Pikaia* [a Burgess Shale chordate] survived the Burgess decimation.... The survival of *Pikaia* was a contingency of "just history." I do not think that any "higher" answer can be given, and I cannot imagine that any resolution could be more fascinating. We are the offspring of history, and must establish our own paths in this most diverse and interesting of conceivable universes—one indifferent to our suffering, and therefore offering us maximal freedom to thrive, or to fail, in our own chosen way.[51]

Did Gould really think that this vision of history, morality, and human autonomy can be harmonized with Christianity, Judaism, Islam, or most other religions?

Apparently NOMA is more a strategy to dissuade religious people from making pronouncements about empirical reality, than a serious restriction on scientists promoting their own vision of religion (often materialism) or moral philosophy masquerading as science. NOMA is a ploy to get religious people to keep their mouths shut about scientific or historical reality. The message is something like this (as the scientist in the white lab coat condescendingly pats the befuddled religious individual on the head): *Yes, it's perfectly fine for you to believe in God, immortality, and your other religious doctrines and creeds, as long as you understand that they are fairy tales to give comfort and meaning to life, and as long as you don't confuse them with reality.*

✻

As we can see from Gould's forays into moral philosophy, many Darwinists do not believe that objective morality or human rights are consistent with Darwinian theory. Darwin recognized that explaining morality was one of the greatest hurdles to overcome, if he wanted to convince his contemporaries that humans had evolved. Morality does seem to set us humans apart from other animals, and most of his contemporaries considered this an insurmountable problem for any theory of human evolution. Not Darwin. He valiantly proposed ways to minimize the differences between human morality and the instincts and behavior of other animals. In 1838 he expressed in his research notebooks many of his ideas about morality that he would publish much later. He thought that human moral sentiments were based primarily on social instincts that had evolved from other social animals. Morality was thus not fixed and unchanging, for instincts (and thus moral sentiments) evolved. He also rejected the universality of morality, claiming that in one of her books Harriet Martineau "argues with examples very justly there is no universal moral sense." He followed this up by alleging "that the conscience varies in different races.—no more wonderful than [that] dogs should have different instincts."[52] It is pretty clear, then, that by 1838 Darwin did not believe in the existence of objective morality.

When he published *Origin of Species* in 1859, Darwin barely mentioned humans, so he did not overtly discuss morality. Aside from his discussion of the self-sacrifice of neuter ants, only one other brief passage in *Origin* alludes to his views about morality. "It may be difficult," Darwin stated,

> but we ought to admire the savage instinctive hatred of the queen-bee, which urges her instantly to destroy the young queens her daughters as soon as born, or to perish herself in the combat; for undoubtedly this is for the good of the community; and maternal love and maternal hatred, though the

latter fortunately is most rare, is all the same to the inexorable
principle of natural selection.[53]

This statement is revealing, because here Darwin divulged the relativistic implications of his view of morality. He clearly believed that whatever behavior benefits an organism so that it can survive and multiply—even killing one's own offspring—is morally praiseworthy. If applied to humans—as Darwin would do later—this would pose a radical challenge to Christian ethics (or many other forms of ethics that believe in objective morality).

In 1871 in *The Descent of Man* Darwin finally divulged in great detail his views on the evolution of morality. He explained that morality had come into existence entirely through naturalistic processes, which included both natural selection and the inheritance of habits. Because self-sacrificing morality did not provide an advantage to individuals, Darwin thought that group selection could account for the increase in social instincts, which were the basis for morality. Specifically, he theorized that competition between primitive tribes, including warfare, gave a selective advantage to those with greater social instincts. He stated,

> When two tribes of primeval man, living in the same country, came into competition, if the one tribe included (other circumstances being equal) a greater number of courageous, sympathetic, and faithful members, who were always ready to warn each other of danger, to aid and defend each other, this tribe would without doubt succeed best and conquer the other. Let it be borne in mind how all-important, in the never-ceasing wars of savages, fidelity and courage must be.[54]

The tribe with the greatest measure of "patriotism, fidelity, obedience, courage, and sympathy" would supplant the one with weaker moral sentiments, and this would eventually lead to the Golden Rule.[55]

Darwin clearly recognized that his biologizing of morality meant that morality was contingent, based upon evolutionary events that could have produced something quite different. He illustrated this with the following example: "If, for instance, to take an extreme case, men were reared under precisely the same conditions as hive-bees, there can hardly be a doubt that our unmarried females would, like the worker-bees, think it a sacred duty to kill their brothers, and mothers would strive to kill their fertile daughters; and no one would think of interfering."[56] Not only did Darwin think that morality was species-specific, but he also argued that not all humans had the same moral sentiments, either. He claimed that primitive races were inferior morally to the higher Europeans.[57] He stated, "Nor is the difference slight in moral disposition between a barbarian, such as the man described by the old navigator Byron, who dashed his child on the rocks for dropping a basket of sea urchins, and a Howard or Clarkson."[58] (Darwin admired Howard and Clarkson as philanthropists for their leading role in the anti-slavery movement—but ironically, while opposing slavery, Darwin thought the white European anti-slavery crusaders were biologically superior to other races in their morality.) Darwin also denied the universality of morality another way. He did not believe that the constant warfare among tribes counted against his view of human social instincts, since "social instincts never extend to all the individuals of the same species."[59] Darwin gave examples of so-called "savages" practicing morality within their tribes, but exulting in killing, robbing, and otherwise harming those outside their society.[60]

One of the most obvious elements of Darwin's discussion of the evolution of the social instincts and morality is that he thought morality changed over time. To give only one example among many, in *Descent* Darwin discussed at length his view on the evolution of marriage. He explained that the differences in sexual morality and marriage institutions throughout human history were the result of pressures to survive and reproduce, thus making clear that morality changes during and because of the evolutionary process.[61]

Many proponents of Darwinism in the late nineteenth and early twentieth centuries agreed with Darwin that his theory relativized morality and obliterated human rights. On the basis of his Darwinian worldview,

U.S. Supreme Court Justice Oliver Wendell Holmes Jr. completely rejected natural rights philosophy in favor of a conflict model for determining rights. He explicitly denied that anyone has the "right to life," stating, "The most fundamental of the supposed pre-existing rights—the right to life— is sacrificed without a scruple not only in war, but whenever the interest of society, that is, of the predominant power in the community, is thought to demand it."[62] Holmes's rejection of natural rights, including the right to life, manifested itself not only in his glorification of brutal competition, including war, but also in his embrace of a radical eugenics ideology that included killing those deemed unfit.

In 1927 Holmes delivered the famous *Buck v. Bell* decision that gave legal sanction in the United States to compulsory sterilization laws, which many states had enacted to promote eugenics. Holmes was a passionate supporter of eugenics, so much so that he wrote to a friend shortly after *Buck v. Bell* that he thought compulsory sterilization "was getting near to the first principle of real reform."[63] He thought the only way out of the pitiless struggle for existence was artificial selection or eugenics, including killing those deemed less fit. He stated this position numerous times in his private correspondence. In September 1921 he wrote to Felix Frankfurter that he advocated "restricting propagation by the undesir- ables and putting to death infants that didn't pass the examination."[64] He had already publicly articulated this position in 1895.[65]

Holmes thus approved of humans rationally deciding which of their fellow citizens they should kill.

Apparently killing innocent people was not only justifiable, but laudatory, in the eyes of this Supreme Court "Justice" who rejected such abstract notions as justice and human rights. In private correspondence he overtly dismissed the "sanctity of human life" and the "sacredness of human life," and he advocated "substitut[ing] artificial selection for natural by putting to death the inadequate."[66] In another letter he told a colleague that he had "too profound a contempt for the bases of all socialisms not prepared to begin with life rather than with property and to kill everyone below the standard."[67] What? "Putting to death the inadequate" and "kill[ing] everyone below the standard"? I hope you find this as shocking as I do, for I was blown away when I discovered that this U.S. Supreme Court Justice—who is highly respected today by many progressives—displayed such a shocking lack of sympathy for those in society whom he scorned as "below the standard." Apparently the ideals of human equality and the right to life—enshrined in the Declaration of Independence and the Constitution—meant nothing to Holmes, even though he had pledged to uphold the Constitution.

Holmes understood his rejection of the sanctity of human life in overtly evolutionary terms. He wrote to a colleague in 1926, "As I don't believe the postulate [of a book he had being reading about justice]—and think morality a sort of higher politeness, that stands between us and the ultimate fact—force—I am not much edified. Nor do I see how a believer in any kind of evolution can get a higher formula than organic fitness at the given moment."[68] Holmes thus believed that the evolutionary struggle for existence trumped morality. "Organic fitness" was more important than abstract notions of justice. Force was the ultimate arbiter between people, so morality was ephemeral and inconsequential. Since he viewed human history as an inescapable contest between humans that is decided by force, it is little wonder that privately he rooted for the strong and mighty. The weak would perish in any case, he thought, but this was not enough for him. He hoped the strong would take evolution into their own hands by consciously delivering the deathblow to the weak. In other words, in private Holmes encouraged murdering people he did not consider up to snuff.

Julian Huxley, one of the most important figures in constructing the neo-Darwinian synthesis in the mid-twentieth century, would likely not have agreed with many elements of Holmes's worldview. However, he did agree with Holmes that evolution undermined any fixed morality. In his famous 1943 speech on "Evolutionary Ethics," he rejected the Nazi form of evolutionary ethics, claiming—without offering any cogent reasons— that evolution tilts toward cosmopolitan, not racist ethics. Nonetheless, he was not endorsing any kind of natural human rights or objective morality. He stated clearly that ethics should be viewed, "not as a body of fixed principles, but as a product of evolution, and itself evolving." He criticized those who believe in objective, unchanging moral principles, stating, "The theologian and the moralist will be doing wrong so long as they cling to any absolute or unyielding certitude." Unlike Darwin, who thought that evolution had produced the Golden Rule, Huxley specifically criticized the Golden Rule as impractical.[69] In a later essay, "The Humanist Frame," he explained that his form of humanism would not allow for any absolute morality. He also rejected human equality, stating, "Our new idea-system must jettison the democratic myth of equality. Human beings are not born equal in gifts or potentialities, and human progress stems largely from the very fact of their inequality. 'Free but unequal' should be our motto."[70] Huxley exalted liberty over equality, but I suspect that freedom would not last very long in a society that embraces inequality and moral relativism.

⁂

One of the most prominent evolutionary biologists of the mid-to-late twentieth century, Ernst Mayr, agreed with Huxley about the implications of evolution for human equality and morality. In 1969 he stated,

> Much in man's conceptual framework is based on the thinking of pre-science or pre-biological science. Terms like "progress," "perfection," "equality," "rights of the individual," etc. were coined and conceptually shaped when everybody still believed in the *scala naturae*, in the concept of a *tabula rasa* [blank slate], and in a biological (=genetic) identity of individuals. It is sometimes a traumatic experience to try to reconcile ethical and political principles that have become dear to our hearts with the realities of scientific advances.[71]

Mayr clearly thought that anyone continuing to believe in outmoded ideas like human equality or individual human rights has simply not grasped the implications of biological science. Apparently in his view believers in human rights are in the thrall of irrational emotional attachments that keep them from confronting reality.

The belief by Darwinists that their biological theory has undermined any objective basis for ethics is still prominent today. At the 2009 conference I mentioned above, just before Ghiselin gave his lecture, a young rapper, Baba Brinkman, performed some rap songs about evolution. Between songs he told us that in some species, such as praying mantises and black widows, the females kill their mates immediately after procreating. This is supposedly an evolutionary adaptation (though most species survive just fine without eating their mates, so it is unclear why this adaptation helps them survive better). Brinkman then informed us that it is only chance—like the flip of a coin, he said—that our own species does not exhibit the same behavior. A random mutation could have turned human females into spouse killers, too. If this had happened, he declared, our moral systems and religions would revolve around women killing their mates. The take-home lesson from Brinkman's discourse was that morality is the contingent product of mindless processes. Interestingly, if one compares Brinkman's perspective on spouse-killing with Darwin's understanding of infanticide (discussed above), there is not much difference. In both cases the moral force of the prohibition, "Thou shalt not kill," loses its potency.

At the same conference I spoke with a philosophy graduate student who told me that because empathy and thus morality were traits produced by evolution, he was convinced that morality was relative. I asked him how far he was willing to go with his moral relativism: What did he think about Hitler—was he evil or not? Clearly uncomfortable with the question, he told me that even though he personally finds Hitler repugnant, that repugnance has no objective validity; it is a subjective response inculcated by evolutionary processes. Finally, in order to be ruthlessly consistent with his position, he uttered the jarring words, "Hitler was okay." He then told me that he does not want his rational belief in relativistic morality to influence his own morality, but he still considers his moral standards evolved traits that are purely subjective. I told him that I thought the reason his "instincts" and philosophy about morality were at odds was because morality really is objective, but he refused to see it that way.

If you think that this student was just off his rocker, then consider how Richard Dawkins responded when Larry Taunton asked in an interview if his rejection of external moral standards meant that Islamic extremists might not be wrong. Dawkins replied, "What's to prevent us from saying Hitler wasn't right? I mean, that is a genuinely difficult question." Taunton admitted that he was stupefied by Dawkins's answer—as he should have been.[72] Anyone who thinks that making a moral judgment about Hitler is difficult has lost their moral compass completely and has no business pontificating about any moral issue (or proclaiming that he has discovered the "root of all evil"—which is what he called religion, of course).

I attended a conference at Oxford University in 2011 on "The Evolution of Morality and the Morality of Evolution." One of the keynote speakers at the conference was Michael Ruse, one of the most prominent philosophers of science today. In a 1985 article co-authored with E. O. Wilson, the founder of sociobiology, they famously wrote: "Ethics as we understand it is an illusion fobbed off on us by our genes to get us to co-operate." Ruse has reaffirmed this position many times since then. In 1994 he explained, "Morality is an ephemeral product of the evolutionary process, just as are other adaptations. It has no existence or being beyond this, and any deeper meaning is illusory (although put on us for good biological reasons)."[73] Ruse argues, on the one hand, that we cannot derive specific moral standards from evolution, because that would violate the naturalistic fallacy, i.e., the fallacy of arguing from nature to morality or from "is" to "ought." However, despite his own warnings, at times he commits the naturalistic fallacy by criticizing specific moral standards for not being in harmony with the evolutionary process. For instance, he argues in *The Darwinian Paradigm* that the command to turn the other cheek is maladaptive and contrary to natural selection; thus it is in "conflict with the implications of modern evolutionary thought."[74] In any case, at the Oxford conference and in all his writings, he repeatedly insists that morality is non-objective and illusory.

Provine agrees with Ruse that Darwinism undermines objective ethics. When Provine jettisoned his belief in design in nature, his belief in human free will also vanished, replaced by the view that "humans are wholly determined by heredity and environment."[75] In a 1994 debate at Stanford University with Phillip Johnson, a leading figure in the Intelligent Design Movement, Provine concisely explained how Darwinism influenced his worldview:

> There is no intelligent design in the natural world. When mammals die, they are really and truly dead. No ultimate foundations for ethics exist, no ultimate meaning in life exists, and free will is merely a human myth. These are all conclusions to which Darwin came quite clearly. Modern evolutionary biology not only supports Darwin's belief in evolution by descent, and his belief in natural selection, but all of the implications that Darwin saw in evolution have been strongly supported by modern evolutionary biology.

Provine's philosophy is remarkably consistent with itself, but unfortunately it does not correspond with the reality of what it means to be human. It also has disturbing consequences for our human lives. In an interview with Ben Stein, Provine admitted that because his evolutionary perspective had rid him of any belief in God or an afterlife, he would not "just sit around" like his brother, who died an agonizing death. Rather, Provine stated, "I don't want to die like that. I'm going to shoot myself in the head long before then."[76]

Alex Rosenberg, a philosophy professor at Duke University, agrees with Provine's rejection of morality and free will, and he criticizes those who shy away from nihilism. In a co-authored article from 2003, "Darwin's Nihilistic Idea: Evolution and the Meaninglessness of Life," he explained, "*Darwinian* nihilism is the thesis that the theory of natural selection and its application to biological data explains why morality is at most an instrumentally useful illusion." No need to fear, however, because Rosenberg assures us that nihilism will not affect our behavior because "Most of us just couldn't persistently be mean, even if we tried."[77] Rosenberg should know better than this, because many of his relatives were murdered in the Holocaust. But wait a minute. Why does it matter if we are mean or not, and why does it matter if the Nazis exterminated millions? On Rosenberg's account of morality, there is nothing objectively wrong about being mean, so why does he need to assure us that nihilism won't lead to meanness? Also, apparently it does matter to Rosenberg that the Nazis killed his relatives, because when debating William Lane Craig at Purdue University in 2013 he stated that because of his family's experience in the Holocaust he found some of Craig's arguments "morally offensive." How can something be "morally offensive," if morality does not exist? Why does Rosenberg appeal to morality, when he claims it is merely an illusion?[78]

�֎

Finally, Darwin introduced an entirely new view of death into Western thought when he published his theory. The prevailing view of death in Darwin's time was based on Christianity, which taught that death was an enemy that had entered the world when Adam and Eve sinned against God. Death would ultimately be overcome in the final resurrection, but in the present age death is completely the result of evil. Darwin contradicted these cherished beliefs by claiming that death occurred for eons before humans ever came on the scene. His theory of natural selection only functioned through multitudes of organisms (the "less fit") dying, because it presupposed that far more progeny are produced than can possibly survive. The survival of the fittest was a competition to the death. Adrian Desmond in his biography of T. H. Huxley is not exaggerating when he claims that according to Darwin's theory, "only from death on a genocidal scale could the few progress."[79]

Darwin not only believed that death had occurred for eons, but he also considered death an engine for biological progress. Death may be bad for the individual, but it clears the way for progeny with better adapted traits, so ultimately it fosters biological improvement. Darwin stated in the penultimate sentence of *The Origin of Species*: "Thus, from the war of nature, from famine and death, the most exalted object which we are capable of conceiving, namely, the production of the higher animals, directly follows."[80] Darwin's jubilation at the power of natural selection to wrest victory from the jaws of death is reminiscent of the biblical promise, "Death is swallowed up in victory."[81] This secular substitute for the Christian view of death provided inspiration for many Darwinists, who now understood death as a progressive force. Many Darwinists came to see death as a good thing.

One of the early proponents of involuntary euthanasia in Germany, the psychiatrist Alfred Hoche, embraced this Darwinian view of death. In his autobiography he explained that to nature, "the continued existence of the species is everything, the individual is nothing; she [nature] carries on an immense waste of seeds, but the individual, after she has given it—the mature one—opportunity to pass on its seed to the future, she heedlessly lets die; it is for her purposes without value."[82] This view was widespread among eugenics proponents, and Robby Kossmann, a medical professor with a doctorate in zoology, explained this connection between Darwinism and the devaluing of individual humans clearly in an 1880 article in a popular periodical. He stated,

> We see that the Darwinian world view must look upon the present sentimental conception of the value of the life of the human individual as an overestimate completely hindering the progress of humanity. The human state also, like every animal community of individuals, must reach an even higher state of perfection, if the possibility exists in it, *through the destruction of the less well-endowed individual,* for the more excellently endowed to win space for the expansion of its progeny.... The state only has an interest in preserving the more excellent life *at the expense of the less excellent.*[83]

Since many Darwinists began interpreting death as a useful and even beneficial force producing evolutionary progress, it was only a short step to considering the killing of the "less well-endowed" with equanimity. As Kossmann's statement suggests, some even began to think that killing the "less well-endowed" was beneficial or even a moral imperative. They thus turned the Judeo-Christian prohibition against killing on its head.

The University of Chicago evolutionary biologist Jerry Coyne stridently denies that Darwinism leads to inhumane acts, such as the Columbine massacre, and I suspect he would agree with those scholars who deny that Nazi ideology had anything to do with Darwinism.[84] However, he admits that biological evolution undermines the importance and purpose of life, as well as morality. He exults in the way that evolution challenges people's religious faith, because it

> strikes them in the idea that they are specially created by God, because evolution says you are not. It says that there is no special purpose for your life, because it is a naturalistic philosophy. We have no more extrinsic purpose than a squirrel or an armadillo. And it says that morality does not come from God. It is an evolved phenomenon. And those are three things that are really hard for humans to accept, particularly who were brought up in a religious tradition.[85]

But in light of his philosophy that human life has no value, purpose, or meaning, it seems strange that Coyne does seem to care far more for the slain Columbine students than for the myriads of squirrels and armadillos being shot or run over every day. Why does he care that Columbine students got massacred? If all our actions are ultimately meaningless, then why is it more horrific for Eric Harris to gun down fellow students than for a coyote to devour a squirrel? Why does he feel a need to distance himself and his worldview from this particular action? Isn't it because he knows deep down that humans really are more valuable than animals and that humans really do have a purpose for their lives? Maybe he understands that morality is more than just a randomly evolved trait, and that love really is objectively superior to hatred, even though he stridently denies it.

In a response to a Ross Douthat column in the *New York Times* that critiqued secularism, Coyne complains that critics of secularism conflate a purposeless universe with a purposeless human life. He writes:

> Secularists see a universe without apparent purpose and real-ize that we must forge our own purposes and ethics, not derive them from a God for which there's no evidence.
>
> Yes, secularism does propose a physical and purposeless universe, and many (but not all) of us accept the notion that our sense of self is a neuronal illusion. But although the uni-verse is purposeless, our lives aren't. This conflation of a purposeless universe (i.e., one not created by a transcendent being for a specific reason) with purposeless human lives is a trick that the faithful use to make atheism seem dark and nihilistic. But we make our own purposes, and they're real. Right now my purpose is to write this piece, and then I'll work on a book I'm writing, and later I'll have dinner with a friend. Soon I'll go to Poland to visit more friends. Maybe later I'll read a nice book and learn something. Soon I'll be teaching biology to graduate students. Those are real pur-poses, not the illusory purposes to which Douthat wants us to devote our only life.[86]

I'm mystified as to why Coyne thinks this line of reasoning rescues atheism from seeming "dark and nihilistic." Coyne—or is it Coyne's "neuronal illusion"?—is the one who is playing sleight of hand in this instance. He uses the word "purpose" in two different ways (the techni-cal term for his mistake is the fallacy of equivocation). When people want to know if their lives have a purpose, they are not referring to self-invented, day-to-day purposes that we all have, such as the mundane purposes that Coyne enumerates. No one is disputing that we have such purposes. No one denies that "we make our own purposes" in this sense. People who are asking about human purpose want to know if there is any purpose outside ourselves, beyond our own creation. If not—as Coyne clearly thinks—then atheism is indeed "dark and nihilistic."

Far from rescuing atheism from its nihilistic implications, Coyne's philosophy is a powerful illustration of the problem. If, as Coyne claims, "we must forge our own purposes and ethics," there is a problem. Coyne seems to bite the bullet by claiming that morality is self-invented, in which case it would not be objective or universal. He acknowledges that altruism exists in the universe, but he states,

> As for where altruism comes from, who knows? My own suspicions are that it's partly genetic and partly cultural, but what's important is that we feel it and can justify it. I can justify it on several grounds, including that altruism makes for a more harmonious society, helps those in need, and, as a selfish motive, that being altruistic gains you more respect. None of this justification has anything to do with God.[87]

First, Coyne is betraying his own philosophy by feeling a need to justify altruism in the first place. This presupposes that altruism is objectively better than selfishness. Since Coyne rejects the idea that any objective morality exists, however, altruism has no claim to being superior to selfishness, so Coyne is assuming a point that contradicts his own worldview.

Also, Coyne's three justifications for altruism commit one of two fallacies; they are either circular or beg the question. Justifying altruism because it makes society harmonious and helps the needy assumes that a harmonious society and helping the needy are morally good. Coyne's worldview provides no reason to suppose that having harmony in society or helping the poor is objectively moral, because someone could just as easily choose—as multitudes of humans have throughout history—to fight their fellow humans or steal from the needy. If we truly "forge our own purposes and ethics," then Hitler's purposes and ethics are no better or worse than Mother Teresa's or Jerry Coyne's. As for the selfish motive of gaining more respect, multitudes of people have gained great respect from people, despite trouncing on the poor and committing atrocities. Mongols had the utmost respect for Genghis Khan. Perhaps altruism is another path to gaining respect, but why do we even care about the respect of our fellow humans? Might it be because we do indeed have a higher purpose for our lives than just working, dining, and travelling, as Coyne seems to think? Maybe loving our neighbor as ourselves is part of our purpose in life, so we respect people who live according to their God-given destiny.

Coyne is far from alone in making these kinds of arguments. Evolutionary biology has exerted a powerful influence in Western culture in convincing many people that humans are nothing more than sophisticated animals with no purpose or destiny. Many evolutionists have not only denied the specialness of humans, but they have whittled away at belief in morality and human rights. In the first century or so after Darwin published his theory, many evolutionists also stressed human inequality and devalued the lives of people with disabilities. Thus, scientists and physicians promoting an evolutionary worldview have been on the forefront of the eugenics and euthanasia movements. They not only brushed aside the Christian prohibition on murdering the weak and sick, but they claimed that such killing was morally praiseworthy, because it benefitted society and contributed to evolutionary progress.

The materialist philosopher Daniel Dennett exults in *Darwin's Dangerous Idea* (the title of his book), in which he rejoices that Darwinism has clobbered religion. While reassuring us that Darwin's dangerous idea will "put our most cherished visions of life on a new foundation," he actually strips away the foundation for valuing human life. Little wonder then that he argues "there are gradations of value in the ending of human lives," and implies that infanticide is acceptable for some disabled babies.[88] Darwin's idea certainly is dangerous, since many take it as encouragement to rid the world of the weak and helpless, the so-called "unfit." Since our society is being taught that we are simply animals with no objective morality to restrain us, why should we be surprised when hatred and violence rear their ugly heads?

THREE

My Genes Made
Me Do It
Biological Determinism

I n 1997 news broke about some shocking infanticides by teenage
mothers. In one notorious case a pregnant teenager went into
labor at her high school prom, delivered her baby in the bath-
room, threw the baby into the trash, and returned to the dance floor.
Many Americans wrung their hands, trying to make sense of this and
similar tragedies. The prominent evolutionary psychologist Stephen
Pinker, who was then at MIT but is now at Harvard, provided a supposedly scientific answer: Their genes made them do it. In an article in *The
New York Times Sunday Magazine* Pinker assured the American public
that infanticide was a hereditary behavior, part of women's "brain circuitry." He claimed that infanticide provided a reproductive advantage
for some women, at least for our ancient forebears. He recognized this
is counterintuitive, because "Even a biologist's cold calculations tell us
that nurturing an offspring that carries our genes is the whole point of
our existence." (Pinker, like so many other secular intellectuals we have

already discussed, apparently sees no ultimate purpose or meaning in life.)[1]

So how would killing your baby help you reproduce more prolifically? Like many other sociobiologists and evolutionary psychologists, Pinker believes that in primitive societies women had difficulty raising all their offspring to maturity, so they had to be selective. Instead of waiting for natural selection to take its course, they had to be proactive and kill those children whom they could not raise or whom they deemed inferior. According to Pinker, in such situations, "A new mother will first coolly assess the infant and her current situation and only in the next few days begin to see it as a unique and wonderful individual. Her love will gradually deepen in ensuing years, in a trajectory that tracks the increasing biological value of a child (the chance that it will live to produce grandchildren) as the child proceeds through the mine field of early development." Did Pinker actually interview new mothers who told him that they coolly assessed their newborn infants and their situation before deciding whether to kill them or not? Well, no. But it makes a good story, and Pinker has a convenient fallback position: our brain circuitry evolved long ago, so presumably our more primitive ancestors felt that way. Since we cannot interview them to find out, Pinker's speculations are thus unassailable. And unverifiable. They certainly do not correspond to my experience, because my wife and other new mothers I have known have been thrilled about their newborn babies and loved them even before they were born. In any case, Pinker's speculations are certainly not scientific. The cases of infanticide that spawned his article were clearly not cases of cool deliberation, but rather acts of frantic desperation. Pinker is misguided to think that infanticide is a genetic tendency that functions as a reproductive strategy.[2]

In his article Pinker dehumanizes newborns by refusing even to call them infants or babies. Rather they are merely "neonates," and killing them is not murder, but "neonaticide." Pinker claims that the reason we are so lenient on "neonaticide" is because we "are not completely sure whether a neonate is a full person." Apparently "we" means those who share with Pinker the theory that human lives are not intrinsically

valuable, but only have value in proportion to some particular characteristics they have. Even newborn infants do not have a right to life,
Pinker claims: "No, the right to life must come, the moral philosophers
say, from morally significant traits that we humans happen to possess,"
such as consciousness and rationality. "And there's the rub: our immature
neonates don't possess these traits any more than mice do." So "neonates" (a.k.a. newborn babies) are not "persons," any more than mice
are, apparently.[3]

Even after denying that newborn infants are "persons" with an
intrinsic right to life, Pinker does not suggest that we should legalize
infanticide, because "It seems obvious that we need a clear boundary to
confer personhood on a human being and grant it a right to life. Otherwise, we approach a slippery slope that ends in the disposal of inconvenient people or in grotesque deliberations on the value of individual
lives."[4] Too late, Professor Pinker. Anyone who thinks that we have the
prerogative to "confer personhood on a human being" (or not confer it)
and that we have the right to "grant it a right to life" (or not to grant it
a right to life), rather than recognizing the inalienable rights that all
human beings possess because they are humans, has already pushed us
over the edge of the slippery slope.

Pinker is a textbook example of the dehumanizing tendencies of
biological determinism, the view that human behavior is mostly hereditary. His book, *The Blank Slate: The Modern Denial of Human Nature*
(2002), declares war both on human free will and on environmental
determinism, the view that human behavior is shaped mostly by the
environment (upbringing, education, the social and economic system,
etc.). Despite Pinker's claim that his view leads to "a realistic, biologically
informed humanism," his view of the human mind and behavior is, in
my view, completely dehumanizing. He is committed to a reductionist
account of all human mental functions and behavior.[5]

So why do we think we are not machines? Why have most people
throughout history believed they had immaterial souls? Pinker replies that
this (allegedly false) intuition arose through evolutionary processes and
became biologically ingrained. "The belief that bodies are invested with

souls is not just a product of religious doctrine but embedded in people's psychology and likely to emerge whenever they have not digested the findings of biology." Pinker believes science has demolished the idea that humans have souls: "But science is showing that what we call the soul—the locus of sentience, reason, and will—consists of the information-processing activity of the brain, an organ governed by the laws of biology."[6] According to Pinker, then, even some of our thoughts and beliefs are biologically determined. How convenient. Explaining that other people's beliefs are simply illusions dictated by their genes (while presumably Pinker's own ideas swing free of biological determinism) is a condescending way to dismiss beliefs without providing arguments against them. To be sure, neither Pinker nor other biological determinists deny that the environment plays some role in human behavior. Nonetheless, many determinists tilt more toward one side or the other of the nature-nurture debate, and Pinker stresses nature.

The debate between nature and nurture is based on the false premise that humans have no free will. Those wanting to explain reality solely by science are forced to embrace some form of determinism, because only if human behavior is determined entirely by natural causes can science provide valid explanations for all human behavior. After all, free will would throw off scientific experiments. Thus many secular intellectuals believe human behavior is determined either by the environment, by heredity, or by some combination of the two. We must remind those who insist that determinism is scientific—as many determinists do—that determinism is on the contrary an assumption, a philosophical presupposition, not a conclusion reached through scientific experimentation. It is based on a worldview that denies a priori that humans have free will and moral responsibility, not on empirical data.

Determinism is more often than not a hidden assumption, guiding much of the current debate over human nature and human behavior. For instance, how many times have you heard intellectuals refer to the nature versus nurture debate? I am not denying that it can be helpful to examine the relative contributions of heredity (nature) and the environment (nurture) on human behavior. However, we do not need to accept the hidden deterministic assumption that nature and nurture are the only factors. Offering only these two alternatives—when others exist—constitutes a philosophical fallacy known as a false dichotomy. What if human behavior is not just the sum total of heredity and the environment?

Some biological determinists—such as Pinker—advance a brilliant argument against free will. Some of them argue that our belief in free will is itself simply a biologically ingrained concept. It is supposedly the product of random genetic mutations, just like the rest of our genetic makeup. Kim Wombles put it rather starkly in a 2011 article in the leading journal, *Science*: "Our very wiring, our neurobiology, makes it almost certain that most will reject the idea that they are not in control, that their identity can be reduced to a three pound pink jello-like substance that is an electrochemical soup."[7] To anyone opposing her views, Wombles could patronizingly proclaim: *Of course you don't believe me; your brain is hardwired to reject my position.* See how easy it is to dismiss belief in free will?

So what is the scientific evidence that our brain circuitry predisposes us to believe in free will? I have not seen any yet. Have scientists identified any genes or neurons that influence us to believe in free will? No. But tagging other people's beliefs as biologically hard-wired is so convenient and dismissive. After all, a belief that is based on nothing but the arrangement of the atoms and molecules in your brain has no rational foundation. But where did the belief that free will does not exist come from? From a chance combination of chemicals? Belief in determinism undermines itself, because the determinists' own belief in determinism would then be determined, so there would be no purely rational grounds to believe it. It has no more claim to be the objective truth than any other belief that determinism tries to dismiss (such as belief in free will). If determinism is true, the determinist has no rational grounds to believe in determinism, because the belief in determinism must be caused by material, non-rational, random events.

In any case, if nature and nurture were all there is behind human behavior, then science could—in principle at least—provide a full explanation for all human behaviors. If one wanted to explain why I am writing this book, a determinist would have to insist that some set of genetic factors together with environmental influences caused the neurons in my brain to fire in such a way that I produced this book. Handel's *Messiah*, da Vinci's *Mona Lisa*, Shakespeare's *Hamlet*, and Mother Teresa's charitable activities could all be explained as the product of material processes. Likewise Hitler's atrocities and all kinds of immoral behavior—including racist slurs, religious violence, rape—are determined by the sum total of biology plus environment. As many determinists freely admit, praising people for their altruistic behavior or blaming others for their immorality is misguided, because praise and blame implies people have the ability to decide otherwise. It only makes sense if people have free will. Apparently, neither Mother Teresa nor Hitler could have done otherwise. So there is no point congratulating those who sacrifice to help the poor, nor is there any reason to despise mass murderers of Jews.

This deterministic view that strips humans of all moral (and criminal) responsibility continues to gain ground among secular intellectuals. In 2006 Richard Dawkins lampooned the "unscientific" idea of free will by recounting a spoof by Basil Fawlty, a comical British television character who got frustrated when his car would not start. Instead of being rational and investigating the cause of the problem, Fawlty sternly warned the car. Naturally, it did not heed his warning, so he promptly began beating it with a tree branch. We laugh, because we know that he should have investigated the problem to figure out what part of the car was defective. The car was only obeying the laws of physics. However, Dawkins, since he is a materialist, then asks—seriously, it seems—why we treat humans differently from cars! (Maybe because we are not machines?) He asks, "Why do we not react in the same way to a defective man: a murderer, say, or a rapist? Why don't we laugh at a judge who punishes a criminal, just as heartily as we laugh at Basil Fawlty?... Isn't the murderer or the rapist just a machine with a defective component? Or a defective upbringing? Defective education? Defective genes?"

Dawkins also ought to ask: Why don't we laugh at materialist philoso-phers who take credit for authoring books and making scientific discov-eries (when the laws of physics did not allow them to do otherwise)? What would Dawkins think if his foes—those who consider his ideas mistaken—pronounced that Dawkins is "a machine with a defective component"?[8]

Also, why does Dawkins use the term "defective"? This word implies that somewhere there is a standard by which to measure human behav-ior, such as murder or rape. However, Dawkins's worldview does not have any moral resources to establish any standard or provide any valu-ations, so I am mystified about why he would call such behavior "defec-tive." Human behavior can only be defective if it is not fulfilling its purpose (for which it was created). Even though Dawkins strenuously and repeatedly denies that humans (or anything in the cosmos) have any purpose or meaning, he smuggles purpose back into his worldview to avoid the dehumanizing consequences of his philosophy. Fortunately, he rightly recognizes that murder and rape are contrary to the way things should be. However, his commitment to materialism drives him to deny that there is any "way things should be."

Of course, many people might laugh at Dawkins just as much as they would at Basil Fawlty. While Fawlty is hilarious because he tries treating a machine like a human, Dawkins errs in the opposite direction by ask-ing us to treat humans like machines. Yet this reversal, in reality, is not humorous, because Dawkins's philosophy has traction in Western thought and real people's lives are in the balance. People are not merely random conglomerations of particles controlled by their heredity and environment, as Dawkins thinks. Yes, they can make real moral choices.

Dawkins is not alone in the notion that biological determinism exonerates criminals of their guilt. In fact, an attorney overtly argued this in a courtroom. In one of the most sensational court cases in the early twentieth century the defense attorney Clarence Darrow defended Nathan Leopold and Richard Loeb, two pampered teenagers with rich parents who murdered a boy for the fun of it in 1924 in Chicago. In the closing arguments Darrow argued that both young men were not responsible for their crime, because they had defective heredity and a "diseased brain." Darrow asked,

> Is Dickey Loeb to blame because out of the infinite forces that conspired to form him, the infinite forces that were at work producing him ages before he was born, that because out of these infinite combinations he was born without [normal emotions]? If he is, then there should be a new definition for justice. Is he to blame for what he did not have and never had? Is he to blame that his machine is imperfect? Who is to blame? I do not know. I have never in my life been interested so much in fixing blame as I have in relieving people from blame. I am not wise enough to fix it. I know that somewhere in the past that entered into him something missed. It may be defective nerves. It may be a defective heart or liver. It may be defective endocrine glands. I know it is something. I know that nothing happens in this world without a cause.[9]

Darrow also blamed the boys' upbringing for contributing to their nefarious crime (which we'll discuss at length in chapter four), but he gave their biological makeup more weight. Against these forces the boys did not have a chance. Their act of murder was foreordained and inevitable, given their biology and upbringing. As Darrow phrased it, "They killed him because they were made that way." While Darrow's "philosophy" might be dismissed as the desperate pleas of a defense attorney, he evidently thought these ideas would resonate enough in American society that they might sway the punishment meted out to his clients. Ultimately Darrow's pleas did succeed in rescuing Leopold and Loeb from the death penalty, though Loeb was killed in prison.

Despite the fact that many people in Western societies recognize Dawkins's and Darrow's error and reject reductionism and determinism, it is difficult to overestimate the influence of determinism in Western thought and culture in the past two centuries. Determinism dominates whole fields of inquiry, such as psychology and sociology. To be sure, not every psychologist or sociologist is a dyed-in-the-wool determinist. However, even ones who might reject determinism often have to operate within a deterministic paradigm when publishing in their discipline. They might reject it personally, but professionally they are bound by it.

✻

In the wake of the 1953 discovery of DNA, the advent of sociobiology and evolutionary psychology in the 1970s and thereafter, and the more recent Human Genome Project, it has become fashionable to try to find the gene responsible for just about every imaginable human behavior, whether moral or immoral. Scientists have produced "explanations" (often speculative stories with little empirical support) for a wide variety of behaviors, sometimes even conflicting ones, such as adultery (but also monogamy and polygamy), infanticide (but also maternal and paternal love), rape (but also opposition to rape), nepotism, altruism, loyalty, and many other behaviors. They have searched for the gene for homosexuality, the gene for alcoholism, and even the gene for religion (without much success, it should be noted). However, biological determinism predates the Human Genome Project and even had a significant following before Mendelian genetics became known around 1900.

During the Enlightenment period, from the late seventeenth through the late eighteenth centuries, determinism emerged as a significant movement, especially among the so-called Radical Enlightenment figures, i.e., those rejecting deism in favor of atheism or agnosticism. In the mid-seventeenth century the Continental Rationalist philosopher Baruch Spinoza called himself a pantheist, but his vision of nature was fully deterministic, so his "God" did not have an independent will. Rather, Spinoza stated that "the universal laws of Nature are God's decrees," so God's will is synonymous with the ironclad, inviolable laws of nature. Humans, according to Spinoza, were just as much a part of nature as anything else, so free will is non-existent. Spinoza's deterministic view of human thought and behavior had a profound impact on the subsequent Radical Enlightenment.[10] Denis Diderot, for instance, embraced materialism and rejected free will, stating, "Look at the matter closely and you will see that the word 'liberty' is devoid of meaning. There are not, and cannot be, free beings."[11] This was indeed a radical idea in the century that saw the French Revolutionaries fight at the barricades for "liberty, equality, fraternity." It was nonetheless beginning to resonate in the eighteenth century, at least among some intellectuals.

While most Radical Enlightenment figures leaned toward environmental determinism, the most famous eighteenth-century materialist, La Mettrie, espoused biological determinism. In *Man the Machine* he argued that one's biological constitution or "organization" was more important in shaping character than education and training. He argued that there are "a thousand hereditary vices and virtues which are transmitted from parents to children." One example he provided was a child of a thief and cannibal who was orphaned as a one-year-old baby and raised by morally upright parents; at age twelve he followed in his biological father's steps.[12] La Mettrie not only believed that behavior is biologically ingrained, but he also thought that one's outward physical appearance reflected inner qualities. He claimed that "you can always distinguish the man of talent from the man of genius, and often even an honest man from a scoundrel."[13] Because of his biological determinism, La Mettrie stressed human inequality more than most of his contemporaries.[14]

La Mettrie approved of physiognomy, the attempt to read people's inner character from their facial features, which became a popular enterprise in Europe in the late eighteenth through the early twentieth centuries. Though today we might consider it kin to palm-reading, in the nineteenth century many intellectuals and scientists thought it was an objective scientific undertaking. Around the turn of the nineteenth century Franz Joseph Gall, a physician from Vienna, tried to improve on physiognomy. He insisted that the skull shape, not the face, was the key to discovering a person's inner qualities. Gall's technique of analyzing the bumps and features of the skull to determine one's intellectual and moral character became known as phrenology. Though Gall's position was controversial, he won many influential disciples among materialists and positivists, including Auguste Comte himself, who considered Gall one of his most important predecessors.[15] Not only were phrenology and physiognomy the subject of serious scholarly inquiry, but they also served as a popular parlor game among the educated elites in Europe, fostering biological determinism along the way.[16]

Despite the popularity of these parlor activities, during the first half of the nineteenth century in Europe, it was actually environmental not biological determinism that was more influential. In the late nineteenth century, however, biological determinism gained in prevalence and by the 1890s was a formidable intellectual current. Two of the most prominent figures peddling biological determinism in the mid-to-late nineteenth century were the British polymath Francis Galton, who is best known today for founding the eugenics movement, and the Italian psychiatrist Cesare Lombroso, who established the field of criminal anthropology.

Galton's first major work promoting biological determinism was *Hereditary Genius* (1869), which used genealogies to investigate the heredity of intellectual and moral traits. Scientists in Galton's day had no idea how hereditary traits passed from one generation to the next. Nonetheless, he discovered in the course of his genealogical studies that certain families seemed to have similar intellectual and moral traits. Prominent musicians tended to have more musically talented children, grandchildren, and great grandchildren. Professionals of all kinds tended to have offspring excelling in the same profession. Galton concluded that the intellectual and moral traits that allowed these men and women to succeed must be primarily hereditary.

Galton's ideas about eugenics first came to him while reading his cousin Darwin's book *Origin of Species*. His real passion was to improve humanity, to make people evolve to higher levels. This implies human inequality, and he rated some humans better and more valuable than others. Since he was a biological determinist, what better way to advance evolution than to "breed better humans"? Galton proposed that procreation should be regulated, so that talented individuals would be encouraged to reproduce more prolifically, while the inferior human specimens would be hindered from procreating. Galton was not too concerned about the rights of individuals, explaining, "If, however, we look around

at the course of nature, one authoritative fact becomes distinctly prominent.... It is, that the life of the individual is treated as of absolutely no
importance, while the race is treated as everything, Nature being wholly
careless of the former except as a contributor to the maintenance and
evolution of the latter."[17] Galton agreed that individuals are not so important, especially those he condescendingly dismissed as inferior. However,
he did hope he could improve on Nature's harsh methods.

Eugenics, Galton thought, should become a "new religion" that
would humanely improve humans biologically. He explained, "What
nature does blindly, slowly, and ruthlessly, man may do providently,
quickly and kindly." However, he ominously branded as enemies of the
state—his utopian state in which eugenics was law—any inferior people
who dared defy reason by procreating; he intoned that such people "have
forfeited all claims to kindness."[18] Since he considered some races decidedly inferior, such as the Africans he encountered in his explorations in
Namibia, he lamented that "there exists a sentiment, for the most part
quite unreasonable, against the gradual extinction of an inferior race."[19]
Galton's attitudes were a recipe for inhumanity.

Like earlier physiognomists, Galton hoped that he would be able to
discover a link between mental and physical traits. He developed a technique of composite photography—overlaying multiple photos to get an
"average" photo—to try to detect physical indicators of criminality. After
compiling composite photos of criminals in three different categories—
murder, forgery, and sexual crime—he initially reported that he had
detected differences in their physiognomy. Later, however, he admitted
that his experiment had failed.[20]

Lombroso, however, concentrated even more energy on discovering
physical traits to identify the "born criminal," a phrase encapsulating his
perspective. In his 1876 book, *Criminal Man*, Lombroso not only argued
that criminal behavior was hereditary, but he considered it an atavistic
trait, that is, an evolutionary throw-back to characteristics of more primitive ancestors. Because Lombroso believed that most criminals' moral
behavior was ape-like, he also thought their physical features would

exhibit simian characteristics. After his death in 1909 his autopsy showed that his brain was smaller than an average man of his height, leading some of his critics to wonder publicly if perhaps he was an example of evolutionary atavism. In 2009 Lombroso ignited controversy anew when his collection of skulls and other artifacts went on display in Turin at the Museum of Criminal Anthropology. Some Italians were outraged by this move to honor Lombroso, arguing that "Lombroso is the real criminal."[21]

Though Lombroso's claim that criminals are ape-like did not win the day, his biological determinism became the standard doctrine among psychiatrists in the late nineteenth and early twentieth centuries. By the first decade of the twentieth century, multitudes of psychiatrists, scientists, and physicians in Europe and the U.S. were convinced that human behavior was shaped mostly by one's biological makeup. Eugenics organizations and eugenics research institutes sprang up in various countries at this time, and in 1907 Indiana passed the first compulsory sterilization legislation in the world. Eugenics advocates popularized the notion that moral character is inborn, not based on human choices.

Many scientists and anthropologists around 1900 believed that different races had different innate mental and moral characteristics. Usually, of course, they portrayed Europeans as possessing such admirable moral traits as loyalty, diligence, honesty, and kindness, while so-called inferior races were deceitful, lazy, cowardly, and ruthless. Darwin advanced this idea in *Descent of Man*, in which he argued that humans evolved an innate sense of morality through natural selection. Darwin had already embraced biological determinism much earlier, stating in his 1838 notebooks, "Our descent, then, is the origin of our evil passions!!— The Devil under form of Baboon is our grandfather!"[22] In *Descent* he applied this perspective to races. Since he considered some human races closer to our ape-like ancestors, he depicted them as biologically more prone to immoral behavior. In one passage he expounded at length on the "immorality of savages," specifically rebutting those who thought that "savages" had high moral character.[23]

Darwin was by no means the first to disseminate the view that races differed in their biologically innate behavior. Just a few years before Darwin published *The Origin of Species*, a French aristocrat, Joseph Arthur Comte de Gobineau, published one of the most influential racist tracts of the nineteenth century: *Essay on the Inequality of Human Races* (1853–1855). He divided humanity into three main races: yellow, black, and white. He portrayed the yellow race as materialistic and lacking metaphysical thought. Because of this, they excel in commerce and thus correspond to the European bourgeoisie. The black race, he judged, has little intelligence but overdeveloped senses. Thus it is suited for manual labor and corresponded to the rabble. Finally, the white race embodies the virtues of nobility, freedom, honor, and spirituality—traits of the European aristocracy.[24] For Gobineau race was the key to understanding all historical developments. The white aristocratic race had dominated European society for centuries, but in the past couple of centuries it had declined, because it interbred with the other racial elements. Gobineau's ideas did not catch on very quickly, especially in France, but in the 1890s Ludwig Schemann established the Gobineau Society in Germany to promote biological racism.

Schemann, like many other racist theorists around the turn of the twentieth century, merged Gobineau with Darwinism and eugenics to concoct a potent brew of racist ideology that would have a profound impact on the twentieth century. Under the influence of Schemann and many other like-minded racist ideologues, the notion that races had different biologically innate mental and moral dispositions became widespread by the early twentieth century. This racial determinism came to dominate German anthropology by the 1910s and 1920s, but it exercised a profound influence elsewhere, too.

By the first decade of the twentieth century biological determinism was well-entrenched in Western thought and culture. The American Eugenics Society displayed exhibits at state and county fairs, proclaiming that "Some people are born to be a burden on the rest." The display distinguished between "high grade" people, which "America needs more of," and "defectives," which "America needs less of." The American Eugenics Society also sponsored "Fitter Family" competitions at fairs. While farmers and ranchers were showing off their best cattle, hogs, and sheep, why not also show off the best breed of people, too? These competitions were not only dehumanizing by putting humans on par with animals, but they also stressed human inequality and implied that some humans are more valuable than others, their value resting on their biological traits.

Thousands were forcibly sterilized in the U.S., Scandinavia, and elsewhere in the first half of the twentieth century as a result of eugenics legislation aimed at improving the human species, not only physically, but also mentally and morally. But nowhere was biological determinism more fanatically applied to society than under the Nazi regime, whose primary goal was to improve the biological characteristics of humans. The Nazis sterilized 350,000–400,000 people deemed inferior because of their cognitive or physical disabilities. German schoolchildren were taught using a poster in the biology classroom that nature eliminates the weak and sick. The Nazi regime was simply helping nature out by getting rid of the "unfit."

Hitler, like many scientists and physicians of his time, believed that moral character and behavior flowed from one's biological constitution. Certain races, especially the Jews, were allegedly innately immoral, manifesting a biological tendency toward greed, deceit, laziness, sexual promiscuity, and other disgusting behaviors. On the other hand, Hitler believed the Nordic or Aryan race had biological proclivities toward honesty, diligence, loyalty, and cooperation.[25] Because Hitler and his fellow Nazis believed that immorality was part of the Jews' biological fabric, he strenuously opposed their assimilation into German culture. This would only result in the Jews' "defective" hereditary traits corrupting German blood. Jews—and other "inferior races"—needed to be eliminated, one way or another. Eliminating these immoral biological types while encouraging the reproduction of the morally upright Nordic people would bring about an overall increase in morality. Thus Hitler

"Elimination of the Sick and Weak in Nature," a Nazi school poster that
was used to promote compulsory sterilization, but ominously featured
death to the weak. *Alfred Vogel,* Erblehre und Rassenkunde in bildlicher
Darstellung *(Stuttgart, 1938)*

and his minions believed they were making the world more moral by
committing some of the worst atrocities the world has ever known.[26]

It is important to understand that many elements of Nazi ideology—
biological determinism, racism, and eugenics—were not just the hare-
brained delusions of uneducated Nazi leaders and functionaries coming
from the fringes of society. Biological determinism, racism, and eugenics
were mainstream in German academe. Hitler and other Germans learned
these things from reputable German professors, and many scientists and
physicians cooperated with the Nazi regime once it came to power. German physicians were active participants in the Nazi atrocities, performing
sterilizations on people with disabilities, running the centers set up to kill
the disabled, conducting the "selections" and supervising the mass killing
at the death camps, and performing brutal experiments on camp inmates.

The unsavory connections between biological determinism and racism and eugenics—especially in their Nazi forms—together with the growing stress on environmental determinism in the fields of psychology and anthropology in the mid-twentieth century, led to a steep decline in biological determinism during the 1940s in Europe and the U.S.[27] The Civil Rights Movement in the U.S., the rise of the New Left, and the cultural shift in the 1960s also militated against biological determinism. However, it never disappeared. Konrad Lorenz, the Nobel Prize–winning biologist who founded the field of ethology (the study of animal behavior), continued pushing biological determinism in the mid-twentieth century. Lorenz grew up in Austria in a scientific milieu impregnated with biological determinism, which was reinforced once the Nazis annexed Austria in 1938. Lorenz found the Nazi views on biology and race harmonized with his own position. In 1940 he wrote an article in the leading German journal for biology teachers, which by that time was controlled by the SS. The primary theme of his article is that evolutionary theory is one of the best pillars supporting Nazi policies, since it corroborates the Nazi view that humans are unequal. Lorenz insisted that evolutionary theory destroys the illusions of religion and instead demonstrates the "complete unimportance of individual organisms in the great evolutionary events of nature." The Nazis were right, he thought, to elevate the race and nation above the "unimportant" individual.[28]

Lorenz is best known for his discoveries of instinctual behavior in animals. He believed that most human behavior is instinctual, too. In his 1966 book, *On Aggression*, he forthrightly applied insights from the animal world to humanity. He recognized that some people regard this an "insult to human dignity," but he remonstrated against them: "All too willingly man sees himself as the center of the universe, as something not belonging to the rest of nature but standing apart as a different and higher being. Many people cling to this error." Lorenz then explained that our human tendency to think of ourselves above the rest of nature is rooted in pride. He identified three obstacles to knowing ourselves as we really are:

Tafel 12.

Die Drohung des Untermenschen.

Es treffen auf:

Männliche Verbrecher: 4,9 Kinder   Eine kriminelle Ehe: 4,4 Kinder

Eltern von Hilfsschulkindern: 3,5 Kinder

Die deutsche Familie: 2,2 Kinder   Akademikerehe: 1,9 Kinder

"Threat of the Subhuman," a Nazi poster that promoted fear of the prolific reproduction of criminals and people with disabilities, who are
depicted as having more children than the average German family or German scholars. *Otto Helmut,* Volk in Gefahr *(1937)*

1. lack of awareness of our evolutionary origin
2. desire to believe in free will and "reluctance to accept the fact that our own behavior obeys the laws of natural causation"
3. setting up a false dichotomy between an external world devoid of values and an inner world of thought that alone has value

This was discussed in a chapter significantly titled "On the Virtue of Humility," in which Lorenz tried to take us humans down a peg by insisting that our human behavior and morality are mostly biological instincts that arose through an evolutionary process. However, Lorenz was conflicted. Just a few pages later in the same chapter he incongruously argued that the evolutionary process has produced animals with greater organization and these organisms have greater value than more primitive ones. He stated, "That the origin of a higher form of life from a simpler ancestor means an increase in value is a reality as undeniable as that of our own existence." He then affirmed that we humans are indeed "the highest achievement reached so far" by the evolutionary process, though he hoped we would be superseded in the future by a yet higher species. Lorenz did not provide any cogent reasons for believing that we have more value than other species, other than to insist that we know it to be true. I agree that we know it, but I suggest that this should give us a reason to question Lorenz's entire worldview, which is inconsistent with this insight.[29]

Another point of tension in Lorenz's worldview is his view of human morality. On the one hand, he explained morality as mostly instinctual and certainly causally determined. On the other hand, he still clung to morality that rises above our natural condition. In the closing paragraph of *On Aggression*, Lorenz called on his fellow humans to love one another, to set aside the instinctual aggression that was no longer beneficial to the species. He claimed that the "bond of personal love and friendship" that had evolved among humans was too limited to encompass all that it should: it prevents aggression only between those who know each other and are friends, while obviously it is all active hostility between all men of all nations or ideologies that must be stopped. The obvious conclusion is that love and friendship should embrace all humanity, that we should love all our human brothers indiscriminately. This commandment is not new. Our reason is quite able to understand its necessity as our feeling is able to appreciate its beauty, but nevertheless, made as we are, we are unable to obey it.[30]

I am happy that Lorenz enjoined us to love one another, as this is indeed one of the highest moral laws. However, where did Lorenz get this imperative? It simply does not fit into his own worldview, so it seems he is importing Christian morality to soften the harshness of his own position. If the evolutionary process has provided us with one set of moral precepts, who is he to say that we should jettison it for another, allegedly superior morality?

Interestingly, Lorenz did not always embrace this universalist view that we should love all humanity. In the 1940 essay I mentioned above, Lorenz claimed that evolution taught the same moral precept as Christianity: love your neighbor as yourself, but he did not think "neighbor" included all humanity: "Since for us the race or Volk [meaning people as an ethnic or racial identity] is everything and the individual is as good as nothing, this command [love your neighbor] is for us a self-evident requirement."[31] At this time, while living under a regime that was already persecuting other races, especially Jews, Lorenz called his fellow Germans to submerge their individual interests to love one another. However, "one another" only included those of one's own race. Thankfully, Lorenz later universalized the love command, even though his worldview did not seem to provide him with any resources to make that move. So again, it seems that he simply appropriated Christian morality without providing any foundation for it.

Lorenz's stress on biological determinism was not widely shared in the 1950s and 1960s, but biological determinism made a sustained comeback beginning in the 1970s, when Harvard biologist E. O. Wilson founded sociobiology. Wilson, an entomologist specializing in ants, studies their instinctual social behavior. In his seminal work, *Sociobiology: The New Synthesis* (1975), Wilson explains, "Sociobiology is defined as the systematic study of the biological basis of all social behavior." He argues that all animal behavior, including that of humans, is controlled by material processes in the brain that evolved through natural selection. He also admonishes scholars to recast ethics on the basis of biological knowledge.[32] After all, as he states in a co-authored article in 1985, "Ethics as we understand it is an illusion fobbed off on us by our genes to get us to co-operate."[33] However, Wilson does not think ethics would ever be completely adequate until biological knowledge advanced to the point that it could provide a complete materialistic explanation of human behavior.[34]

Wilson does not have a very high view of humanity. In *Sociobiology* he stated that "in evolutionary time the individual organism counts for almost nothing." The only significance of an individual organism is to reproduce: "the organism is only DNA's way of making more DNA."[35] Though he was discussing organisms in general here, he always included humans in his analysis (the final chapter in *Sociobiology* was on humans). Three years later he applied sociobiology to humans in a book-length treatise, *On Human Nature*. He argued that despite many variations in human behavior, "Human behavior... is the circuitous technique by which human genetic material has been and will be kept intact. Morality has no other demonstrable ultimate function."[36] At the beginning of his memoirs he explains how his worldview shapes his view of humanity:

When the century began, people could still easily think of themselves as transcendent beings, dark angels confined to Earth awaiting redemption by either soul or intellect. Now most or all of the relevant evidence from science points in the opposite direction: that, having been born into the natural

world and evolved there step by step across millions of years,
we are bound to the rest of life in our ecology, our physiology,
and even our spirit.[37]

Elsewhere he stated that his empirical, scientific worldview "has
destroyed the giddying theory that we are special beings placed by a deity
in the center of the universe in order to serve as the summit of Creation
for the glory of the gods."[38]

Wilson believes that everything about humans—behavior, morality,
and even religion—is ultimately explicable as the result of completely
material processes. Even our most deeply held beliefs are simply products
of mindless evolutionary processes inscribed on our gray matter: "Perhaps, as I believe, it [religion] can all eventually be explained as brain
circuitry and deep, genetic history."[39] Wilson admits that he is a reductionist, and he exudes optimism that scientists will someday explain
everything about human behavior. In *Consilience* (1998), which is a plea
to bring the social and human sciences completely under the sway of
natural science, he asks, "Given that human action comprises events of
physical causation, why should the social sciences and humanities be
impervious to consilience with the natural sciences?" Wilson claims that
ultimately every phenomenon in the cosmos can be reduced to physical
laws, so the human mind is simply physical brain activity, and humans
have no free will.[40]

In 2009, on the bicentennial of Darwin's birthday and the sesquicen-
tennial of Darwin's *Origin of Species*, Wilson pronounced Darwin's
Origin of Species the most important book ever written, because for the
first time it provided us an understanding of humanity based on science
rather than religion. Darwin's theory, according to Wilson, forms "the
best foundation for human self-understanding and the philosophical guide
for human action." Wilson thus believes that what science tells us about
reality can provide moral guidance, showing that he has little regard for
the is-ought divide. Further, he argues that all organic processes—and
here he clearly includes human behavior—are ultimately reducible to the
laws of physics and chemistry. For Wilson evolution has clearly replaced

religion as the source of answers about the purpose and destiny of life. He asserted, "The great questions—'Who are we?' 'Where did we come from?' and 'Why are we here?'—can be answered only, if ever, in the light of scientifically based evolutionary thought." What Wilson does not explain is why these questions have any importance if we are nothing more than the result of mindless material processes.[41]

This problem also permeates Wilson's most recent book, *The Meaning of Human Existence* (2014). Therein Wilson explains that there is no ultimate meaning or purpose in life. Rather, he asserts, the only meaning we have is that we are the product of mindless evolutionary processes. He states,

> We were created not by a supernatural intelligence but by chance and necessity as one species out of millions of species in Earth's biosphere. Hope and wish for otherwise as we will, there is no evidence of an external grace shining down upon us, no demonstrable destiny or purpose assigned us, no second life vouchsafed us for the end of the present one. We are, it seems, completely alone. And that in my opinion is a very good thing. It means we are completely free.[42]

Free to do what? Interestingly, Wilson explains that this freedom gives us options that "empower us to address with more confidence the greatest goal of all time, the unity of the human race."[43]

But why should this human unity be our goal? Wilson explains that everything that makes us human, including morality and religion, is the product of chance mutations and natural selection. He explains that both selfishness and altruism arose through natural selection, because each, in its own way, contributed to human survival and reproduction. He also argues that religion is a trait produced by the evolutionary process. Thus he understands both religion and morality as illusions in the human mind that helped us in earlier phases of evolutionary history. But in modern society, he argues, religion is no longer beneficial, but harmful, so we should dispense with it altogether and face up to the reality that religion is a pernicious fiction. However, while encouraging us to bravely face our loneliness in the cosmos, Wilson is unwilling to jettison his own illusion that he admits was put on him by his evolutionary past: morality. I heartily agree with Wilson's moral desire to forge the "unity of the human race," but given his own worldview, I do not understand why Wilson thinks that he should fight for one illusory product of his evolutionary heritage—morality—at the expense of the other—selfishness. In the end, Wilson is—if his worldview is correct—just as much living a lie as those religionists that he castigates.[44]

In the 1970s when Wilson was creating a splash with his ideas about sociobiology, the evolutionary biologist and atheist Richard Dawkins was also doing his part for biological determinism. In *The Selfish Gene* (1976) Dawkins proclaims, "We are survival machines—robot vehicles blindly programmed to preserve the selfish molecules known as genes." This means that organisms are only DNA's way of making more copies of itself. Dawkins believes that genes code for many behaviors, some very complex, which aid the organism in its quest for replicating its DNA. He states, "By dictating the way survival machines [i.e., organisms] and their nervous systems are built, genes exert ultimate power over behavior." Because individual organisms are competing to replicate their genes as prolifically as possible, Dawkins portrays all behavior as aiming ultimately at reproduction.[45]

Dawkins depicts relationships among organisms, including family relationships, as inherently competitive. He discusses the inherent tensions between siblings, mates, and parents and children, who, he believes, are competing with each other to reproduce as much as possible. He calls mating "a relationship of mutual mistrust and mutual exploitation," because "[e]ach partner can therefore be thought of as trying to exploit the other, trying to force the other one to invest more" in raising the children. If this is applied to humans (and Dawkins makes clear that all these principles do apply to humans), it implies that a husband's and wife's love toward each other is merely a genetically-induced strategy that has worked in the past to reproduce genes. This implication flies in the face of our personal experience, and I sincerely doubt that Dawkins thinks of his own wife in these terms.[46]

In a similar vein, I'm sure Dawkins holds his mother in higher regard than his philosophy implies. When discussing whether mothers ever play favorites with any of their children, Dawkins intones starkly, "I am treating a mother as a machine programmed to do everything in its power to propagate copies of the genes which ride inside it." I hope Dawkins's mother did not read this, because she would have been rightly insulted to be depicted as a "gene machine," whose maternal love is nothing more than a ploy—an act of manipulation—by her "selfish genes" to replicate themselves. Following his own gene machine logic, however, Dawkins argues that of course a mother can play favorites, because some of her children may not be as hardy as others. The mother, Dawkins claims, is well-advised to abandon a "runt," because it has less chance of reproducing. In a bizarre twist, Dawkins also argues that the runt "should die gracefully and willingly," and should "preferably let himself be eaten by his litter-mates or his parents," because this will help his kin to reproduce (and they carry some of his genes).[47]

Dawkins's book, however, is not entirely a sustained argument for selfishness, despite its title and passages like this: "I shall argue that a predominant quality to be expected in a successful gene is a ruthless selfishness. This gene selfishness will usually give rise to selfishness in individual behavior.... Much as we might wish to believe otherwise, universal love and the welfare of the species as a whole are concepts which simply do not make evolutionary sense." Filling his book with myriads of examples illustrating the biological basis of behavior, and insisting that this applies to humans just as to other animals, Dawkins nonetheless recoils. He cautions his readers in the introduction and conclusion that his selfish gene idea does not mean that we have to obey our biological impulses. He closes the book with the momentous words, "We, alone on earth, can rebel against the tyranny of the selfish replicators." Humans are unique, after all, Dawkins admits, because they are the only organism that can resist the genetic imperative to reproduce.[48]

Is Dawkins inconsistent by maintaining that humans can somehow rise above nature and take mastery over their genes? Perhaps not, but let's examine this a little closer. Dawkins defends himself against this charge in *A Devil's Chaplain* (2004), in which he explains that human reason has given us the ability to resist the selfishness inherent in the evolutionary process. He reminds us that a medical scientist could provide a scientific explanation for cancer and then fight against cancer. So why can't an evolutionary scientist explain the evolutionary process and then oppose it? He then states, "For good Darwinian reasons, evolution gave us a brain whose size increased to the point where it became capable of understanding its own provenance, of deploring the moral implications and of fighting against them." He then concludes that only we humans have the "gift of understanding the ruthlessly cruel process that gave us all existence; the gift of revulsion against its implications."[49]

While Dawkins might be right that there is nothing inherently contradictory in his opposition to the evolutionary process, he has provided no foundation for his position either. He imports "moral implications" from some undisclosed location outside his own worldview to justify his personal struggle against the struggle for existence. He pillories the natural process that "gave us all existence" as "ruthlessly cruel," without explaining why the word "cruel" has any meaning in an amoral, atheistic worldview. Cruel implies a moral judgment, and if that moral judgment is simply the result of evolutionary processes, then how can the evolutionary process itself be "cruel"? Why shouldn't we be exulting in natural selection and trying to sharpen competition, so that we can evolve to even higher levels (as Darwin and other social Darwinists in the late nineteenth century suggested)?

Thankfully Dawkins is contemptuous of such social Darwinism with its dog-eat-dog ethos. Rather he wants "to build a society in which individuals cooperate generously and unselfishly towards a common good." He admonishes us to "try to *teach* generosity and altruism, because we are born selfish,"[50] which is commendable, but where did Dawkins get the idea that cooperation, unselfishness, and generosity are morally superior to selfishness and cutthroat competition? Why does he favor the welfare state helping the poor and disadvantaged, rather than letting them starve? He admits that these moral precepts do not come from nature. Where, then, did he get these extra-natural (dare I say, super-natural?) moral standards that he encourages us to uphold and teach? They certainly did not arise from his own worldview, which denies the existence of any extra-natural morality.

The troubling implications of biological determinism and reduction-ism come into sharp focus when we examine the worldview of James Watson, one of the most famous biologists of the late twentieth century. Watson was co-discoverer of the helix model of DNA, a line of research that appealed to him because he wanted to discover the chemical basis for life. When he was at Harvard in the 1950s he joined a faction of the biology faculty that wanted to direct all biological research toward bio-chemistry. Later he became the first head of the Human Genome Project, which successfully sequenced all the DNA of the human genome.

Watson's genetic determinism has aroused considerable controversy, especially because he has applied it in ways that are politically incorrect. He aroused a firestorm of protest in 2007 when he said that he was pes-simistic about the future prospects for Africa, because he doubts that black Africans are as intelligent (on the average) as Europeans. He explained that "there is no firm reason to anticipate that the intellectual capacities of peoples geographically separated in their evolution should prove to have evolved identically," so people of different races are likely to be unequal in mental ability.[51] Watson also applies his inegalitarian philosophy to people with disabilities and to those with less mental acu-ity than the majority. In a PBS special on DNA, Watson vigorously promotes a new eugenics to deal with the problem of what he calls the "unfit." He suggests that we should use abortion to eliminate disabled people from society.[52] Earlier, in 1973, he had even suggested that babies should not be declared alive until they were three days old, so the parents could decide if they wanted to keep the child or kill it.[53]

By the 1990s sociobiology had penetrated many disciplines and spawned the burgeoning new field of evolutionary psychology. Many scientists and scholars in the past couple decades have tried to explain nearly every human behavior imaginable as a hard-wired biological trait inherited from our ancestors. Biologist Randy Thornhill and anthropologist Craig Palmer stirred up a hornet's nest in 2000 when they published a book with MIT Press arguing that rape is a behavior biologically ingrained in human males through natural selection. According to this line of reasoning, men rape women because it gives them a reproductive advantage—either directly or indirectly. As they explained in the opening pages of A Natural History of Rape, their argument rests on the "understanding of the ultimate (that is, evolutionary) causes of why humans are the way they are." They insist that their project would help us find ways to oppose rape. However, if people's "desires, emotions, and values" are ultimately caused by the mindless process of evolution, as Thornhill and Palmer seem to think, then what could be wrong with rape? Evolution has selected for it, it is part of our biology, so why should we resist it? Thornhill and Palmer can reply that we also have a contrary biological urge, which is to protect our spouse from other males. This is what makes us oppose rape—but only if someone else is doing it.[54] Given their reductionist view of humanity, it is hard to see how they could uphold any objective morality, including prohibitions against rape.

Indeed, in an interview Richard Dawkins once admitted that opposition to rape is arbitrary, meaning that rape is not objectively wrong. When he was asked about the immorality of rape, at first he did not want to answer, but merely stated that rape is not okay in our society. However, he ultimately admitted that his view that rape is immoral is itself only a chance product of natural processes. The interviewer Justin Brierley summed up what he saw as the implications of Dawkins's view of morality, stating, "OK, but ultimately, your belief that rape is wrong is as arbitrary as the fact that we've evolved five fingers rather than six.

Dawkins replied, "You could say that, yes."[55] So, if the view that rape is immoral is a biological trait selected for by evolution, and the propensity to rape is a biological trait also selected for, how can we arbitrate between the two urges? Neither has claim to any objective superiority over the other. Whatever gets you more offspring wins the future, no matter what we regard today as moral. Power—i.e., whatever it takes to win the struggle for existence—determines behavior and morality.

Some sociobiologists and evolutionary psychologists have even interpreted religion as a biologically-based behavior that has evolved because it helps us survive and reproduce better. A few geneticists have even tried to discover a "God gene," a strand of DNA that makes some people religious. Of course, they seem to forget that in the not-so-distant past the vast majority of people were religious, so if it existed, why wouldn't everyone have this gene? Also, if religion is genetic, why do so few children raised by atheists remain committed to atheism (some statistics indicate that only 30 percent of children raised as atheists remain atheists as adults)? An appreciation for historical developments and context could do much to prevent scientists from jumping to conclusions.

For instance, history is not the strong suit of evolutionary biologist David Sloan Wilson, who, despite his own lack of religious faith, argues that religion provides an evolutionary advantage. When he comes to specific historical explanations, however, problems mount. As a typical example, he claims that Calvinism triumphed in sixteenth-century Switzerland and elsewhere because it provided group cohesion, which in turn gave its adherents a selective advantage. However, when one examines the details of this transformation, the argument breaks down, because all the elements that Wilson thinks are important for giving the Calvinists group cohesion were already present in Catholicism. Also, Catholicism remained dominant in many parts of Europe. His "explanation" simply does not explain the relevant historical events.[56]

Even more problematic are the views of the evolutionary psychologist Kevin MacDonald, who claims that both Judaism and anti-Semitism are evolutionary strategies for group cohesion. MacDonald slyly remarks at the beginning of *Separation and Its Discontents: Toward an Evolutionary*

Theory of Anti-Semitism, that "the charge that this is an anti-Semitic book is…expectable and completely in keeping with the thesis of this essay."[57] In other words, if you charge me (MacDonald) with anti-Semitism for the positions I take in this book, then you are only corroborating my thesis. Heads I win, tails you lose. According to MacDonald, even anti-Semitism is in "our" genes. Again, this explanation runs aground when one examines the history of anti-Semitism. In the course of one or two generations after World War II, most Germans have turned against anti-Semitism. Is it really plausible to think that they experienced radical genetic change in this short period of time?

Sociobiology and biological determinism found a ready audience far beyond the guild of professional biologists. *Time* magazine ran a cover story on sociobiology in August 1977, and E. O. Wilson won two Pulitzer Prizes for his writing. Though sociobiology spawned considerable controversy and opposition, it also gained many adherents. Popular culture has become infected with biological explanations for human behavior. In August 1994 biological determinism was splashed on the cover of *Time* magazine, which proclaimed rather sensationally, "Infidelity: It May Be in Our Genes." The science writer Robert Wright wrote the accompanying article, which was one of many he wrote popularizing evolutionary psychology. Wright's story explained that scientists now understand why humans—especially males—commit adultery: it is hardwired into our genes. Our male ancestors who committed adultery bequeathed more genes to the next generation, and guess what? Those genes carried instructions that predisposed them to follow the adulterous behavior of their fathers and grandfathers. The lesson here seems to be: adultery is not a sinful action that people choose; rather it is a biological predisposition that helps the adulterer's "selfish genes" to multiply. Adultery is a way to win the struggle for existence against other rivals. Don't blame men and women for committing adultery; they cannot help themselves.[58] In contrast to the male "mating strategy" of marital infidelity and perhaps even polygamy, many sociobiologists argue natural selection has determined women's best "mating strategy" is to select males who will remain faithful and help provide for their children. Women thus favor monogamy and select males who are more monogamous. Other sociobiologists argue that we humans are not genetically hard-wired for monogamy at all because the lifespan of our ancestors was so brief that most marriages did not last very long. The Oxford University philosopher Julian Savulescu has recently echoed this position. He claims that the present average length of marriage and the high divorce rate is a biological tendency inherited from our ancient short-lived forebears. Aside from the fact that no gene has been identified that causes humans to divorce each other, this argument completely ignores major historical developments, such as the fact that monogamous marriages and much lower divorce rates have characterized many societies throughout history. The average length of marriage was much higher in the United States and Europe before the Sexual Revolution of the 1960s altered sexual mores.

As I have already demonstrated in my discussion of Pinker, some sociobiologists and evolutionary psychologists have even brought infanticide and abortion under their microscope. Despite their pretensions to scientific objectivity, their biological explanations for why people kill their babies often result in normalizing such behavior. The anthropologist Sarah Blaffer Hrdy pioneered infanticide studies, when she controversially suggested that langur monkeys committed infanticide. Since then, she has become the leading figure arguing that infanticide is hard-wired in primate and human brains. In 1984 she co-edited a book called *Infanticide: Comparative and Evolutionary Perspectives*, which uses sociobiology to explain infanticide. In the introduction she and her co-author argue that infanticidal behavior in primates and humans arose through natural selection and is hereditary.[59] Other authors in that volume reinforce this point.[60]

In most of her writings, Hrdy does not directly promote or condone infanticide. However, she argues forcefully that it is a normal part of human behavior that provides reproductive advantage. Far from being pathological or irrational, as most people think, it makes sense in the Darwinian struggle for existence, where survival and reproduction determine biological traits, including behavioral ones. In her 1999 book,

Mother Nature: A History of Mothers, Infants, and Natural Selection, however, Hrdy does seem to condone infanticide. After arguing that infanticide is one element of a mother's strategy to control her reproduction, she states, "These consistencies [in mothers' behaviors throughout history] remind us that we descend from creatures for whom the timing of reproduction has always made an enormous difference, and that the physiological and motivational underpinnings of a quintessentially 'pro-choice' mammal are not new."[61] Thus, Hrdy's implicit "normalization" of infanticide in her earlier works becomes more manifest, as she explicitly dubs humans (and their ancestors) "quintessentially 'pro-choice.'" Hrdy's biological explanation for infanticide has become rather commonplace among biologists and anthropologists in the past two decades.

In *Moral Minds: How Nature Designed Our Universal Sense of Right and Wrong* (2006) the evolutionary psychologist Marc Hauser, formerly of Harvard University (but forced to resign in disgrace because of research malfeasance), also promotes Hrdy's position, declaring, "Some animals, in some conditions, are no different than some humans in some conditions: infanticide, siblicide [i.e., killing one's siblings], and even suicide are all options, supported by none other than Mother Nature."[62] Not only does Hauser equate humans with animals here, but he tells us that murder is in our genes. Hauser's main argument in this book is that humans have a moral instinct that "was designed by the blind hand of Darwinian selection."[63] In the evolutionary process, reproductive success determines biological traits, including behaviors. Hauser confesses that his own moral sensibilities (which he considers instinctual) favor euthanasia, and later in the book he provides an evolutionary argument for it:

Do people ever have the moral obligation to die, to cause themselves harm, in effect? Though it may be hard to see how natural selection could ever result in a suicide instinct, further reflection suggests that this sacrifice might pay off in the service of preserving valuable resources for kin. Self-sacrifice may have been selected in certain circumstances. Such selection may, in turn, have generated a psychology of moral obligation. Once we open the door to such moral maneuvers for euthanasia, admittedly abhorrent to many, parallel issues arise for abortion and infanticide, and for notions of harming others more generally.[64]

Hauser then argues that natural selection not only can make suicide and infanticide intelligible and even rational, but can generate moral obligations to kill ourselves or others.

❊

Even if scientists can show—through studying twins, for instance—that some behaviors are more frequent among those with genetic similarities, they are still far from demonstrating that hereditary influence is so powerful that someone simply has no choice but to become an alcoholic or rapist or adulterer (or a kindly saint). I accept without hesitation the notion that some hormones could influence behavior. For instance, testosterone does seem to have an influence on aggression. Does this mean that after an outburst of temper I can excuse and justify my bad behavior by shifting the blame to testosterone levels? By no means. On the contrary, a person with anger problems should struggle all the more against his or her biological tendencies. We need to urge people to control their biological passions, rather than teaching them that they cannot help themselves.

Another point worth mentioning is that behavior also influences one's physiology and hormone levels, so there is not a one-way street from biology to behavior. It is of course true that some people face powerful temptations to indulge in some kinds of immoral behavior, and sometimes there are physiological causes behind these urges. However, by controlling what we see and hear, we can alter ourselves. For instance, those who consume a diet of sexual smut are activating hormones that lead to greater sexual temptation. If one wants to control one's sexual behavior, then, one needs to control one's eyes and mind. Our behavioral choices can control our biological dispositions and tendencies to some extent. We are not simply captive to every carnal urge.

Another problem with biological determinism is that scientists do not have a clue if there really is a strand of DNA (or some combination of strands) that codes for alcoholism, rape, adultery, or xenophobia. Despite all the hype over the "gay gene," scientists have never identified any clear links between specific genes and most behaviors, including homosexuality. In other words, much of the biological determinism in human sociobiology and evolutionary psychology is speculative, based on "just-so stories" that have little or no empirical support. Some scientists might retort: give us time and we will find the genetic causes of behavior. My response is this: Since when is scientific knowledge based on discoveries of the future? This seems an odd way to do science. Would you accept payment from someone with a check handed to you that that was post-dated ten (or twenty or thirty) years in the future? Neither would I. Why then should anyone believe a scientific theory based on discoveries in the future that may or may not pan out?

I do not doubt that our biology influences our behavior, but this does not mean that we are slaves to our physical body and its desires. Biological determinism, however, wrongly preaches that heredity is a destiny that we cannot rise above. This vision of humanity is built on a materialistic worldview that denies free will and human responsibility. It presupposes that humans have no independent moral agency and cannot conquer their biological urges. Thus it demotes humanity to the level of animals who have no choice but to obey their instincts or even reduces us to machines that simply do what we are programmed to do. Biological determinism has thus contributed to the devaluing of human life that pervades our culture, especially in intellectual circles.

FOUR

My Upbringing Made Me Do It

Environmental Determinism

As we mentioned in chapter three, one of the most shocking and highly publicized crimes of the early twentieth century was the premeditated murder of a fourteen-year-old boy in 1924 in Chicago by Nathan Leopold and Richard Loeb. The two young men pleaded guilty, and their famous attorney, Clarence Darrow (who later appeared in the sensational Scopes Trial), pulled out all the stops to keep them from being executed for their horrific crime. These two intellectually brilliant teenagers with wealthy parents seemed to have a very auspicious future—Leopold had been accepted to Harvard Law School, and Loeb was the youngest graduate ever from the University of Michigan. As far as anyone could figure out, Leopold and Loeb had no other motive than the thrill of trying to perpetrate a perfect crime. Their rosy future abruptly unraveled because their intellectual brilliance deceived them (a not uncommon occurrence, as we demonstrate throughout this work). Their belief that they could perpetrate the "perfect crime" was obviously unfounded, because they were caught. The cold-blooded, shocking nature of the crime, together with the social and educational level of the murderers, fascinated the public, for whom the murder seemed inexplicable. Why had they done such a despicable deed?

Since the prosecution (and the public) was clamoring for the death penalty, Darrow had to explain what motivated his clients, and the explanation had to mitigate their personal responsibility. Inspired by secular ideologies gaining currency in psychology and the social sciences in his day, Darrow insisted that the "old view" that humans commit crimes "willfully, purposely, maliciously and with a malignant heart" is as outmoded as the notion of demon possession. He then explained the "new" scientific way of viewing moral responsibility:

Science has been at work, humanity has been at work, scholarship has been at work, and intelligent people now know that every human being is the product of the endless heredity back of him and the infinite environment around him.[1]

Darrow repeatedly insisted that Leopold and Loeb—like all humans—are completely helpless before the forces of nature. Their behavior is shaped entirely by natural causes, either through heredity or through environmental influences. On this basis Darrow argued that his clients should not be executed. If they were merely the product of their biology and environment, then why blame them? They had no choice.

In his closing arguments, Darrow used the term "diseased" over twenty times to describe his clients' minds or brains. In addition to blaming their "diseased brains" and thus their biological makeup, he also explained the culpability of their upbringing. Loeb, he explained, had an overly strict governess and read too many crime novels. Leopold read Nietzsche and as a result fancied himself a Nietzschean superman. How can society condemn these two boys for their behavior, when they had no control over their upbringing? Darrow argued, "I know that every influence, conscious and unconscious, acts and reacts on every living organism, and that no one can fix the blame." Their crime, according to

Darrow, simply flowed from the working of nature. It was natural cause
and effect, Darrow explained: "Their parents happened to meet, these
boys happened to meet; some sort of chemical alchemy operated so that
they cared for each other, and poor Bobby Franks's dead body was found
in the culvert as a result." He further claimed, "Nature is strong and she
is pitiless. She works in her own mysterious way, and we are her victims.
We have not much to do with it ourselves. Nature takes this job in hand,
and we play our parts." According to Darrow, anyone who thought these
young men should be held responsible for their actions was backward
and unenlightened. He stated, "And yet there are men who seriously say
that for what Nature has done, for what life has done, for what training
has done, you should hang these boys."[2]

As Darrow correctly suggested, those who reject free will and moral
responsibility as outmoded ideas of a backward, unscientific age have
three alternatives: biological determinism (my genes made me do it),
environmental determinism (my upbringing made me do it), or some
combination of these two. Some secularists recognize the dehumanizing
character of biological determinism, especially in light of its unsavory
associations with racism and sexism, not to mention Nazism. They mis-
takenly suppose that environmental determinism is friendlier and more
humane, so they take sides with nurture in the nature-nurture debate.
As victims of Stalin, Mao, or Pol Pot can attest, however, belief in environmental determinism is no guarantee of kinder treatment and is no
more immune to atrocities than belief in biological determinism. Of
course, just as biological determinism does not lead inevitably to the
Holocaust, neither does environmental determinism always lead to communist atrocities. On the contrary, many non-Marxist proponents of
environmental determinism promise that their views will lead to a blissful democratic utopia (but remember that Marxists promised this, too).

Unfortunately the reverse it true, because environmental determinism
undermines the dignity and value of human life. Humans become passive
cogs in nature without any creative power or free will to extricate themselves from the predetermined chain of natural causation. In this view,
freedom and dignity are fictions that hinder humans from reconstructing

society and achieving universal bliss. The behaviorist psychologist B. F. Skinner, for instance, insisted that those believing in free will and human dignity are not only misguided, but are dooming humanity to a miserable existence of war, poverty, greed, and ultimately destruction. What Skinner and other environmental determinists do not seem to understand is that stripping humans of their dignity and value paves the way for those willing to ride roughshod over humane considerations. Rather than saving us from misery, as most proponents of environmental determinism clearly hope, it results in further degradation.

The Enlightenment was a pivotal intellectual event in the rise of environmental determinism, as it was for materialism and biological determinism. John Locke's empiricist philosophy in the seventeenth century spawned associationist psychology, the view that all human ideas and human behavior are shaped by external influences. Locke's philosophy was not only dominant in the Anglo-American intellectual world, but was also prominent among French Enlightenment philosophes, such as Voltaire.

One of the most thorough-going environmental determinists of the Enlightenment was Claude Adrien Helvétius, who took Locke's idea of *tabula rasa* (blank slate) seriously. "No individual is born good or bad," Helvétius proclaimed, so "There is nothing impossible to education." Our character is entirely shaped by upbringing and education. However, Helvétius also claimed that government and laws are perhaps the most significant influences on our upbringing, thus playing a crucial role in shaping human behavior. He did not believe that humans are responsible for their own conduct, but rather maintained "that the virtue and vices of men are always the effects of their different situations, and the different instruction they receive." He expressed faith that perfect legislation would produce perfect people, and he thought such enlightened legislation was within reach. With good government, everyone would be virtuous and happy. Indeed, he thought that an enlightened legislature would create laws so that "men will be forced to be virtuous."[3]

In light of this vision of government-created human virtue, the famous intellectual historian Isaiah Berlin branded Helvétius an enemy of human liberty. Berlin perceptively explained:

> One thing is clear: in the kind of universe which Helvétius depicts there is little or no room for individual liberty. In his world men may become happy, but the notion of liberty eventually disappears. It disappears because liberty to do evil disappears, since everyone has now been conditioned to do only what is good. We have become like animals trained to seek only that which is useful to us.[4]

To be sure, Helvétius was not a fan of a despotic absolutist monarchy, under which he lived. However, as Berlin points out, he substituted the despotism of technocracy, which no matter how well-intentioned, still robs humans of their individual liberty and rights, because it denies them the ability to make their own choices.

Helvétius, like so many other Enlightenment thinkers, snobbishly considered most of his fellow citizens unenlightened, so he had to find a way to circumvent their influence on the next generation and his strategy to mold a new society. Thus he advocated removing children from their families whenever possible to remove any harmful parental influences, especially religious influences. He stated, "In general, that education is best where the child, most distant from his parents, has least opportunity of mixing incoherent ideas with those which he ought to acquire in the course of his studies. It is for this reason that a public education will always excel a private [one]." Instead, children should be abandoned to their peers, who will (allegedly) correct defects in each other, thereby producing model citizens. For this peer-directed education to be most effective on a child, "it is necessary that he be almost always absent from the paternal dwelling; and that he do not return in the vacations and holidays, to catch again, from a conversation with the people of the world, the vices his fellow-pupils had effaced." As we shall see, Helvétius would not be the last environmental determinist to see the family as a retrograde institution corrupting the next generation.[5]

No one stressed the importance of the environment for determining human behavior more than Robert Owen, a textile mill owner who became the leading British socialist of the early nineteenth century. Owen was inspired by Enlightenment rationalism (and anticlericalism) to seek a scientific solution to human misery and vice. Thus it is ironic that Friedrich Engels later contrasted his own allegedly scientific socialism (i.e., Marxism) with Owen's utopian (thus implicitly unscientific) socialism. In his many writings, including his autobiography, Owen repeated over and over again that the guiding principle on which he based his entire worldview was that humans have no control over their own beliefs or behavior. Rather, he claimed, their behavior is shaped almost entirely by their upbringing and environment. In his autobiography he admitted, "I was a man of one fundamental principle and its practical consequences...that 'the character of man is formed *for* and not *by* him.'"[6] In *The Book of the New Moral World*, he stated that man is not "responsible for his will and his actions.... it will be known that man is, altogether, a being whose organization, feelings, thoughts, will and actions are predetermined for him by the influence of external circumstances acting upon his original constitution, and that he is, therefore, irresponsible for the character formed for him, whatever it may be."[7]

As the full title of this work indicated—*The Book of the New Moral World, Containing the Rational System of Society, Founded on Demonstrable Facts, Developing the Constitution and Laws of Human Nature and of Society*—Owen believed that his views were based on laws of nature that he had discovered through reason. He was a true child of Enlightenment rationalism, and he jubilantly proclaimed that his view that humans are shaped by their circumstances or surroundings was "the greatest discovery that man has made for the universal happiness of his race through all future time."[8] He continually remonstrated against the opposing view—that humans have the power to make choices and shape their own character—as "the true and sole origin of evil. It generates and perpetuates ignorance, hatred, and revenge, where, without such error, only intelligence, confidence, and kindness would exist. It has hitherto been the Evil Genius of the world."[9] Owen rejected the Christian teaching of original sin and human depravity, claiming instead that humans are neither good nor evil, but "universally plastic."[10] Raised in good surroundings, they become good; subjected to evil circumstances, they become evil. According to Owen, if people would only lay aside their superstitious religious belief that humans have freedom to choose their behavior, we could rationally shape human behavior, so everyone would be virtuous.

Since he considered human behavior the result of one's upbringing and surroundings, Owen had great confidence that he could rationally refashion society, so that everyone would be cooperative, sober, industrious, prosperous, and happy. If only we would properly educate and train our children, he thought, we could eliminate all crime, vice, and even wars. In order to test his ideas and prove that they were practicable, he improved the living and working conditions of his employees at his New Lanark textile mill, while continuing to turn a profit. Owen had grandiose hopes for his model community in New Lanark, later calling it "the most important experiment for the happiness of the human race that had yet been instituted at any time in any part of the world."[11] His self-proclaimed success at engineering a model community for his employees at New Lanark was not repeated in the subsequent experimental communities, where Owen had less control over the inhabitants. In 1825 Owen spent much of his fortune to buy the community of New Harmony, Indiana, where his disciples settled to blaze the path to utopia. Less than one year later separatist tendencies divided New Harmony, and in 1827 Owen abandoned his failed experimental community.[12]

Rather than admit that he may have made some miscalculations about human nature, Owen insisted that the fault lay in the upbringing of the other people involved in the community. He confessed that his experiment may have been a bit premature, given the human material he had to work with. However, he did not budge one inch from his faith that human nature was completely plastic, and that he was ordained to bring humanity to a higher state of happiness and bliss. Even toward the end of his life, as he wrote his autobiography, he saw himself as an almost messianic figure in his attempt to bring heaven to earth, stating, "Society has never yet put it into my power to show the world an example of these conditions,—although it is the highest and most permanent interest of all that this example should be given in my lifetime, because my experience in scientific practical arrangements for superseding evil by good conditions, is the only experience of that character yet known to the world."[13]

The solution was so simple that all he had to do was get people to understand it, and everything would fall into place. He often referred to his ideas as self-evident, and anyone not seeing the truth of his position was obviously in the thrall of irrational superstitions or ingrained prejudices. Indeed he once remarked that anyone who is rationally educated will recognize that all human laws are either unnecessary or contrary to natural laws.[14] His anarchist tendencies colored his view that society could dispense with all punishment, once it properly educated and provided for its children. He proposed setting up educational institutions for very small children, where each would be instructed upon entering (and presumably reminded when necessary) "never to injure his playfellows, but that, on the contrary, he is to contribute all in his power to make them happy." This simple precept, as Owen called it, "will be easily taught, and as easily acquired," because as much as possible the children would be removed from their families, where they might contract false beliefs and develop troublesome behaviors. He wanted older children rather than parents to be the mentors of the younger generation, because the parents were more likely to have been raised with superstitions and beliefs contrary to reason, which they might pass on.[15] Indeed Owen considered marriage itself an irrational institution that would be superseded in his utopian society, so this made the communal raising of children all the more necessary.[16]

Owen's writings exuded an overweening confidence that his viewpoint was absolutely rational and even self-obvious, while all his opponents were steeped in falsehood, prejudice, and superstition. Ironically, he complained bitterly and incessantly about the dogmatism of religions, blinded to his own dogmatism. He insisted that all religions must be false, since there are so many different, mutually incompatible views about religion. He did not seem to reflect on the fact that there are many different views about politics and society, as well, so how could he insist that his alone was the right one?

Further, since Owen argued that all beliefs were formed by one's circumstances and surroundings, he recognized that his own views were also the product of his upbringing. He never quite seemed to understand that this made his own philosophy suspect. Why should anyone believe his ideas, since—if he is right—his own beliefs are every bit as much the product of his surroundings as everyone else's are? This contradiction—between his insistence that his own views were formed by his surroundings, and his claim that his views were rational and absolutely true—shines through clearly in this passage from his autobiography, where he rejected all religions for teaching that individuals form their own character:

My own reflections compelled me to come to very different conclusions. My reason taught me that I could not have made one of my own qualities,—that they were forced upon me by Nature;—that my language, religion, and habits, were forced upon me by Society; and that I was entirely the child of Nature and Society;—that Nature gave the qualities, and Society directed them. Thus was I forced, through seeing the error of their foundation, to abandon all belief in every religion which had been taught to man.[17]

Owen was raised in a very pious Christian household, so the religion that was "forced upon [him] by Society" was Christianity. However, oddly, through "reflection" and "reason" Owen broke with the religion of his family and society. Somehow he transcended his education and upbringing, all the while insisting that he was "entirely the child of Nature and Society." Where did he get this power to use his "own reflections" and his "reason" to break with the dominant beliefs of his society? And even if some element in his upbringing did cause him to break away from the dominant religious, political, and social doctrines of his society, why should anyone suppose that his ideas constituted the truth, while everyone else's upbringing had produced error? It is unclear why his upbringing should accidentally have led him to the truth, while the vast majority in his society—many with upbringings remarkably similar to his—were shrouded in error.

Owen was a true philanthropist with genuine benevolence for humanity. We cannot say for sure, but it seems likely that this universal benevolence, which he attributed to his rationalistic anti-religious philosophy, was ingrained in him early in life through religion. Despite preaching to others about the power of one's childhood training, Owen did not always understand the power of his own upbringing. His work ethic and his disdain for drinking, gambling, and prostitution seem to derive from his straitlaced religious upbringing. Whether this is the case or not, Owen surely did not understand the dehumanizing tendencies inherent in his worldview, in which people are entirely passive, not creative, and they have no ability to make free choices. He once stated, "Children are, without exception, passive and wonderfully contrived compounds; which . . . may be formed collectively to have any human character. And although these compounds, like all the other works of nature, possess endless varieties, . . . " For Owen, children are "compounds," a conglomeration of chemicals that are simply a part of nature. Like chemicals, their behavior is entirely determined by the laws of nature, and they have no ability to change their destiny.[18] Some of Owen's contemporaries understood the dehumanizing thrust of his position, nicknaming him "reasoning machine," because they understood his philosophy as reducing humans to nothing more than a machine.[19]

✤

Other socialists in the nineteenth century agreed with Owen that human nature is shaped mostly by the environment. Many of these socialists were compassionate men who commiserated with the plight of the impoverished urban factory workers, whose exploitation they rightly decried. They deplored the inhumane and miserable living and working conditions inflicted upon factory workers in the early Industrial Revolution. However, while accurately sensing and critiquing the dehumanizing effects of industrialization, they simply substituted a different form of dehumanization. Their rescue attempts failed miserably and often produced even worse exploitation and misery than the capitalist system they despised.

Indeed one of the most influential forms of socialism in the nineteenth century, Marxism, became one of the most pernicious ideologies ever to plague the world, contributing to untold millions of deaths in the twentieth century. Mao had the highest body count of any of the communist leaders: ten million executed directly, about twenty million perished in Mao's labor camps, and about twenty million more died in 1959–1961 in the largest famine in history, which was engineered by Mao with his Great Leap Forward program. Pol Pot's Khmer Rouge communist regime more than decimated the Cambodian population, since one out of every seven Cambodians perished in that genocide. Estimates vary, but Stalin killed about six million Soviet citizens in his collectivization campaign in the early 1930s, and about seven hundred thousand more in the purges in the late 1930s (in two years the NKVD executed an average of over nine hundred people per day, seven days a week). Multitudes more died in the Soviet Gulag or during forced deportations of various ethnic groups. Though Leninist atrocities were eclipsed by Stalin, those who cling to the fiction that Lenin's style of communism was kind and gentle need to explain the hundreds of thousands of executions for political opposition during his regime (in the entire century preceding the Bolshevik Revolution, by contrast, the tsars executed fewer than seven thousand people for political opposition, and most of these were during the Russian Revolution of 1905). Once we add in the killing sprees of other communist regimes—no communist regime seemed to be immune from them entirely—the total number of people slain in the name of communism approaches 100 million.[20]

Ironically, Karl Marx considered his philosophy a liberating form of humanism that would elevate humanity and rescue people from the misery of the Industrial Revolution. However, like most early socialists (many of whom influenced him), Marx's worldview was tainted by environmental determinism. He believed that historical developments were not subject to the whims of humans, because history was shaped by technological and economic change. These changes were subject to economic laws, so historical developments were inevitable. Thus Marx could confidently predict the inevitable collapse of capitalism and the triumph of the proletarian revolution. Marx not only encouraged revolution to inaugurate a communist society; he insisted it could not fail to happen. People have no real choice.

Marx's economic determinism was evident already in some of his early writings, such as *The Communist Manifesto* (1848), co-authored by Friedrich Engels, who bankrolled Marx's work with the profits he earned from managing textile factories. Therein Marx and Engels argued, "The history of all hitherto existing society is the history of class struggles," and the two classes currently struggling for supremacy were the bourgeoisie (business owners) and proletariat (laborers). Instead of free individual personalities shaping history, people are little more than manifestations of their class. These nameless, faceless classes were formed by "a series of revolutions in the modes of production and of exchange." Economic developments, in Marx's view, are not shaped by individuals making free choices, but rather they are inevitable developments based on present technology. Marx's claim that the fall of the bourgeoisie and "the victory of the proletariat are equally inevitable" implies that human choices are not ultimately consequential.[21] Marx thought he could predict the future, because he had grasped the *"economic law of motion of modern society,"* as he called it in *Capital*.[22]

The preface to Marx's *Contribution to the Critique of Political Economy* (1859) contains one of the pithiest explanations of his "materialist conception of history," as his view of history came to be known. There he claimed that the "guiding thread" for his study was this:

> In the social production of their life, men enter into definite relations that are indispensable and independent of their will, relations of production which correspond to a definite stage of development of their material productive forces. The sum total of these relations of production constitutes the economic structure of society, the real foundation, on which rises a legal and political superstructure and to which correspond definite forms of social consciousness.... With the change of the economic foundation the entire immense superstructure is more or less rapidly transformed.[23]

By using the phrase "independent of their will" Marx denied that human choices play a significant role in shaping historical developments. Rather than individuals shaping society, classes drive historical development, and classes are the inevitable product of the economic base or foundation.

In his earlier unpublished manuscript on *Poverty of Philosophy* (1847), Marx explained that society was shaped by economics and ultimately by technology. He stated, "Social relations are closely bound up with productive forces. In acquiring new productive forces men change their mode of production; and in changing their mode of production, in changing the way of earning their living, they change all their social relations. The hand-mill gives you society with the feudal lord; the steam-mill society with the industrial capitalist."[24] This statement about the power of the hand-mill and steam-mill to shape history suggests that technologies determine the shape of society.

Some might object that this is too facile a view of Marx's philosophy. There are scholars who portray Marx as an economic determinist, but others deny that he was a strict determinist, and some see him as conflicted. Indeed, especially in his earlier writings, Marx seemed to understand some of the problems inherent in deterministic materialism. In his "Theses on Feuerbach" (1845), written early in his career but only published after his death, Marx explained that Feuerbach's materialist

philosophy is defective. He complained that Feuerbach and other materialists ignore human activity or revolutionary praxis. Marx perceptively
pointed to the Achilles' heel of environmental determinism:

> The materialist doctrine that men are products of circum-
> stances and upbringing, and that, therefore, changed men are
> products of other circumstances and changed upbringing,
> forgets that it is men who change circumstances and that it is
> essential to educate the educator himself. Hence, this doctrine
> necessarily arrives at dividing society into two parts, one of
> which is superior to society.[25]

The famous closing line of "Theses on Feuerbach" underscores his
desire to steer clear of strict determinism: "The philosophers have only
interpreted the world, in various ways; the point, however, is to *change*
it."[26]

Despite his emphasis on human activity, as a convinced materialist
Marx never was able to shake free of determinism. This deterministic
side of Marx takes the edge off the more humanistic side of Marx, which
shines brightly in his early unpublished writings, where he attacked
human alienation caused by the capitalist factory system. Throughout
Marx's work there is a tension between his vigorous defense of individual human freedom and humans as merely pawns of social forces over
which they have no control. Marx promised that the future communist
society would be characterized by a classless society "in which the free
development of each is the condition for the free development of all."[27]

Marx's complete confidence that communist society would produce
freedom and bliss for humanity was based upon his understanding of
private property as the root cause of every evil in society. Because he
thought human nature was shaped by the economy, changing the economy could transform human nature dramatically. Not only the political
and legal system, not only religion and culture, but even morality was
merely a reflection of economic conditions. Thus he rejected the reigning
morality of his age as a collection of bourgeois prejudices, as a tool of

bourgeois oppression.[28] However, Marx smuggled morality into his philosophy by constantly using morally loaded terminology, such as oppression, robbery, exploitation, etc. It also seems clear that Marx considered communism morally superior to capitalism, which Eugene Kamenka claims is difficult to reconcile with Marx's relativistic view of morality as historically contingent.[29]

Marx's renunciation of natural law morality, his economic determinism, and his championing of the proletarian cause led him to countenance harsh measures to bring about communist society. He admitted that the bourgeoisie would not roll over and play dead, so even after a successful revolution, the transition to communism "cannot be effected except by means of despotic inroads on the rights of property." We cannot know how much despotism the freedom-loving Marx would have countenanced, since he never had a chance to exercise power. However, every single communist regime that has claimed to rule according to his philosophy has been infamous for its hostility to human liberty (as most of us understand the concept), and the Marxist approach to social engineering has contributed to some of the worst atrocities in all of world history—such as those committed under Stalin, Mao, and Pol Pot.

The fundamental problem with Marx's philosophy, the core idea that contributed to these atrocities and oppression, was not its desire to socialize property or promote greater socio-economic equality. Rather, it was its flawed and impoverished vision of humanity. Alexander Solzhenitsyn portrayed this poignantly in his famous novel, *One Day in the Life of Ivan Denisovich* (1962), in which the protagonist, Ivan Denisovich Shukhov, describes the fruitless efforts of the Soviet communist regime to alter human nature. Shukhov and his fellow prisoners are being rehabilitated so they can return as good communists to Soviet society—although most of them were imprisoned on trumped-up charges, never having actually challenged the communist regime. Moreover, the prison camp does not achieve its purpose of transforming them into faithful communists. Shukhov and many of his fellow inmates continue to think and act like non-communists. When his squad leader told him to throw out some mortar so the squad could make it to formation on time,

Shukhov refuses, not wanting to waste the mortar. The narrator then states, "Shukhov wasn't made that way—eight years in a camp couldn't change his nature."[30] Even the guards and administrators of the prison camp do not seem especially socialist, since they are corrupt and live off of bribes. Solzhenitsyn knew first-hand the degrading existence in the Stalinist Gulag, and it certainly did nothing to reshape him into a loyal communist citizen.

❊

The leader of the first successful Marxist revolution, Vladimir Lenin, took seriously his task of reformulating the environment—especially the economy—to reshape humanity. He had complete confidence that the communist economic system would lead to a classless society free from oppression. But he believed that the first step to this communist society was to establish a "dictatorship of the proletariat," which became the centerpiece of his political philosophy. According to Lenin,

> During the dictatorship of the proletariat, it will be necessary to re-educate millions of peasants and petty proprietors, hundreds of thousands of employees, officials, and bourgeois intellectuals; to subject them all to the proletarian State and to proletarian guidance; to rid them of bourgeois habits and traditions.... In like manner, it will be necessary, in the course of a long struggle and under the aegis of the dictatorship of the proletariat, to re-educate the proletarians themselves.[31]

Re-education may sound benign, but it masked a harsher reality, because Lenin did not promise re-education would be a peaceful, painless process. Many times—both before and after taking power in Russia—he stressed the need for a newly-founded communist regime to employ coercion, force, and violence to suppress the bourgeois elements of society. After seizing power he stated, "What dictatorship implies and means is a state of simmering war, a state of military measures of struggle against the enemies of the proletarian power."[32] He was prepared to fight and kill whenever necessary to establish a communist regime.

Most historians today recognize that Lenin trampled on the rights of multitudes—including their right to life—with the hope of bringing bliss to future generations. The historian Richard Pipes calls Lenin a "heartless cynic" with "utter disregard for human life." Pipes uncovered and published newly-discovered documents by Lenin that reinforce his verdict:

> Lenin is revealed in these documents as a thoroughgoing misanthrope. They corroborate what Gorky wrote of him on the basis of long and close acquaintance: that Lenin "in general" loved people but "with abnegation. His love looked far ahead, through the mists of hatred." That is, he "loved" humankind not as it really was but as he believed it would become when the revolution triumphed and produced a new breed of human beings.[33]

Communism never achieved the promised "new breed of human beings" with a new, improved human nature, free from oppression. All we are left with, then, is Lenin's oppressive means—the killing of political opponents, bourgeois elements, priests, and other "enemies of the state." The ends that were supposed to justify these harsh measures never arrived.

The Terror that Lenin unleashed on Russia was aimed not at individuals, but at an impersonal economic class. A leading official in Lenin's secret police force explained: "We are not carrying out war against individuals. We are exterminating the bourgeoisie as a class. We are not looking for evidence or witnesses to reveal deeds or works against Soviet power. The first question we ask is—to what class does he belong, what are his origins, upbringing, education or profession? These questions define the fate of the accused. This is the essence of the Red Terror."[34] Lenin and his Marxist colleagues had no sympathy whatsoever for individuals and individual rights. Lenin's close associate Leon Trotsky once overtly repudiated what he called the "Kantian-clerical, vegetarian-Quaker chatter about the 'sanctity of human life.'"[35] No wonder then that Lenin and Trotsky presided over the deaths of hundreds of thousands.

Lenin's ruthless successor, Joseph Stalin, outstripped even Lenin in his zeal to crush the bourgeois opposition and establish a communist society. It may seem bizarre in light of his atrocities, but Stalin was an intellectual. His life and thought were fully immersed in Marxist philosophy. Based on his materialist convictions, he insisted that thoughts were merely the product of material causation, so humans are subject to scientific investigation. "Hence," he stated, "social life, the history of society, ceases to be an agglomeration of 'accidents,' and become the history of the development of society according to regular laws, and the study of the history of society becomes a science." Like other Marxists, Stalin saw communism as a fully scientific enterprise. Thus he stated that his activity "must not be based on the good wishes of 'outstanding individuals,' not on the dictates of 'reason,' 'universal morals,' etc., but on the laws of development of society and on the study of these laws.... Hence socialism is converted from a dream of a better future for humanity into a science." Scientific socialism thus trumps individual rights, rationality, and morality.[36]

The connections between Stalin's materialism and his amorality are evident in some brief notations he made on the flyleaf of the 1939 edition of Lenin's *Materialism and Empiriocriticism*, Lenin's defense of dialectical materialism. There Stalin jotted,

If a person is:
   1) strong (spiritually)
   2) active
   3) intelligent (or capable),
then he is a *good* person regardless of any other "vices".
   1) weakness
   2) laziness
   3) stupidity
are the only thing [sic] that can be called vices.[37]

For Stalin, materialist philosophy upended traditional morality, and he thought "revolutions made by oppressed classes are a quite natural and inevitable phenomenon" and "the class struggle of the proletariat is a quite natural and inevitable phenomenon."[38] They are facts of nature, not human-directed events to moralize about. However, presumably the "strong, active, intelligent" individuals (such as himself) would cooperate with the forces of nature, even if it required them to commit violent deeds that the "weak, lazy, and stupid" might morally condemn.

In his recent book *Stalin's Genocides*, Norman Naimark forcefully argues that Stalin's atrocities are rightly labeled genocide since he targeted specific groups for mass murder and annihilation. Stalin was willing to carry out this campaign against his fellow countrymen, according to Naimark, because "The lives of Soviet citizens that were entrusted to his leadership were to Stalin—for all intents and purposes—without inherent value." Thus Stalin rejected the view that humans have intrinsic value and that individuals are important and have inalienable rights. One victim group Stalin considered worthless (or maybe worse than worthless) was the kulaks, whom he considered prosperous peasants infected with bourgeois ideals (though in reality they were often only slightly more prosperous than their neighbors and probably no more bourgeois than their fellow peasants). Naimark explains how kulaks were stripped of their human status by Soviet propaganda in the 1930s: "Gorky described them [kulaks] as 'half animals,' while Soviet press and propaganda materials sometimes depicted them as apes. Kulaks in this sense were dehumanized and racialized into beings inherently inferior to others—and they were treated as such." In the early 1930s, Stalin deported millions of kulaks to "special settlements" and seized food from peasants in Ukraine, resulting in mass famine, even as the Soviet Union exported grain to pay for Stalin's industrialization program. Later in the 1930s, Stalin had his NKVD police forces conduct purges that resulted in seventeen hundred executions per day for sixteen months. Ultimately Stalin's quest for a communist utopia was responsible for the deaths of about seven to nine million people (some estimates are even higher).[39]

*

Socialists were not the only ones to embrace environmental deter-minism in the nineteenth and early twentieth centuries. The increasing secularization of European and American intellectual life, together with the growth of materialism and positivism among scholars, led to wide-spread efforts to bring humans under the purview of scientific investiga-tion. While Marx wanted to pursue "scientific socialism," non-socialist scholars hoped to create the "social sciences." For the most part the budding new disciplines of psychology and sociology dispensed with belief in free will or an immaterial soul, insisting that all human behav-ior must be subject to scientific laws.

One of the best examples of the secularization of psychology in the early twentieth century was the growth of behaviorism, which came to dominate American psychology in the early twentieth century. The founder of behaviorism, John B. Watson, was a psychology professor at Johns Hopkins University from 1908 to 1920. He claimed that "behav-iorism is a true natural science" because it rejects body-soul dualism and investigates human psychology just as scientists would study animals. He rejected introspection, focusing his psychology exclusively on what he could observe and experiment on: human behavior. He founded behaviorism on an environmental determinist view of humanity, stating, "The rule, or measuring rod, which the behaviorist puts in front of him always is: Can I describe this bit of behavior I see in terms of 'stimulus and response'?" According to Watson, all human behavior can be traced back to some stimulus from the environment that evokes a (completely determined) response from the human. He denied that humans have instincts that shape our behavior, so heredity is inconsequential. All behavior is learned behavior. The human is merely a stimulus-response machine, and yes, Watson did sometimes refer to humans as machines.[40]

Watson admitted that his behaviorism had no room for human free-dom: "You have already grasped the notion that the behaviorist is a strict determinist—*the child or adult has to do what he does do. The only way he can be made to act differently is first to untrain him and then to retrain him*." Any flaws in an individual's behavior (if a deterministic universe can be said to have "flaws") are entirely the fault of his or her parents and teachers. Watson had supreme confidence that with full power over the environment, he could transform humanity. He asserted, "Give me a dozen healthy infants, well-formed, and my own specified world to bring them up in and I'll guarantee to take any one at random and train him to become any type of specialist I might select—doctor, lawyer, artist, merchant-chief and, yes, even beggar-man and thief, regardless of his talents, penchants, tendencies, abilities, vocations, and race of his ancestors."[41] This promise did not seem to work out so well in practice, because one of his sons, Billy, angered his father by choosing psychiatry as his profession. Watson considered his son's choice a slap in the face, and relations between the two remained strained thereafter.[42]

The dehumanizing implications of Watson's philosophy come into even clearer focus when we examine his views on child-rearing. When discussing child training, Watson once again flaunted his lab coat, claiming that parenting is a science "which must be worked out by patient laboratory methods." Watson was so contemptuous of the "unscientific" child-rearing methods of his contemporaries that he stated, "It is a serious question in my mind whether there should be individual homes for children—or even whether children should know their own parents. There are undoubtedly much more scientific ways of bringing up children which will probably mean finer and happier children." He did not think the family would disappear any time soon, but he strove to minimize its impact.[43]

When we turn to Watson's specific instructions to parents, some of them are so ludicrous one is tempted to wonder if Watson was writing a parody (alas, he was not). One of the more bizarre recommendations is that parents refrain from showering their infants and children with affection and kisses. Watson believed that one of the most serious problems confronting young people was their inability to function well in society once they left home, because their mothers coddled them instead of preparing them to face the real world. "Mothers just don't know, when they kiss their children and pick them up and rock them, caress them and jiggle them upon their knee, that they are slowly building up a human being totally unable to cope with the world it must later live in." This is not just a minor point in his book, but a theme he hammers on repeatedly, insisting, "There are serious rocks ahead for the over-kissed child." According to Watson, too much parental love and affection contributes to "invalidism," divorce, and suicide.[44]

Watson hoped to replace this "over-coddling" with a more "scientific" way of raising children that would turn them into more efficient, adjusted adults. He explained, "There is a sensible way of treating children. Treat them as though they were young adults. Dress them, bathe them with care and circumspection. Let your behavior always be objective and kindly firm. Never hug and kiss them, never let them sit in your lap. If you must, kiss them once on the forehead when they say good night." He suggested that if possible children be raised by nurses, and he recommended rotating nurses so the child could not become attached to any of them. (He also added: "Somehow I can't help wishing that it were possible to rotate mothers occasionally too!") If mothers cannot afford nurses and "cannot leave your child, put it out in the backyard a large part of the day. Build a fence around the yard so that you are sure no harm can come to it. Do this from the time it is born." (Notice Watson called the child "it.") Thus Watson's recipe for caring for your child psychologically is to spend as little time as possible with him or her and refrain from hugging and kissing him or her. Despite Watson's scientific pretensions, his book contains no scientific data to back up his outrageous and harmful proposals.[45]

Watson based his faulty view of child-rearing on his flawed vision of humanity—that a person is nothing more than a stimulus-response machine. Not only fear and anger, he thought, but even love are merely emotional reactions conditioned by stimuli. Love is just matter in motion over which the individual has no control. According to Watson, "Only one thing will bring out a love response in a child—stroking and touching its skin, lips, sex organs and the like. It doesn't matter at first who strokes it. It will 'love' the stroker. This is the clay out of which all love—maternal, paternal, wifely or husbandly—is made."[46] Notice the quotation marks

Watson put around the verb "love," which has no place in his reality. It is purely a physical response to a physical cause over which humans have no control. He thought humans would be better off with less love, so they could function more efficiently as the machines they are.

And what happens if the machines do not function properly? What happens when they misbehave (whatever that could possibly mean when they are completely determined)? Watson recognized that people commit crimes, but he denied that they should be held individually responsible for their behavior, since "only the sick or psychopaths (insane) or untrained (socially untrained) individuals commit crimes." Punishment is out of the question. If the person is sick, we should try to heal them, if possible, or else institutionalize them where they cannot harm others. Or kill them: "The question as to whether the hopelessly insane should be etherized has of course been raised time and time again. There can be no reasons against it except exaggerated sentiment and mediaeval religious mandates." Watson's suggestion that we should toss a human being on the scrap heap when "it" malfunctions is entirely consistent with his view of humans as machines. However, if the criminal's behavior is the result of improper training rather than a biological problem, Watson suggested that a behaviorist psychologist be assigned to remold their behavior.[47]

In an essay in which he sketched his view of "The Behaviorist's Utopia," Watson dreamed of a future time when technocrats would remold humans to make them efficient, productive citizens in modern society. One of his biographers, Kerry Buckley, considers his vision of future society nightmarish, and with good reason, since love, human warmth, feeling, and the arts are banished. In his utopia, Watson wanted children to be raised "as much as possible under laboratory control. Mothers would not know the identity of their children. Breast feeding would be prohibited, and children would be rotated among families at four-week intervals until the age of twenty." Watson also desired a future where all women are beautiful, so "ill-favored" women would not be permitted to reproduce. The insane would fare even worse than the ugly in this allegedly ideal world, for physicians "would not hesitate to put them to death."[48] Watson's "utopia" is a frightening example of the devaluing of human life that occurs when materialist metaphysics masquerades as science, especially in the human sciences.

One of the key problems for Watson's behaviorist psychology, of course, was that it was self-defeating. Why should we take seriously his ideas, if they are merely conditioned responses shaped entirely by his upbringing and training? Why should we regard his recommendations for child-rearing as "scientific," when they more likely reflect his own experiences, including the neglect of his alcoholic, absentee father? Environmental determinists seem to think that they can hover above their circumstances with scientific objectivity, but their own theory of mind cries out against this. Ultimately, they have no way to extricate themselves from their own environment. If environmental determinism is true, then belief in environmental determinism is environmentally determined. This undermines any rational reason to believe it is true.

Also, for someone so intent on controlling emotion through conditioned responses, Watson displayed a remarkable lack of control of his own emotions. He ingloriously sank his academic career at Johns Hopkins in 1920 by having an affair with a graduate student, which led to salacious articles in the national press and a highly-publicized divorce. He then married this student and took up a career in advertising. He also lectured at the New School for Social Research in the 1920s, but in 1926 they terminated his lectures, again because of sexual improprieties. He also drank heavily. Apparently the controller needed some controlling.

Not only that, but his own child-rearing experiences are not much of an advertisement for behaviorism. In an ad for his child-rearing book, he included photos of his two sons, calling them children "who [sic] adults like to be around," because they sleep when they are put to bed and eat what they are given. He stated, "They are free from fears and temper tantrums—*they are happy children.*" This surely sounded good to parents tired of struggling with their children over food and bedtime. However, in the course of researching her biography Buckley interviewed the younger son and found that "their childhood was far from happy. Watson's youngest son later remarked that growing up with his father was 'like a business proposition.' Their relationship was 'devoid of emotional interchange.'" Another of Watson's sons committed suicide four years after his father's death. In Watson's own family, behaviorism did not seem to contribute to happiness and human thriving.[49]

Nonetheless Watson won many disciples in the scholarly community, and behaviorism dominated American psychology in the early-to-mid twentieth century. Bertrand Russell admired Watson's child-training philosophy, but it does not seem to have worked particularly well in his case, either.[50] Despite her love for her father, Russell's daughter Katharine Tait lamented that her father had practiced on her "that early behaviorism whose clockwork efficiency embittered the infancy of so many of my generation." At the time Russell was convinced that behaviorist child-rearing methods were fully scientific. Tait explained that this fixation on science actually misled her father: "My father's respect for science, coupled with his rejection of all old-fashioned orthodoxy, led him into absurdities that a greater confidence in his own good sense might have avoided." Indeed, later Russell recognized that his methods had been too harsh and mechanical, but only after his children had endured them. Tait resented having been treated as an automaton being manipulated as if in an experiment, even though her parents' intentions were to improve her life. She complained, "I do not like to think of myself being treated with such austere benevolence, as raw material to be shaped rather than as a person to be enjoyed." Interestingly, Tait noticed that while her father denied free will and believed in the omnipotence of the environment in determining human behavior, he always seemed to make an exception for himself: "He may have thought that the right conditioning of his children would produce the right kind of people, but he certainly didn't consider himself the inevitable result of his own conditioning." Ultimately, Watson's behaviorism stripped people of their humanity and robbed children of the love and affection they need.[51]

✺

One of the most important proponents of behaviorist psychology in the twentieth century was B. F. Skinner, professor of psychology at Harvard University. Skinner embraced materialism as an undergraduate in the 1920s, in part from reading the materialist biologist Jacques Loeb's writings on brain physiology. He stated later that in his view, "Mind is a myth." Shortly before beginning graduate school in psychology at Harvard in 1928, he read John Watson's writings and became a zealous behaviorist.[52]

Even before going off to college, Skinner had become somewhat skeptical about religion. A concerned high school teacher who was also a devout Catholic sensed Skinner's anti-religious tenor and once lent him a work opposing evolution. Just before his graduation, his teacher told him privately, "You were born to be a leader of men. I just want to say one thing. Never forget the value of human life." This teacher probably correctly understood the way that evolution was guiding Skinner's thoughts. Just a few months before he died, Skinner stated, "I think evolution is random, accidental, no design in it at all." He viewed humans as nothing more than products of an impersonal nature and thus accidental, unplanned beings with no intrinsic value. His Catholic teacher would no doubt have been disappointed that Skinner once paid for a girlfriend's abortion, but would likely have been pained even more by Skinner's philosophy.[53]

Skinner opened his bestselling book, *Beyond Freedom and Dignity* (1972), by evoking fear that humans are on the verge of annihilating themselves by their bad behavior, especially through rapid population growth, the proliferation of nuclear weapons, and rampant pollution. His behaviorist psychology, then, was not just an esoteric exercise in ivory-tower theorizing, but of the greatest practical importance and even urgency. According to Skinner, the solution to the problems spawned by technological developments (nuclear power, industrialization, etc.) is to introduce "a technology of behavior." He derided what he considered the pre-scientific view of humanity, which insists on purpose, free will, and the responsibility of individuals for their behavior. The scientific view of humanity, he asserted, is that "a person does not act upon the world, the world acts upon him." Psychology, he claimed, has "moved forward by dispossessing autonomous man, but he has not departed gracefully," since many scholars in many fields still invoke him (or her). Skinner was determined to push him (and her) off the cosmic stage for good.[54]

How did Skinner justify his position? Why did he think this environmental determinism was scientific, and what scientific experiments proved it? Skinner admitted in a very telling passage that his views were not scientifically proven, intimating that his belief was based more on his chosen philosophy of science rather than any empirical scientific facts. He stated:

> In what we may call the prescientific view (and the word is not necessarily pejorative) a person's behavior is at least to some extent his own achievement. He is free to deliberate, decide, and act, possibly in original ways, and he is to be given credit for his successes and blamed for his failures. In the scientific view (and the word is not necessarily honorific) a person's behavior is determined by a genetic endowment traceable to the evolutionary history of the species and by the environmental circumstances to which as an individual he has been exposed. Neither view can be proved, but it is in the nature of scientific inquiry that the evidence should shift in favor of the second.[55]

The reason he thought that "evidence should shift in favor" of his position and against his opponents was because he saw free will as a miraculous event, and he believed science was opposed to any kind of miracles. His materialistic philosophy underpinned his view of science and humanity.

Skinner enunciated this point again in the conclusion of *Beyond Freedom and Dignity*, stating, "Krutch [one of his articulate critics] has argued that whereas the traditional view supports Hamlet's exclamation, 'How like a god!,' Pavlov, the behavioral scientist, emphasized 'How like a dog!' But that was a step forward. A god is the archetypal pattern of an explanatory fiction, of a miracle-working mind, of the metaphysical. Man is much more than a dog, but like a dog he is within the range of a scientific analysis." Skinner's goal was to subject humans to scientific investigation by denying they have any power to rise above natural processes. He remonstrated against the anti-determinist Christian intellectual C. S. Lewis, who complained that determinism leads to the *Abolition of Man*. Skinner denied that he wanted to abolish man, but confessed, "What is being abolished is autonomous man—the inner man, the homunculus, the possessing demon, the man defended by the literatures of freedom and dignity. His abolition has long been overdue.... Science does not dehumanize man, it de-homunculizes him, and it must do so if it is to prevent the abolition of the human species. To man *qua* man we readily say good riddance."[56] He was battling to destroy the vision of humanity that Lewis sought to preserve, a vision of humans as creative agents with the ability to make real choices and shape their own personality.

In his 1948 novel *Walden Two*, Skinner sketched a utopia that could develop if people would just see things his way. The founder of the utopian community, T. E. Frazier, explains to some visitors the philosophical underpinnings and practical working of the community, which is a model of cooperation, economic productivity, and artistic excellence. Frazier, whose perspective is usually identical to Skinner's, told his guests, "The fact is, we not only *can* control human behavior, we *must*.... I deny that freedom exists at all. I must deny it—or my program would be absurd. You can't have a science about a subject matter which hops capriciously about. Perhaps we can never *prove* that man isn't free; it's an assumption. But the increasing success of a science of behavior makes it more and more plausible."[57] Once again Skinner shows that his desire to bring human behavior under the banner of science—rather than the empirical evidence flowing from scientific experiments—drives his determinism. Frazier is, of course, correct that "You can't have a science about a subject matter which hops capriciously about." However, this insight leaves us with another viable option that Frazier (and Skinner) is loath to consider: perhaps human behavior is in principle not entirely subject to scientific investigation.

Walden Two is a technocracy that thrives by practicing "behavioral engineering." Interestingly, Skinner—like Helvétius and Owen before him—recommended the abolition of the family unit. In Walden Two children are raised communally, and most of the time the older children train the younger ones. The children grow up programmed to be well-behaved, free from animosity, pride, and envy. The whole community's penchant for cooperation allows them to work only about four hours per day, leaving them ample leisure time to cultivate the arts. The members of the community are free, yet they are controlled at the same time, as Frazier explained, "Our members are practically always doing what they want to do—what they 'choose' to do—but we see to it that they will want to do precisely the things which are best for themselves and the community. Their behavior is determined, yet they're free."[58] The "we" who see to it that community members always want what is best are the six Planners who set the policies for Walden Two.

Ominously—especially since Skinner penned his utopia sandwiched between Stalin and Hitler on the one hand and Mao and Pol Pot on the other—Frazier (and presumably Skinner) rejects democracy, which, Frazier states, "isn't, and can't be, the best form of government, because it's based on a scientifically invalid conception of man. It fails to take account of the fact that in the long run *man is determined by the state*."[59] The two great experiments in anti-democracy in the twentieth century— fascism and communism—do not seem to bother Skinner at all. Possibly this is because Skinner has no use for history. In fact, as Frazier explained, "History is honored in Walden Two only as entertainment. It isn't taken seriously as food for thought." Later Frazier said that in Walden Two "we discourage any sense of history."[60] Of course, as a historian I find this appalling. However, I also wonder why a scientist studying human behavior would simply dismiss the vast bulk of data available about actual human behavior. I guess it just did not give him the results he wanted.

Like most utopians, he hoped he could make a radical break with history. He saw his mission in almost messianic terms. In a bizarre passage toward the end of the novel, Frazier is conversing with a visitor, Prof. Burris, who is still a bit skeptical about Frazier's project. When Burris remarks to Frazier that he must take great satisfaction in having created a "world of your own making," Frazier replies with words taken from the Genesis creation story: "I look upon my work and, behold, it is good." Then Burris notices that Frazier's "beard made him look a little like Christ. Then, with a shock, I saw that he had assumed the position of crucifixion." Surprised, Burris hastens to make sure Frazier does not regard himself as God, but Frazier responds, "There's a curious similarity." Frazier then states that Walden Two was "an improvement on Genesis," and remarks, "I like to play God! Who wouldn't, under the circumstances?" Remarking on this deification of Frazier, a biographer of Skinner opined, "The novel may also have been an attempt to isolate and control his own God complex. Indeed, Skinner often, mockingly but half-seriously, saw himself as a sort of savior to humanity."[61]

Despite Skinner's messianic complex and his three-volume autobiography, both testimony to what some called his "opinionated arrogance," Skinner did not even think his own life had any special value or significance. He claimed he wanted his autobiography to be "the autobiography of a nonperson."[62] Indeed his philosophy did militate toward stripping people of their personality and personhood, or what he called the "autonomous man." Perhaps it should come as no surprise, then, that Skinner joined the Hemlock Society and helped them popularize their support for suicide and assisted suicide. A 1984 article in *Hemlock Quarterly* quoted him comparing humans to animals, stating that "we dispose of an old dog in a way that is called humane.... Many old people, living in pain or as a burden to others, would be glad to be put to death caninely."[63] For Skinner, humans were no more valuable than dogs.

�֍

In the mid-twentieth century Marxist forms of environmental determinism gained ground in Eastern Europe, China, and several other countries, while other forms of environmental determinism (together with Marxism, too!) dominated Western academe. The earlier powerful influence of biological determinism over biology, anthropology, and psychiatry waned during the middle third of the twentieth century. The collapse of the Nazi regime, the rising popularity of leftist political views in Western Europe, the anti-racist views of the burgeoning Civil Rights Movement in the United States, and the nationalist movements in Africa and Asia all converged to overthrow the view that biology is destiny. The New Left of the 1960s, together with the rising tide of feminism, reinforced the view that nurture was more important than nature in shaping human character. By the 1960s–1970s nurture seemed to reign supreme.

The dominance of nurture began eroding in the 1970s under the onslaught of sociobiology and evolutionary psychology in the sciences and postmodernism in the humanities. However, environmental determinism is still a powerful force in many disciplines, especially in the social sciences. Many social scientists still view human behavior as nothing more than the inevitable response to one's upbringing or environment. As with biological determinism, this reduces humans to merely physical beings with no independent mind or will or consciousness. Humans are only hunks of flesh to manipulate by altering their education or training. They are no more important than a circus animal trained to do impressive tricks. Thus environmental determinism, despite its efforts to rescue humanity from the degradation of biological determinism, still ends up in the same ditch.

FIVE

The Love of Pleasure

But know this, that in the last days perilous times will come. For men will be lovers of themselves, lovers of money,...lovers of pleasure rather than lovers of God.
—Paul[1]

When the eighteenth-century French writer Marquis de Sade promoted sexual libertinism and waxed eloquent about the delights of inflicting pain and torture on his fellow human beings, he was institutionalized as insane. For Sade his own individual pleasure—even if it meant hurting and oppressing others—trumped any other consideration. In the late twentieth and early twenty-first centuries, however, some of Sade's disciples are not only considered intellectually respectable, but one of them is perhaps the most famous philosopher of the late twentieth century. As a young man Michel Foucault became such a devoted disciple of Sade that he scorned his fellow students who were not conversant with Sade. Foucault, who is feted by countless intellectuals today as a brilliant philosopher, was a harsh critic of Western society's view of madness and incarceration, thus exonerating his idol. Sade would undoubtedly have been proud at the way that this revered intellectual reveled in sado-masochism and the ecstasy of a drug-induced stupor.[2]

Most Americans would not countenance Sade's misanthropic philosophy. However, even among those not disposed to follow Sade's twisted vision, the single-minded pursuit of pleasure and sexual profligacy are becoming mainstream in American culture, as the historian James Collier explains in his profound book, *The Rise of Selfishness in America* (1991). Not only are Hollywood, the media, and the internet saturating American culture with a pleasure-seeking, sex-saturated mentality, but universities are purveying the same values. At Yale University's Sex Week (held biennially since 2002), porn stars have been invited to discuss their trade and students can attend workshops that explore themes like sado-masochism, incest, and bestiality. On the west coast, scholars assembled in February 2013 at the University of California, Berkeley, for the International Academic Polyamory Conference, where psychologists and social scientists promoted the pleasures of sexual relations with multiple partners. For the sake of moral purity, I have refused to follow all the salacious details of these events, and I will endeavor in this chapter to avoid any titillating content. Nonetheless, anyone whose head is above ground in the U.S. could hardly fail to notice that our culture worships pleasure—and not just sexual pleasure. Twenty-first century Americans are pleasure junkies, as is evident from the growing problems with obesity, diabetes, binge drinking, eating disorders, and lack of self-restraint of all sorts. Our fixation on entertainment reflects this problem, too, as we seem to be constantly seeking sensory stimulation and excitement to satisfy our craving for pleasure.

As we shall see, many philosophers and pundits since the Enlightenment have insisted that pleasure is the measure of morality, just as the ancient Greek philosopher Epicurus did. This philosophy elevates pleasure to the *summum bonum*, the highest good, so pleasure becomes the sole purpose of life and thus the chief human pursuit. Indeed this Epicurean philosophy experienced a resurgence in early modern Europe, partly through the rediscovery in 1417 of the Roman poet Lucretius's eloquent *On the Nature of Things (De rerum natura)*, which became very popular with European intellectuals. The Harvard literary scholar Stephen Greenblatt recounts the importance of this rediscovery for modern thought, rightly noting that the Epicurean principles that Lucretius propagated were "an abomination to right-thinking Christian orthodoxy." Greenblatt closes his book by indicating that Lucretius's influence reached American shores, too. Thomas Jefferson, who owned at least five Latin editions and three translations of *On the Nature of Things*, once informed a correspondent, "I am an Epicurean." No wonder, then, that he insisted in the Declaration of Independence that one of the inalienable human rights is "the pursuit of happiness."[3]

Perhaps you are wondering why today's propensity to pursue pleasure is germane to a study of the devaluing of human life in Western culture. First, those promoting a moral philosophy based on pleasure have typically been atheists and agnostics, who have reduced humanity to pleasure-seeking machines or animals. They deny the intrinsic goodness of self-sacrificial love or creativity or many other endeavors that make us human. Contra these secularists, I maintain that these and many other human pursuits are good, whether or not they result in pleasure or keep us from pain.

Second, our current idolization of pleasure has powerful ramifications for bioethics. The notion that the value of a human life can be measured by how much pleasure a person can experience, and the concomitant idea that pain is a moral evil, opens the door for the permissibility—and perhaps even the encouragement—of suicide, assisted suicide, and maybe even involuntary euthanasia. Many bioethicists today argue that we have a moral obligation to rid the world of pain and suffering, even if that means killing the people who are experiencing it. In this confused view, the lives of people who experience more pain than pleasure are not worthwhile, so death is preferable to a painful life. In addition, many people experiencing chronic suffering are considered a drag on their fellow human beings, who have to sacrifice pleasure and suffer pain to serve them. These suffering individuals "get in our way." Also, the rampant increase of abortions in the late twentieth century is linked to the Sexual Revolution, so the unrestrained pursuit of sexual pleasure has resulted in over fifty million babies being killed in the United States—and hundreds of millions more worldwide—before they had the chance to be born.

The Enlightenment witnessed a critical shift in thinking about pleasure. In the Christian tradition, pleasure had never been identified with morality, but instead Christianity had traditionally taught self-denial. Some branches of Christianity even idealized asceticism. Christian churches, before and after the Reformation, insisted that pleasure had to be evaluated, because it could be a temptation to immorality. In any case, it was certainly not viewed as a way to determine what is moral and what is immoral. Many Enlightenment thinkers remonstrated against many elements of Christianity, including its focus on self-denial and asceticism, embracing instead an Epicurean view of morality. This was so pronounced that the eminent historian Roy Porter asserted, "The Enlightenment's great historical watershed lay in the validation of pleasure." He perceptively continued, "The new science [during the Enlightenment] promoted mechanical models of man essentially as a machine motivated to pursue pleasure and avoid pain."[4] Recently Oxford historian Faramerz Dabhoiwala, who calls the Enlightenment the "First Sexual Revolution," explains how important this Epicurean attitude was in the Enlightenment: "It is sometimes remarked that the Enlightenment's greatest triumph was its elevation of the pursuit of happiness as the most important aim in life.... Nothing epitomizes the advance of this general idea than changing attitudes towards sexual pleasure."[5]

One of the most radical Enlightenment figures to resurrect Epicureanism forthrightly was Julien La Mettrie. In 1750 he wrote *System of Epicurus*, in which he expressed complete approval of Epicurus's hedonistic philosophy. Exalting pleasure as the supreme good, he indicated that his chief pursuits in life were good food, good company, joyfulness, study, and the seduction of women.[6] He followed up this work with *Anti-Seneca* (1748), in which he blasted the Greek and Roman Stoics for focusing on their souls rather than their bodies. He disdained their stress on self-control, believing that the path to happiness lies elsewhere. Instead, he believed that we should give freer rein to the passions. He stated that "we shall not try to control what rules us; we shall not give orders to our sensations. We shall recognize their dominion and our slavery and try to make it pleasant for us, convinced as we are that happiness in life lies there."[7] When La Mettrie discussed pleasure, erotic pleasure was often at the forefront, and after a brief, unhappy marriage, he became a profligate womanizer. He devoted an entire work, *The Voluptuousness*, to extolling sexual pleasure.

La Mettrie scandalized his contemporaries, including many who sympathized with his materialist metaphysics and his hedonistic bent. They sensed that his moral philosophy, with its stress on the pursuit of happiness and pleasure, would end up discarding all moral values. The historian Lester Crocker blames La Mettrie for "develop[ing] the first theory of nihilism in the eighteenth century."[8] In the introduction to his collected philosophical works, La Mettrie explained that according to his moral philosophy, "nothing is absolutely just, nothing absolutely unjust. There is no true equity, there are no absolute vices, no absolute greatness and no absolute crimes."[9] As if this amoralist stance were not radical enough, he also provocatively indicated that those deemed immoral by society could achieve happiness, too, just as well as the morally upright.[10] He tried to allay his critics' fears by claiming that philosophy, even moral philosophy, has no impact on anyone's actions. As a determinist, he believed that behavior was shaped entirely by heredity and the environment (mostly the former). Thus, La Mettrie assured his opponents, there is nothing to fear. The philosopher—even a materialist philosopher such as La Mettrie—"is a model of humanity, frankness, gentleness and probity; while writing against the law of nature, he follows it rigorously, and while arguing about what is just, he nevertheless behaves justly in relation to society."[11]

In *Man the Machine*, La Mettrie had likewise denied that his philosophy would lead to the moral breakdown of society. He claimed that those sharing his views would not destroy others, but

will love human character even in his enemies.... In short, the
materialist, convinced, in spite of the protests of his vanity, that
he is but a machine or an animal, will not maltreat his kind,
for he will know too well the nature of those actions, whose
humanity is always in proportion to the degree of the analogy
proved above [between human beings and animals]; and following the natural law given to all animals he will not wish to
do to others what he would not wish them to do to him.[12]

This passage seems to imply that La Mettrie had derived the Golden
Rule (at least the negative form of it) from "natural law." However, when
La Mettrie used the term "natural law," he did not mean what most
Enlightenment thinkers meant. He did not think natural law was an
objective moral law laid down by a deity. Rather, for La Mettrie natural
law was an inborn feeling that probably arises out of fear that what we
do to others might redound on us sometime down the road.[13]

In sum, La Mettrie construed humans as pleasure-seeking machines.
Happiness is the only goal in life, since "Nature has created us all solely
to be happy."[14] So how do we achieve happiness? According to La Mettrie, "To have everything one wants—a favorable organisation, beauty,
science, wit, grace, talents, honours, wealth, health, pleasure and glory—
is true, perfect happiness." Of course, in the hierarchy of pleasures, La
Mettrie ranked sexual pleasure at the apex, stating, "there is no Sovereign Good as exquisite as the great pleasure of love."[15] Judging from his
writings and his lifestyle, it is clear that he was not thinking of Christian
self-sacrificial love (*agape*) in this context, but rather erotic love. In his
pursuit of happiness, La Mettrie lived a life of self-indulgence and hedonistic debauchery centered on wine, women, and song (and intellectual
stimulation).[16] He admitted in *The Voluptuousness*, "Pleasure, sovereign
master of men and gods, before whom everything disappears, even reason itself, you know how much my heart adores you, and all the sacrifices
it has made at your altar."[17] Pleasure had become his god. No wonder
historian Jonathan Israel calls him the "self-proclaimed prophet of pleasurable indulgence."[18]

La Mettrie's message of the primacy of pleasure found a ready audience in the eighteenth century, even though almost everyone rejected the amoral bent of his philosophy. Indeed, even other leading figures of the Radical Enlightenment distanced themselves from La Mettrie. Most of the philosophes—even the more radical ones—hoped to find a rational basis for morality, rather than dispensing with it altogether. Jonathan Israel argues that this made La Mettrie out of step with the Radical Enlightenment: "This amoralism of his last works sets La Mettrie firmly at odds with the neo-*Spinosistes* [followers of Spinoza] and materialists and hence with the Radical Enlightenment."[19]

The most notorious of La Mettrie's disciples was undoubtedly the Marquis de Sade, a late eighteenth-century French writer who spent much of his adult life in prison or in an asylum, first because of rape and attempted murder, and later because of his obscene and shocking novels and essays. Though some considered him insane, it seems that his main crime was to take La Mettrie's nihilistic, pleasure-seeking philosophy seriously. According to Crocker, "The similarities of La Mettrie's thinking to Sade's are so obvious that we can understand why the marquis called him one of his spiritual godfathers."[20] Sade believed that the universe is amoral and cruel, so when humans are brutal to each other, they are actually acting in harmony with the cosmic order (or to be more consistent with Sade, I should say, "cosmic disorder").[21] Furthermore, Sade recognized that if materialism is true and the universe is amoral, then there is no reason for an individual to sacrifice his own pleasure for the good of anyone else. Indeed, if an individual gains pleasure through the suffering of another—either directly or indirectly—then Sade saw no problem with it. He stated, "the action which serves me by hurting another is perfectly indifferent to nature," and since in his view nature is all that exists, hurting others is permissible.[22]

Of course, Sade, whose name was immortalized in the word sadism, found pleasure in directly inflicting suffering and torture on his fellow human beings. He claimed that human life had no particular importance, once remarking that a human life is no more important than a blade of grass.[23] Sade did not believe that humans could love one another, not even their own family members. Concerning paternal love, he wrote,

> It is false that one loves his father; it is false that one can love him; we fear him, but we do not love him; his existence irritates us, and does not please us; self-interest, the holiest of nature's laws, invincibly urges us to desire the death of a person whose fortune we are awaiting; and in this regard, it is doubtless true that it not only would be easy to hate him, but still more natural to kill him.[24]

Indeed, Sade thought it was perfectly reasonable to kill, torture, and harm others, if that was what brought one pleasure. War between humans was normal and natural. He delighted in cruelty and oppression, murder and sexual abuse. Pleasure was the touchstone of his moral philosophy, and he found pleasure in exercising power over others, no matter how much suffering it caused.

The strong, he stated, "is equally right when he tries to despoil the weak and obtain pleasure at his expense.... The more atrociously he harms the weak, the more voluptuously he is thrilled; injustice is his delectation, he enjoys the tears that his oppression snatches from the unfortunate wretch; the more he grieves him, the more he oppresses him, the happier he is."[25] Sade gave a black eye to the hedonistic impulse of the Enlightenment in the same way that the Great Terror provided a warning to those enthusiastic about the French Revolution.

*

Most philosophes, however, even those in the Radical Enlightenment, rejected La Mettrie's nihilistic conclusions, and they were even more horrified by Sade's brutality. They tried to build a more humane morality out of Epicureanism. Helvétius was one of the luminaries of the

Radical Enlightenment who hoped to establish a more sure footing for morality rather than dispense with it. He wanted to construct a scientific morality based on reason rather than revelation. He founded his moral philosophy on his view of human nature. Even though he was an avowed environmental determinist, he still thought that one element of human nature was permanent—our self-love, which he identified as the pursuit of pleasure and the avoidance of pain. "Self-love makes us totally what we are," he asserted in his influential *Treatise on Man* (1773). Indeed he interpreted self-love, or the pursuit of pleasure, as the motive of all human behavior: "The springs of action in man are corporeal pains and pleasures.... Pleasure and pain are, and always will be, the only principles of action in man."[26] As signaled by the adjective "corporeal" in this quotation—and reinforced elsewhere in his writings—Helvétius's vision of pleasure was primarily physical.[27]

The term "self-love" did not carry negative connotations for Helvétius. He considered it perfectly just and right (and unavoidable, since he was a determinist) that people should seek their own pleasure. Even though he probably did not believe in God, nonetheless he stated, "The will of God, just and good, is that the children of the earth should be happy, and enjoy every pleasure compatible with the general welfare."[28] As with La Mettrie, Helvétius found sexual pleasure the highest form of pleasure: "Now, among all the pleasures, that which without doubt acts the most forcibly on us, and communicates the greatest energy to the soul, is the love of women. Nature, by attaching the greatest intoxication to the enjoyment of them, intended to make them one of the most powerful principles of our activity."[29] Crocker called Helvétius an "apologist of free love" who called for the dissolution of marriage and the family.[30] He lived accordingly by chasing women.[31] However, Helvétius also acknowledged that people strive for power, presumably because this abets them in their pursuit of pleasure. Even the love of virtue, or the desire for equity and justice, he thought, is simply a means for people to gain more pleasure for themselves.[32]

Despite his emphasis on self-love and his relativizing of morality, Helvétius was not abandoning virtue altogether, nor did he think that every individual should pursue his or her own untrammeled desires. Rather he wanted to establish a morality that would produce true human happiness. He considered the Golden Rule insufficient and wanted to replace it with a higher principle: "That the public good is the supreme law."[33] He exuded optimism that universal happiness was within the grasp of an enlightened society guided by reason. All that was necessary was wise legislation. Especially conducive to happiness would be laws that would even out the inequities in the distribution of wealth, so that everyone could work moderately, provide for their own needs, and have a reasonable amount of leisure. The legislature can achieve this universal happiness, he thought, by passing proper laws that reward virtue with pleasure and punish vice with pain. Thus, by adopting his deterministic pleasure-pain principle in legislation, "men will be forced to be virtuous."[34]

It is unclear, however, why Helvétius thought that a body of human legislators would abandon their own pursuit of self-love, pleasure, and power—which he insisted all humans were constrained to follow—to pass such wise laws. Given Helvétius's view of human nature, why would the rich and powerful give way politically to create a system that would distribute wealth more equitably? Helvétius had clearly stated, "Man, solely anxious for himself, seeks nothing but his own happiness."[35] Why, then, would legislators care enough about the happiness of everyone else to pass laws intended to benefit all of humanity? I agree with Helvétius that we should aim to benefit all humanity and find ways to make others happy. Universal happiness is indeed a wonderful goal.

However, his own philosophy contradicts any such attempt to legislate happiness, because it would seem that the individuals who would have to force everyone (else) to be virtuous would somehow have to extricate themselves from their own self-love in order to care about the happiness of others. But the legislators presumably seek nothing but their own happiness. Further, if Helvétius had simply applied his philosophy to himself, he would have recognized that Helvétius "seeks nothing but his own happiness." Why, then, should others follow his self-serving philosophy, which is—if he is to be consistent—nothing but the expression of his own pursuit of happiness, pleasure, and power? How did Helvétius think that he and some wise legislators alone could overcome the determinism and the pleasure-pain principle inherent in his system?

Many philosophes rejected Helvétius's hedonistic ethic, which did not comport well with the natural law morality that was prominent in the mainstream of the Enlightenment. The Radical Enlightenment was more receptive, but even some of its prominent figures—such as Denis Diderot—were wary of Helvétius's moral philosophy. Diderot was absolutely appalled by La Mettrie's nihilistic philosophy, but he was conflicted about Helvétius. Diderot, co-editor of the magisterial *Encyclopedia*, a compendium of human knowledge and a powerful tract for enlightened rationalism, was a closet materialist. After a brief stint in prison for his radical views, he only divulged his most radical thoughts in his private writings (and probably in conversations at the salons he frequented). He entrusted these manuscripts to a fellow materialist to publish posthumously. In his private writings he evinced sympathy for Helvétius's deterministic view of humanity. In 1773–1774 he read Helvétius's *Treatise on Man* four times. The reason he had to grapple so intensively with this book was that Helvétius seemed merely to be spelling out the conclusions of many of Diderot's own views. However, Diderot could not bring himself to accept all the conclusions that Helvétius reached. He agreed with Helvétius's materialism and determinism, and before reading *Treatise on Man* he seemed to accept Helvétius's Epicureanism. Diderot even wrote the article on Epicurus in his *Encyclopedia*, and though it purports merely to be relating Epicurus's own views, it was "full of loving fondness" for the Greek philosopher.[36] Diderot was also sharply critical of sexual continence and wrote pornographic works encouraging free sexuality, so he certainly endorsed a hedonistic lifestyle.[37]

However, even though Diderot the rationalist embraced a philosophy similar in many ways to Helvétius's, he balked at following the logic of Helvétius's moral philosophy. Some scholars have noted that Diderot struggled to reconcile his logical, rational side with his emotions and sentiments. After intensively studying and reflecting on *Treatise on Man*, his sentimental side came to the fore, causing him to reject his own previous views on morality. According to D. W. Smith, Diderot "was so appalled by Helvétius's extreme conclusions that his sentimental nature reasserted itself and forced him to refute his own materialistic ethics." Before 1773 the prevailing thrust of Diderot's ethical philosophy implied that "Man had no exceptional status: he was simply 'un animal un peu plus parfait qu'un autre' [an animal (only) a little more perfect than another]." However, deep down he somehow knew that this was not true, so he was repelled by Helvétius's vision of humanity, a vision that he shared to some extent. As Smith explains, "Diderot's 'Réfutation' of *De l'homme* [Refutation of *Treatise on Man*] is thus also a refutation of Diderot's own ethics, an attempt to convince himself as well as Helvétius that man was something special in nature, quite distinct from animals in the realm of moral causation."[38] In his novel *Jacques the Fatalist* (completed in 1780, but only published in the 1790s), Diderot expressed his continued belief in determinism, but also insisted that humans have some autonomy to change themselves. According to Arthur Wilson, "*Jacques le fataliste* (*Jacques the Fatalist*) affirms the dignity of man and the paradox of moral autonomy in a deterministic universe."[39] Diderot could not figure out rationally how to square determinism with human autonomy, so he simply asserted both and left his readers to sort out the paradox.

❧

Despite the problems with his ideology, Helvétius gained some influential disciples and allies, who would catapult his ideas into even greater prominence in the nineteenth century. Inspired by Helvétius's claim that legislation was the key to achieving human happiness, the British thinker

Jeremy Bentham devoted his life to devising legislative reforms that he hoped would benefit humanity. Indeed Bentham had grandiose aspirations to become the most "effectively benevolent" person ever to live. After formulating detailed plans for pauper and penal reform, he felt slighted that the British monarch did not see fit to commit all the paupers and prisoners of Britain to his supervision. As directed in his will, his skeleton was preserved and—filled out with straw and topped with a wax head—it is on display at University College, London. Bentham thought the display of his image would inspire future generations to emulate his beneficence.[40] Humility was apparently not one of Bentham's stronger moral qualities.

The opening words of one of Bentham's most important works, *An Introduction to the Principles of Morals and Legislation* (1789), explained the centrality of pleasure to his moral philosophy: "Nature has placed mankind under the governance of two sovereign masters, *pain* and *pleasure*. It is for them alone to point out what we ought to do, as well as to determine what we shall do."[41] Bentham thus used pain and pleasure as the only criteria for defining what is morally good, and he called this the principle of utility. He stated, "Now, pleasure is in *itself* a good: nay, even setting aside immunity from pain, the only good: pain is in itself an evil; and, indeed, without exception, the only evil; or else the words good and evil have no meaning."[42] Even though he exalted pleasure to the highest good, Bentham was not thereby endorsing the unrestrained pursuit of each individual for his or her own pleasure. Rather he taught that the supreme goal of morality was the greatest happiness for the greatest number—with happiness being defined as experiencing the greatest amount of pleasure and the least amount of pain.

Bentham's moral philosophy based its judgments about the morality of actions or rules on their consequences: Do they yield more pleasure and avoid pain, or not? Followers of Bentham have divided over whether to apply this principle of utility to specific actions (act utilitarians) or moral rules (rule utilitarians), but in either case, morality is measured by the total amount of happiness they bring to everyone affected by them. Bentham, rationalist that he was, believed that at some point in the future humanity would be able to practice "felicific calculus," i.e., the mathematical calculation of pleasures and pains. The value of pleasures and pains for each individual affected by an action or rule would be tallied to figure out its contribution to the total happiness for humanity. The value of a particular pleasure would be measured by factors such as intensity, duration, certainty (or uncertainty), and nearness (or remoteness).[43] Bentham did not think pleasures should be ranked qualitatively, affirming instead that "the game of push-pin is of equal value with the arts and sciences of music and poetry."[44] "Felicific calculus" would bring legislation and morality under the sway of reason and turn it into a veritable science.

Because he insisted that only the consequences of actions or rules justified them as moral or condemned them as immoral, Bentham denied that a person's intentions played any role in judging the morality or immorality of an action. Nor did he think that individuals had any inherent rights that should not be violated. He rejected natural law or natural rights moral philosophy, once deriding natural rights as "nonsense upon stilts."[45] As part of his attack on the notion of natural rights, Bentham even denied that anyone had an inherent right to life. He did maintain murder was immoral, but only because he did not think it would produce the greatest happiness for the greatest number. As the Bentham scholar John Dinwiddy explains, "What made *murder* in his view, a very serious offence was not the extinction of a human life, nor (principally) the pain suffered by the person who was killed, 'for that is commonly less than he would have suffered by a natural death': it was 'the terror which such an act strikes into other men.'"[46] In Bentham's view, then, murder was not wrong because it violated someone's rights or some objective moral standard, but because it would make everyone in society afraid that they might become the target of murder, which was not conducive to the greatest happiness of the greatest number.

Bentham's moral philosophy undermined the Judeo-Christian sanctity-of-life ethic, not only because it reduced humans to seekers of happiness and pleasure, but because it denied the intrinsic value of an individual life. Bentham recognized this, because in his private papers he explicitly condoned infanticide. He reasoned that killing infants would not inspire terror, because those who understood what was happening could not be the victims. Nor would it cause distress in the infants, because they would not know anything about it. Thus it would not reduce human happiness, and since he did not think anyone had an intrinsic right to life, infanticide was morally justified. Presumably infanticide would not only be permissible, but morally praiseworthy (in Bentham's view), if it would increase the pleasure of other people or reduce the suffering of the infant. As long as the infant died painlessly, its interests were irrelevant.[47]

Bentham's hedonistic philosophy also caused him to reject Judeo-Christian sexual morality, which he considered irrational and a hindrance to pleasure. Like many other Enlightenment figures, Bentham considered sexual pleasure one of the greatest pleasures in life. Though circumspect in his published writings, Bentham revealed his sexual libertinism in his private manuscripts. There he stated that any consensual sexual relationship was morally permissible, including homosexuality, bestiality, and sex between teachers and their pupils. In order to foster greater sexual freedom and its accompanying pleasures, Bentham favored the toleration of contraception, abortion, infanticide, and divorce.[48]

Not only did he castigate Christianity for upholding an allegedly irrational sexual morality, but he also revised the story of Jesus to suit his own purposes. In the gospel according to Bentham, Jesus was an Epicurean who abolished the Jewish law, including its prohibitions against sexual immorality. He explained that Jesus' real message was: "sexuality not discouraged but rather encouraged." He further claimed that Jesus was not celibate, but had a sexual relationship with Mary Magdalene and possibly with John.[49] Of course, Bentham simply ignored all of Jesus' condemnations of sexual immorality, such as his teaching that it is impermissible to even look on a woman with lust, as well as his rather frequent fulminations against adultery, fornication, and even divorce. Instead he painted an image of Jesus that looks a lot more like some Enlightenment philosophe—or Bentham himself—than the real, historical Jesus.

＊

Among Bentham's most influential disciples was John Stuart Mill, one of the most famous British intellectuals of the nineteenth century. His father, a well-connected economist, became a close friend of Bentham in 1809 and spent a great deal of time with him and his associates, so the young Mill grew up surrounded by Benthamites. In his zeal to become a great Benthamite crusader for reform, Mill formed a circle of like-minded intellectuals in 1822 called the Utilitarian Society. The group was small and short-lived, but it gave a new name to the Benthamite moral philosophy: utilitarianism. In 1826 Mill, whose father had rigorously educated him to accept the principles of science, logic, rationalism, and the omnipotence of the environment in shaping human character and conduct, faced an intellectual crisis. He despaired of ever achieving happiness, recognizing that even if he achieved his goals, he would not be happy. Mill admitted in his autobiography that "my love of mankind...had worn itself out," and he suffered a prolonged period of melancholy.[50]

Two considerations lifted him out of his depression. First, he came to understand that the way to achieve happiness is not by dwelling on one's own happiness, but rather by seeking other people's happiness, or by pursuing some art or other pursuit as an end in itself. Pursuing one's own happiness would not make one happy. Second, Mill was deeply impressed by reading William Wordsworth's poetry in 1828. Thereafter he found solace in poetry from the Romantic movement, finding that it touched his emotions in ways that the cold logic of Enlightenment philosophy could not. Mill's father had not been tender or emotional, and he viewed humans through the lens of science, as the objects of rational inquiry, completely subject to the laws of nature. After 1828 Mill integrated emotion into his philosophy to such an extent that he wrote "cultivation of the feelings became one of the cardinal points of my ethical and philosophical creed."[51]

Nonetheless, despite this transition, Mill remained firmly committed to utilitarianism. In 1863 he published his most important statement on moral philosophy, *Utilitarianism.* Therein Mill defended Bentham's greatest happiness principle:

> The creed which accepts as the foundation of morals, Utility, or the Greatest Happiness Principle, holds that actions are right in proportion as they tend to promote happiness, wrong as they tend to produce the reverse of happiness. By happiness is intended pleasure and the absence of pain; by unhappiness, pain and the privation of pleasure.[52]

Mill rejected natural law morality, arguing against the view that "the Just must have an existence in Nature as something absolute." He considered natural law morality a moral intuition that is not always binding, explaining, "That a feeling is bestowed on us by Nature does not necessarily legitimate all its promptings."[53] However, despite overtly rejecting moral sentiments as a reliable guide to morality, Mill did smuggle into his utilitarianism the view that moral sentiments can receive moral consideration, because he maintained that following one's moral sentiments, as well as intellectual pursuits, can bring pleasure to people. Indeed Mill modified Bentham's moral philosophy by asserting that following one's intellectual and moral inclinations was qualitatively superior to sensory pleasures.[54]

Mill also tried to make his utilitarianism compatible with Christian morality, asserting, "In the golden rule of Jesus of Nazareth we read the complete spirit of the ethics of utility. To do as you would be done by, and to love your neighbour as yourself, constitute the ideal perfection of utilitarian morality."[55] However, unlike Jesus, for Mill love was not the highest principle (and of course he completely ignored what Jesus called the Greatest Commandment—to love God). For Mill love was only a means to an end, and the highest end was happiness or pleasure. Like Bentham, Mill was completely unimpressed with Jesus' teaching about sexual morality, and he expressed sympathy with the Utopian Socialists Robert Owen and Charles Fourier, who advocated the abolition of marriage and free sexual relationships.[56]

✻

The early French socialist Fourier was even more radical than Mill or Bentham, though in some respects they were kindred spirits. Fourier wrote most of his works in the first quarter of the nineteenth century, though his influence increased in the 1830s and 1840s, as his disciples established utopian agrarian communities in the United States and elsewhere. Fourier harshly criticized civilized society, because it repressed human passions, rather than finding ways to give freer rein to our instincts. Civilization, he insisted, thus breeds unhappiness and stymies human flourishing, producing poverty, frustration, ennui, and misery. Fourier laid out a vision for a utopian society called Harmony that would throw off the shackles of conventional society to allow more untrammeled pursuit of pleasure.

Many features of Fourier's blueprint for Harmony seem bizarre (rising at 3 a.m., for instance, after having had less than five hours of sleep), but like so many socialists, he insisted that his views were scientific. Fourier scholars Jonathan Beecher and Richard Bienvenu admit that Fourier's "bizarre style, his extravagant cosmogony, and his quaintly precise specifications concerning rose-growing and animal-breeding in Harmony have all helped perpetuate his reputation as a harmless and entertaining crank.... But Fourier conceived of himself as the 'Messiah of Reason' who had come to save mankind."[57]

Fourier based all his speculations on the universal "law of attraction," which he considered just as applicable to human affairs as the law of gravitation was to the physical world.[58] Subsumed under this law of attraction were twelve human passions, and Fourier thought he could mathematically calculate the passionate attractions.[59] The twelve passions are the five senses, friendship, love (usually meaning sex in Fourier's usage), paternity or family, ambition, cabalism (desire to intrigue), butterfly (desire for varied pleasures), and composite (the meshing of all the passions).[60]

Fourier did not believe that all humans had exactly the same amount of each passion, so there were many different passional types: 810 different ones to be precise. The ideal community, or phalanstery as he called it, should have two of each passional type, so Harmony would ideally need 1,620 members (though he made allowance for experimental communities of fewer people in early phases of development). Fourier did not seem to think industrial or commercial activity was consistent with human passions, so Harmony's economy would be primarily agricultural. The diligent denizens of Harmony would engage in jobs based on the principle of attraction. Even filthy jobs could be attractive, Fourier claimed, to young boys who delight in getting dirty. Everyone's work schedule would be varied to prevent boredom and keep the work attractive.

Fourier was especially indignant at the poverty endemic in early nineteenth-century French society, so he imagined a community "in which the least of men will be rich, polished, sincere, pleasant, virtuous and handsome (excepting the very old); an order of things in which marriage and our other customs will have been forgotten, their very absence having inspired a host of amorous innovations which we cannot yet imagine."[61] In Fourier's utopia, everyone's passions would be accommodated, because everyone would be guaranteed a minimum of basic necessities, creature comforts, and even sexual liaisons. For tactical purposes, Fourier kept his sexual libertinism secret during his lifetime, but in 1817 he penned a secret manuscript, *The New Amorous World*, which divulged his views. Therein he derided monogamy and Christian sexual norms, arguing that they are incompatible with human passions and thus lead to unhappiness. He promoted more freewheeling sexual liaisons and amorous adventures with multiple partners, which reflected his own private life. Fourier recognized that publicizing his radical views on sexuality would evoke a backlash against his socialist experiment, so he kept quiet publicly about them. However, he privately wrote that the unleashing of the amorous passions was fundamental, indeed "the mainspring of all works and of the whole of universal attraction."[62]

✻

Fourier's stress on passion, especially sexual passion, and the role of civilization in repressing passions, makes him seem a harbinger of

Sigmund Freud, founder of psychoanalysis and popularizer of the idea
that the unconscious plays a powerful role in the human psyche. Freud
probably never read Fourier, but both men were heirs of the Enlightenment, not only in its focus on scientific rationalism, but also in its stress
on happiness and pleasure. Even though Freud explained human behavior by appealing to irrational drives and instincts, especially the libido
or sexual instinct, he insisted that all human behavior and the operations
of the psyche were strictly determined. Thus the mind could be explored
scientifically, and Freud posed as a logical scientist conducting empirical
research to plumb the depths of the human psyche. Today, however,
many scholars see his psychology as highly speculative and given to
flights of fancy.

In *Civilization and Its Discontents* (1930) Freud claimed that human
life has no purpose—at least none that we can know—but we know that
people seek happiness. Like Bentham and Mill (and Epicurus), he defined
happiness as avoiding pain and experiencing pleasure. He stated, "As we
see, what decides the purpose of life is simply the programme of the
pleasure principle. The principle dominates the operation of the mental
apparatus from the start."[63] As is evident in most of his writings, for
Freud the sex act was "the greatest pleasure attainable by us," and was
one of the most powerful motivations behind human behavior.[64] Nonetheless, after the horrors of World War I, Freud also posited the importance of an aggressive instinct, which he called the death instinct, in
shaping human behavior.

Freud was much more pessimistic than Bentham that humans could
ever attain happiness, because he believed that humans had to repress
their instinctual drives in order to live in civilized society. Unlike Fourier,
he did not think it possible to cast off all the restraints of present society
to fulfill the passions. He had a more positive view of civilized society as
a necessary evil and thought that some repression was unavoidable. He
admitted it was a trade-off, but one that he thought worth making.
Nonetheless, he urged his society to reduce the amount of repression and
loosen its sexual mores, which he considered too restrictive. Despite his
pessimism about achieving happiness, Freud still thought that the quest

for happiness and pleasure was inescapable. He stated, "The programme of becoming happy, which the pleasure principle imposes on us, cannot be fulfilled; yet we must not—indeed, we cannot—give up our efforts to bring it nearer to fulfillment by some means or other."[65]

Freud explained that morality consisted of social conventions that allowed humans to live together in society. Some of these have become ingrained in our psyche as a conscience, or what Freud called the super-ego. The super-ego tries to restrain the instincts (the Freudian id), which, if given free rein, would undermine social life. But why do humans need to live in society? Freud answered by pointing out two factors that make social life necessary: the compulsion to work and the power of love. Humans need to cooperate in their work, and sexual love draws a man and woman together, forming a family.

While emphasizing the importance of sexual love in binding society together, Freud had no appreciation for loving all humanity. In *Civilization and Its Discontents*, he criticized those who embraced a universal love for all mankind, objecting that "not all men are worthy of love."[66] A few pages later he remonstrated against Jesus' allegedly impossible command to love your neighbor as yourself, because "If I love someone, he must deserve it in some way." Indeed Freud thought it would be morally wrong to love a stranger who "cannot attract me by any worth of his own." Worse yet, he considered it more rational to hate strangers than to love them, stating, "Not merely is this stranger in general unworthy of my love; I must honestly confess that he has more claim to my hostility and even my hatred." Freud's contempt for at least some parts of humanity also comes through clearly when he explained, "But if I am to love him [a stranger] (with this universal love) merely because he, too, is an inhabitant of this earth, like an insect, an earth-worm or a grass-snake, then I fear that only a small modicum of my love will fall to his share—not by any possibility as much as, by the judgement of my reason, I am entitled to retain for myself." Comparing humans with insects and other vermin in the midst of an argument about why we need not love strangers—and probably should hate them—was a tragic corollary to Freud's atheistic worldview.[67] Unfortunately, it would come back to haunt him. In 1938, after the Nazi annexation of Austria, Freud was forced to flee from a regime that refused to love its Jewish neighbors and compared them to noxious vermin.

*

Despite the many differences between Freud's and Fourier's perspectives, both contributed—directly and indirectly—to the Sexual Revolution and the youth counterculture of the 1960s. Fourier's complete works were published in France in the 1960s, with his New Amorous World becoming public for the first time in 1967. In 1971 Beecher and Bienvenu published an English translation of excerpts from Fourier's work. They recognized that Fourier's socialist and sexual utopia of passionate attraction would appeal to the anti-capitalist, anti-industrial, anti-Establishment counterculture, whose motto was, "If it feels good, do it," and "Do your own thing." (The Sixties crowd, like most earlier Fourierists, simply ignored Fourier's detailed, picayune prescriptions for society that seem rather authoritarian and oppressive, rather than individualistic and liberating.) Freud's works likewise enjoyed cult status among young intellectuals who exulted in his plea for greater sexual freedom. Also, Freud and Fourier influenced some of the leading figures in the Sexual Revolution, such as the famous philosopher Herbert Marcuse, who was acclaimed as the "father of the New Left" in the 1960s.[68]

In his book-length discussion of Freudian psychology, Eros and Civilization (1955), Marcuse challenged Freud's claim that civilization is necessarily built on the repression of instincts, especially the sex drive. In this work Marcuse largely adopted a Freudian perspective, wedding it to his version of Marxist socialism.[69] However, he argued that Freud was wrong to think that a "non-repressive civilization" is impossible. Marcuse believed that a future socialist society could eliminate repression, clearing the way for the pleasure principle to have greater sway than Freud had thought possible. Marcuse wanted to jettison many of the sexual taboos in modern society, while replacing the capitalist system with socialism. The transformation of work relations and sexual relations would lead, according to Marcuse, to a re-sexualization of every individual's entire body (whatever that means), so that the "body in its entirety would become an object of cathexis, a thing to be enjoyed—an instrument of pleasure."[70] This new development, Marcuse explained, would lead to the disintegration of the social institutions that have supported repression in civilization, including monogamy and the family as we know it.

Marcuse's focus on the importance of pleasure shaped the way he viewed death and dying. In the final two pages of *Eros and Civilization* he tried to overcome the problem of death, blaming our repressive society for exacerbating the problem: "Not those who die, but those who die before they must and want to die, those who die in agony and pain, are the great indictment against civilization." In a non-repressive society, on the other hand, death would be liberating. Suicide would become an acceptable way of exercising one's freedom. However one died, though, he hoped "it can be made rational—painless." Marcuse implied in this passage that neither death nor even suicide is evil, but pain is the real enemy.[71]

Marcuse's problematic view that pain is worse than death would reverberate throughout the bioethics community in the late twentieth and early twenty-first centuries, though not primarily through Marcuse's influence. Rather, utilitarian ethical philosophy experienced a resurgence in the late twentieth century. Probably the most famous bioethicist promoting utilitarianism today is Peter Singer. For decades Singer has been advocating a form of utilitarianism more nuanced—but still just as problematic—as the classical utilitarianism of Bentham and Mill. Like the classical utilitarians, Singer dispenses with natural law morality and natural rights, arguing that only the consequences of actions matter in determining the rightness or wrongness of conduct. Unlike the classical utilitarians, Singer embraces "preference utilitarianism," a view that takes the interests or informed preferences of individuals—not just the sum total of their pleasure and pain—as the primary moral criteria.

Singer explains, "According to preference utilitarianism, an action contrary to the preference of any being is, unless this preference is outweighed by contrary preferences, wrong." He then applied this insight to the moral question of murder: "Killing a person who prefers to continue living is therefore wrong, other things being equal."[72] One major problem with this view is that other things are never equal. Preferences of some individuals are constantly conflicting with preferences of others. How can we decide among conflicting preferences? Thankfully, Singer clearly rejects the idea that morality is determined by whatever the majority of society prefers. However, what then arbitrates between conflicting preferences? In the case of killing others, anyone's preference to live could easily be "outweighed by contrary preferences." Genghis Khan and his Mongol hordes preferred that everyone living in cities that opposed his conquest should be killed—and because they had superior numbers or superior military prowess, they carried out their preferences. Genghis Khan claimed that he found happiness—and presumably bequeathed a similar happiness to multitudes of fellow Mongols—by trampling on the lives, fortunes, and families of others. He stated, "Man's highest joy is in victory: to conquer one's enemies, to pursue them, to deprive them of their possessions, to make their beloved weep, to ride on their horses, and to embrace their wives and daughters." Undoubtedly Singer would argue that Genghis Khan brought more pain than pleasure to the world and violated the preferences of multitudes. However, what if he made millions happy by tromping on hundreds, or even thousands? Would this make it morally acceptable and even praiseworthy?

Thus the problem remains: Whose preference counts? Maybe a better example would illustrate this problem: In societies where the overwhelming majority of people practice a particular religion, they often believe that religious dissent is harmful. If they then prefer that heretics be executed, are they justified in killing them? This is not merely theoretical, but describes the Roman Catholic Inquisition, the Islamic persecution of infidels in many Muslim societies throughout history, and many other examples of religious intolerance. In these cases, executing a few individuals who prefer not to be killed would accord with the preferences of large numbers and would contribute to greater happiness for multitudes. Whose preference counts? Singer recognizes this problem, stating, "Even for preference utilitarianism, the wrong done to the person killed is merely one factor to be taken into account, and the preference of the victim could sometimes be outweighed by the preference of others."[73] Recognizing the problem, however, is not the same as solving the problem, and Singer never explains how to balance preferences and how to decide when some preferences "outweigh" others.

He also never solves another problem that he recognizes: Given Singer's rejection of God and any ultimate meaning in the cosmos, why should we act morally? Indeed, Singer confronts this issue head-on in a chapter of *Practical Ethics* entitled "Why Act Morally?" One would think that he would tackle this crucial problem at the beginning of the book, because if he cannot solve this conundrum, his whole project fails and the rest of the book is without foundation. Instead he relegates this fundamental question to the end of the book. He admits that atheists such as himself "must give up the idea that life on this planet has some preordained meaning. Life *as a whole* has no meaning." Life, he explains, arose and evolved through random processes without any design, purpose, or meaning. Then he tries to rescue purpose and meaning from the abyss: "All this [i.e., the origin and evolution of life] just happened; it did not happen for any overall purpose. Now that it has resulted in the existence of beings who prefer some states of affairs to others, however, it may be possible for particular lives to be meaningful. In this sense atheists can find meaning in life."[74] It seems to me that Singer is conjuring up meaning in life simply by altering the meaning of "meaning." Most people, when they express a desire for meaning in their life, expect that meaning to be some objective purpose beyond themselves. How can a particular life then be meaningful, if there is no overarching purpose or meaning to be found in the cosmos?

Singer overcomes this objection, it seems, by insisting that morality must be universalizable. He rejects the notion that morality has some kind of objective existence, stating, "Ethical truths are not written into the fabric of the universe."[75] However, he also combats moral subjectivity and the pursuit of selfishness, arguing instead that morality must correspond to principles that can apply to everyone. He explains, "To act ethically is to act in a way that one can recommend and justify to others—that, at least, seems to be part of the very meaning of the term."[76] Singer believes that we as humans can find purpose in life by living for others and reducing pain in the world, rather than pursuing our own selfish interests. I applaud Singer for encouraging us to deny our self-interest to help others, and certainly alleviating pain is a worthy cause. However, I still have not figured out why Singer thinks that pursuing morality gives us a "transcendent cause" to give our lives purpose and meaning.[77] If there is no "transcendent" meaning and purpose in the universe, as he has already indicated, how can the cause be "transcendent"? Perhaps he only means that we are transcending our own selfish perspective, but in that case there is no transcendent reason why living for others would be superior to living for ourselves.

Yet Singer does imply at times that the moral good we do does have transcendent value in a way that his own worldview cannot support. In the closing sentence of *How Are We to Live?*, Singer tells us that if we commit ourselves to living morally, "Most important of all, you will know that you have not lived and died for nothing, because you will have become part of the great tradition of those who have responded to the amount of pain and suffering in the universe by trying to make the world a better place."[78] Make the world a better place? This is nonsense in a worldview that denies that the world has any meaning or purpose. It is nonsense if morality has no transcendent existence, because "better" implies an objective standard toward which something is moving.

However, why should an atheist like Singer or any of the rest of us worry about purpose and meaning in life, if the cosmos has no purpose or meaning? Singer answers, "The need for purpose lies deep in our nature," and is rooted in our evolutionary heritage.[79] However, it would seem that this would make "the need for purpose" simply an illusion produced by chance events over eons. But now that science has shown us that the emperor has no clothes, why should we continue pretending that purpose and meaning matter?

Another problem with Singer's preference utilitarianism is that, despite taking a more nuanced position than classical utilitarianism, it still relies heavily on the pleasure-pain principle. Indeed pleasure and pain figure prominently in Singer's utilitarian moral calculations. He explains in *Practical Ethics* (1979):

> The capacity for suffering and enjoying things is a prerequisite for having interests at all, a condition that must be satisfied before we can speak of interests in any meaningful way.... If a being suffers, there can be no moral justification for refusing to take that suffering into consideration.... This is why the limit of sentience (using the term as a convenient, if not strictly accurate, shorthand for the capacity to suffer or experience enjoyment or happiness) is the only defensible boundary of concern for the interests of others.[80]

Indeed Singer continually factors in the amount of pleasure and pain a being experiences when assessing the value of its life. In defending the moral propriety of infanticide, Singer continually appeals to pleasure and pain as the key arbiters, while rejecting the doctrine of the sanctity of human life. He suggests that if some physical or mental condition, such as spina bifida, will give the child a "miserable" life, then that life is "not worth living," and "utilitarian principles suggest that it is right to kill such children." He then argues that if the death of a "defective" infant would lead to the birth of an infant with better prospects for happiness, "the total amount of happiness will be greater if the defective infant is killed. The loss of happy life for the first infant is outweighed by the gain of a happier life for the second." When considering euthanasia for adults who have lost capacities they formerly had, he claims that their lives "have value if they experience more pleasure than pain; but it is difficult to see the point of keeping such beings alive if their life is, on the whole, miserable."[81] In case we did not already get the point that suffering and pain make life worthless, Singer repeated this point toward the end of the chapter on euthanasia: "A life of physical suffering, unredeemed by any form of pleasure or by a minimal level of self-consciousness, is not worth living."[82]

But why should we assume that pleasure and pain are the sole arbiters of happiness, or that they have any role to play in determining the rightness or wrongness of an action? It simply is not the case that those who have the most pleasure and the least pain are the happiest. Many people who are blind or deaf or have Down syndrome are far happier than those without such disabilities. Some people suffering excruciating chronic pain and living in poverty are far happier than others with a robust life of health and wealth. The pediatric surgeon and former U.S. Surgeon General C. Everett Koop, who had considerable experience treating children with disabilities, provided this perspective:

> I am frequently told by people who have never had the experience of working with children who are being rehabilitated into our society after the correction of a congenital defect that infants with such defects should be allowed to die, or even "encouraged" to die, because their lives could obviously be nothing but unhappy and miserable. Yet it has been my constant experience that disability and unhappiness do not necessarily go together. Some of the most unhappy children whom I have known have all of their physical and mental faculties and on the other hand some of the happiest youngsters have borne burdens which I myself would find very difficult to bear.[83]

The utilitarian claim that pleasure leads to happiness and pain to unhappiness is far too simplistic. It does not correspond with many people's experiences.

Another problem with utilitarianism is that it does not take account of the nobility of human courage and fortitude in the face of suffering, or the irreplaceable value of human love and sympathy in serving those who are suffering. It is remarkable that in past ages in Western society, when pain management was non-existent and many people suffered excruciating agony before they died, suicide was much less common, and philosophers were certainly not extolling the virtues of killing oneself and others to avoid pain and suffering. Many people's lives have been enriched and ennobled by their experience with suffering or with helping others in their distress.

Instead of measuring the value of human lives—including our own—by how much pleasure or pain we experience, I suggest that we recognize the intrinsic value of all human lives. Once we understand the intrinsic moral worth of our fellow humans and our objective moral responsibility to love them, we will have all the more reason to endeavor to relieve their suffering and contribute to their pleasure. If we love our neighbors as ourselves, we will seek to alleviate their pain. However, we will not degrade them or any other human being by thinking that a painful life is less valuable than a pleasurable one. Humans are simply not pleasure-seeking machines that can be thrown out if they are not functioning properly, i.e., if they are experiencing pain. We dare not sacrifice our disabled and pain-ridden neighbors on the altar of our own pleasure.

SIX

Superman's Contempt for Humanity

Existentialism and Postmodernism

Die at the right time; thus teaches Zarathustra.... Far too many [people] live and hang much too long on their branches. May a storm come to shake all these rotten and worm-eaten ones from the tree.
—Friedrich Nietzsche[1]

When Clarence Darrow desperately struggled to rescue Nathan Leopold and Richard Loeb from the gallows in their sensational murder trial in 1924, he not only argued that biological and environmental determinism minimized their responsibility (as we have seen in chapters three and four). He also conjured the specter of Nietzsche, who powerfully influenced the thinking of Leopold, an impressionable young intellectual. According to Darrow, Leopold murdered an innocent boy purely for the sake of adventure, in part because Leopold considered himself a Nietzschean Superman not subject to conventional morality. Leopold made the cardinal mistake, Darrow told the jury, of actually taking Nietzsche's existentialism seriously as a philosophy that could be applied to real life. Darrow was not a Nietzsche scholar, but his rendition of Nietzsche's existentialist philosophy was not far from the mark. He explained, "Nietzsche held a contemptuous, scornful attitude to all those things which the young are taught as important in life; a fixing of new values which are not the values by which any normal child has ever yet been reared.... In other words, man has no obligations; he may do with all other men and all other boys, and all society, as he pleases."[2] In other words, Nietzsche effaced conventional morality, so—Darrow asserted—he paved the way for this cold-blooded murder.

Darrow was not the only one to blame Nietzsche and existentialism for contributing to death, destruction, and brutality. During and after World War I, some British and American intellectuals condemned Nietzsche as one of the key intellectual instigators of that horrific war.[3] Just a few weeks after World War I began, Nietzsche's sister contributed to the image of her brother as a fomenter of war, telling the German public:

> If ever there was a friend of war, who loved warriors and those who struggle, and placed his highest hopes on them, then it was Friedrich Nietzsche. "My brothers in War! I love you completely, I am and I was one of your kind". That is why so many young heroes are marching into enemy territory with *Zarathustra* in their pocket. My brother could never sufficiently stress the purifying, uplifting and sublime effect of war, and as I have already mentioned, he received one of his deepest philosophical insights precisely during the period of his war experience.[4]

Nietzsche's influence on the political and military leaders of Austria-Hungary, Germany, and other nations who unleashed the First World War was probably not decisive. However, Nietzsche may have contributed to the war's outbreak in yet another way. Gavrilo Princip, who sparked the war by assassinating the Austrian archduke Franz Ferdinand, was fond of Nietzsche, as were many of his fellow Serb nationalists, who promoted violence against the Austro-Hungarian Empire to attain their goal of a Greater Serbia.[5]

An Italian militarist who urgently exhorted his country to join the First World War, Benito Mussolini, was also infatuated with Nietzsche. Mussolini and many of his contemporaries saw Nietzsche's philosophy as a justification for breaking with conventional morality and values, even if—maybe especially if—it required violence in the streets.[6] Mussolini explained, "In truth, we are relativists *par excellence*, and the moment relativism linked up with Nietzsche, and with his Will to Power, was when Italian Fascism became, as it still is, the most magnificent creation of an individual and a national Will to Power."[7] Mussolini regarded the violent escapades of his black-shirt goons, including murdering political opponents, an exercise of the Nietzschean Will to Power.

Some scholars—both during and after the Third Reich—considered Nietzsche a precursor to Nazi ideology and the atrocities perpetrated by Hitler and his minions. Hitler publicly visited and contributed funds to the Nietzsche Archives to honor the founder of existentialism. He also had his photo taken across from Nietzsche's statue in order to publicly associate himself with Nietzsche. The Nazis appointed the Nietzschean philosopher Alfred Bäumler to a prestigious professorship at the University of Berlin. Debate still rages on the connections between Nietzsche and Nazism, however, since some Nazis rejected Nietzsche, and many Nietzscheans opposed Nazism and fascism of all kinds.[8]

Though Nietzsche died long before the Nazis came to power, one of the most influential existentialist thinkers of the twentieth century—indeed one of the most prominent philosophers of the twentieth century—Martin Heidegger, lived through the Nazi era. Debate still swirls around his relationship with the Nazi regime, too, because he joined the Nazi Party and collaborated with the Nazification of the University of Freiburg. Existentialism was not necessarily fascist, however, since the famous French existentialist, Jean-Paul Sartre, who was enthralled with Nietzsche and Heidegger, favored Marxism, albeit an idiosyncratic form of Marxism. Sartre was a staunch foe of Hitler, Mussolini, and all forms

Hitler posed across from a bust of Nietzsche at the Nietzsche Archive in
Weimar to indicate his admiration for Nietzsche. The caption claims that
Nietzsche was a forerunner of Nazism. *Heinrich Hoffmann,* Hitler wie ihn
keiner kennt *(1938)*

of fascism. However, he threw his full support to that other great master
of brutality: Stalin. Existentialism was equal opportunity when it came
to the choice of dictators.

It is not my purpose to dissect the political commitments of
Nietzsche, Heidegger, Sartre, or later amoralist philosophers (often
known as post-structuralists or postmodernists), except inasmuch as
their ideas and actions impinge on the sanctity of human life and bioethics. At first glance, one might take Nietzsche and his successors to be a
counterweight to the kinds of dehumanizing philosophies that I sketched
in preceding chapters. After all, Nietzsche was a staunch foe of materialism, positivism, and scientism. He upheld individual freedom and creativity. However, unfortunately, Nietzsche jumped out of the frying pan into
the fire. He rejected all human rights and morality, contemptuously
dismissing the masses of humanity as the "herd." He thereby implied
that most people are no better than animals. Nietzsche may have rescued

the aristocratic, creative genius—the so-called Overman or Superman—
from the dehumanizing tendencies of scientific materialism and determinism. However, he consigned the rest of humanity to a state of
inferiority and subservience—or even death.

When Nietzsche sounded the death knell for God, he also announced
the demise of the Christian conception of humanity. He despised the
Christian belief that humans have a soul and exhorted his contemporaries to *"remain faithful to the earth*, and do not believe those who
speak to you of otherworldly hopes!"[9] Despite his ambivalence about
science in general and Darwin's theory of natural selection in particular,
he believed in the animal ancestry of humans. This meant that humans
were not specially created beings, made in the image of God. Rather we
still bear the imprint of our animal ancestors. Nietzsche explained, "You
have made your way from worm to man, and much in you is still worm.
Once you were apes, and even now, too, man is more ape than any ape."[10]
The philosopher Rüdiger Safranski notes that in Nietzsche "this natu-
ralization of the mind and the consequent relativization of the special
status of man, which was in effect a disparagement of man," came from
Darwinian influence.[11]

Indeed, like many nineteenth-century Darwinian-inspired thinkers,
Nietzsche insisted that biological evolution proves that humans are
unequal. According to Nietzsche, Darwin proved that humans are only
"natural beings" who attained their present level, not by treating others
as equals, but by exercising the "privilege of the stronger."[12] If humans
are biologically unequal, Nietzsche reasoned, then some men must be
more valuable than others (and women were far less valuable in
Nietzsche's male-dominated aristocratic hierarchy). Though he had utter
contempt for the emasculated European aristocracy and bourgeoisie of
his own day, he favored some form of aristocracy, because it would reflect
human inequality. In *Beyond Good and Evil* (1886), he explained,
"Every enhancement of the type 'man' has so far been the work of an
aristocratic society—and it will be so again and again—a society that
believes in the long ladder of an order of rank and differences in value
between man and man, and that needs slavery in some sense or other."[13]

Nietzsche rejected the noble and humane ideal, enshrined in the Declaration of Independence, that all humans are equally valuable and have intrinsic rights.

Not only did Nietzsche insist that some superior humans (elsewhere called the Overman) are more valuable than the rabble, but he even endorsed slavery and other forms of oppression. Nietzsche had nothing but disdain for do-gooders who preached human equality and worked for the abolition of slavery. Nietzschean aristocrats should revel in their ability to take advantage of other people. He explained, "The essential characteristic of a good and healthy aristocracy, however, is that it...accepts with a good conscience the sacrifice of untold human beings who, *for its sake*, must be reduced and lowered to incomplete human beings, to slaves, to instruments."[14] Other humans matter little or nothing at all. Unlike Immanuel Kant, who argued that humans must always be treated as ends, not as means, Nietzsche encouraged his readers to make other people mere tools to serve them. The (allegedly) more valuable people should dominate—or even obliterate—the less valuable.

Nietzsche contemptuously rejected Christian morality—with its stress on love, compassion, and humility—deriding it as "slave morality" or even "herd morality." He dismissed it as the creation of a bunch of sickly weaklings who wanted to impose their life-denying and decadent principles on everyone else. Rather, Nietzsche promoted an allegedly life-affirming, "aristocratic morality," which delights in strength, pride, power, dominating others, and oppressing the weak.[15] He explained that oppression and exploitation are what life is all about:

> Here we must beware of superficiality and get to the bottom of the matter, resisting all sentimental weakness: life itself is *essentially* appropriation, injury, overpowering of what is alien and weaker; suppression, hardness, imposition of one's own forms, incorporation and at least, at its mildest, exploitation—but why should one always use those words in which a slanderous intent has been imprinted for ages?

Exploitation, he continued, is simply what it means to live, so there is no use moralizing about it. It "is a consequence of the will to power, which is after all the will to life."[16]

In Nietzsche's philosophy, the will to power was the only guide for the Overman, who lives "beyond good and evil." In *The Genealogy of Morals* (1887), Nietzsche dismissed all moral codes, stating, "To speak of right and wrong *per se* makes no sense at all."[17] However, in his zeal to overturn Christian morality (and most traditional forms of morality), it seems that he did value some kinds of human behavior above others. In the same passage that he dismissed the concepts of right and wrong, he affirmed, "It is an historical fact that the aggressive man, being stronger, bolder, and nobler, has at all times had the better view, the clearer conscience on his side."[18] While claiming to spurn morality, then, he often simply inverted morality, calling good evil and evil good.

Love and compassion, for instance, especially for the weak and sick, was in Nietzsche's view, contrary to the "life-affirming" philosophy of the Overman. Compassion or pity runs contrary to the evolutionary law of natural selection, enervating the instinct for preserving life. "It [compassion] preserves what is ripe for destruction," and favors the "outcasts and condemned."[19] Nietzsche was not just consigning a tiny portion of humanity to death and destruction. In his view the vast bulk of humanity was worthless. He confirmed this in *The Genealogy of Morals*, writing, "To sacrifice humanity as mass to the welfare of a single stronger human species would indeed constitute progress."[20] About the same time he also wrote, "The great majority of men have no right to existence, but are a misfortune to higher men."[21] The great masses of humanity were nothing more than slag, fit for the dump.

Not only did Nietzsche deny the majority of humanity the right to live, but he often implied that his fellow Overmen should not shrink back from delivering the deathblow to their fellow humans, if necessary. In *Ecce Homo* (1888) he expressed hope that in the future some will take upon themselves the glorious task of breeding a higher humanity, which includes the "unsparing destruction of everything degenerate and parasitical."[22] In *Will to Power* (published posthumously) Nietzsche wrote that in the future it would be important "to gain that immense energy of greatness in order to shape the man of the future by means of breeding and also by destroying millions of failures, and not perish from the suffering that one creates; nothing of this sort has ever existed!"[23] Nietzsche was even more explicit in *Twilight of the Idols* (1888), where he defined freedom—which he praised—as the ability to destroy others. Freedom entails, according to Nietzsche, "That one is prepared to sacrifice human beings for one's cause, not excluding oneself. Freedom means that the manly instincts which delight in war and victory dominate over other instincts, for example, over those of 'pleasure.' ... The free man is a *warrior.*" As we see in this quotation, not only should the free individual make war and kill others, but in some cases he might be called upon to kill himself.

In harmony with his life-to-the-aristocratic-few, but death-to-the-masses philosophy, Nietzsche extolled suicide and infanticide as noble acts. In a section of *Thus Spake Zarathustra* (1885) entitled, "On the Free Death," he encouraged his readers to commit suicide at a time of their choosing, rather than dying whenever it is thrust upon them. Apparently, he saw this as another way for individuals to assert their autonomy. He urged them to choose death when they are in a state of victory, rather than later in life, when they are feeble. He lamented that too many people hang on to life too long.[24] In a section of *Twilight of the Idols* on "Morality for Physicians" he not only advocated suicide for those who are sick or whose birth "is a mistake," but he also advised physicians to stop encouraging the sick to continue living, especially if they are "vegetating in cowardly dependence on physicians and machinations, after the meaning of life, the right to life, has been lost." (Remember, this was written long before the use of life-support systems, so he is not referring to artificial technologies and machines that keep people alive.) The new responsibility of the Nietzschean physician "demands the most inconsiderate pushing down and aside of degenerating life—for example, for the right of procreation, for the right to be born, for the right to live."[25] Nietzsche did not say explicitly that physicians ought to kill their patients, but his remarks seem to drive in that direction. What else would it mean to push down or push aside people whose health is not robust?

In *The Gay Science*, he is even more explicit about killing people with disabilities. In a section entitled, "Holy Cruelty," he told a parable about a man who brings a child in his arms to a saint. The child is "miserable [and] deformed," but won't die, so the man asks the saint what he should do. The saint tells him to kill the child, whereupon the man leaves, disappointed. When others rebuke the saint for his cruelty, the saint replies, "But isn't it more cruel to allow it to live?"[26] It seems pretty clear that Nietzsche was using this saint as his own mouthpiece and thus endorsed murdering people with disabilities. Indeed, killing them just makes sense if their lives are worthless, if they are a drag on those whose lives really are valuable, and if compassion and pity are evil.

Since Nietzsche's time, many people have been entranced with his philosophy, seeing it as liberating and exhilarating. They, of course, see themselves as the Overman (or, despite Nietzsche's misogyny, perhaps as the Overwoman), who can break free of the constraints of conventional morality. However, by denying human equality and human rights, and by devaluing the lives of the masses, Nietzsche's philosophy is really a loveless, forlorn philosophy of death, cruelty, and oppression.

Some of Nietzsche's apologists try to craft a kinder, gentler, more tolerant Nietzsche, one who would not hurt a fly. One of the more outrageous examples of this that I recently stumbled across is the strained interpretation of the literary scholar Michael Lackey, a Nietzsche enthusiast. He vehemently denies that Nietzsche's worldview leads to violence or "an anything-goes philosophy." "To the contrary," Lackey contends, "his philosophy mandates an extremely respectful relationship between people, which is calculated to ennoble."[27] Except, Lackey forgot, if those people happen to be sick, weak, disabled, female, or part of the masses— that is, the vast bulk of humanity. Nietzsche scholar and critic Simon

May disagrees with Lackey's untenable position. He notes that some Nietzsche apologists argue that other forms of ethics can also justify inhumanity, so why pick on Nietzsche? May responds,

> To this apologist one would reply that with Nietzsche there is not even an attempt to produce a systematic safety net against cruelty, especially if one judges oneself to be a "higher" type of person with life-enhancing pursuits—and, to this extent, his philosophy licenses the atrocities of a Hitler even though, by his personal table of values, he excoriates anti-Semitism and virulent nationalism. Indeed, to that extent it is *irrelevant* whether or not Nietzsche himself advocates violence and bloodshed or whether he is the gentle person described by his contemporaries. The reality is that the supreme value he places on individual life-enhancement and self-legislation leaves room for, and in some cases explicitly justifies, unfettered brutality.[28]

Of course, Nietzsche might have personally opposed what Hitler or Mussolini did. Nietzsche did not endorse the Nazis' nationalism, anti-Semitism, or biological determinism. However, he still cleared the way for their project by demolishing human rights, love, and compassion.

❧

Two of Nietzsche's most famous followers illustrate this descent into inhumanity. Martin Heidegger, one of the most influential philosophers of the twentieth century, enthusiastically supported Hitler, especially in the early years of the regime. True, he never personally participated in gassing Jews. However, the Nazis appointed him rector (head) of the University of Freiburg in May 1933, and he used his position to remove Jews from university teaching positions, even though he had previously had an adulterous relationship with one of his Jewish students, the brilliant Hannah Arendt. Heidegger's infatuation with Nazism does not imply that either his philosophy—or Nietzsche's—necessarily leads to the horrors of Nazism (especially since Heidegger's initial enthusiasm for Nazism faded after the first couple years of Nazi rule). One of Heidegger's followers, the French philosopher Jean-Paul Sartre, took existentialism in a different political direction, becoming decidedly anti-Nazi and anti-fascist. However, while staunchly attacking the Nazis' worldview and Hitler's atrocities, he became an apologist for Stalin, Mao, and other communist leaders who collectively murdered even more people than Hitler did.

Since existentialists could just as easily embrace left-wing communist atrocities as right-wing fascist ones, perhaps their philosophy was irrelevant to their politics (as some philosophers sympathetic with their philosophy—but not their politics—argue). However, while I acknowledge that neither Heidegger's nor Sartre's philosophy necessarily leads to Nazism or communism, there is still a fundamental question we need to ask: If these thinkers' ideas are so brilliant and insightful, why didn't their philosophies provide them with moral resources to oppose the inhumanity of fascism and communism? Was there something about their philosophies that made them susceptible to accepting inhumanity in its various guises? Indeed, it seems clear to me that their vision of humanity and morality left them vulnerable to the siren song of anti-humanists who scorned human dignity and value.

Heidegger's philosophy is incredibly dense and difficult to comprehend. Even philosophers find his work difficult. His colleague Karl Jaspers wrote to the denazification committee handling Heidegger's case that Heidegger "stands at a remove from true science [*Wissenschaft*]. He often proceeds as if he combined the seriousness of nihilism with the mystagogy of a magician."[29] Heidegger was not as interested in ethics as was Nietzsche or Sartre, but his anti-rationalism and contempt for universal truths had profound implications for morality.[30] Like Nietzsche, he rejected fixed truths and concepts, and moral truths were no exception, so ultimately humans have to create their own way in the universe. In 1937 Heidegger wrote that we have no access to "an objective, universally binding knowledge or power."[31] Instead of relying on moral precepts imposed upon them, individuals should flex their will and make free decisions. Heidegger insisted that each individual should take full responsibility for his or her decisions, rather than acting on the basis of some universal moral code or social pressure. However, since moral rules were passé, individuals cannot rely on any guidance from outside themselves. As the philosopher Yvonne Sherratt has commented about Heidegger's position: "Morality, human rights, pity, these were bygone notions. They should be expelled from philosophy lest Germany be weakened."[32]

Thus, in Heidegger's view, humans are radically free to make their own decisions—including the decision to follow the German Führer. In 1933 Heidegger told the students at his university: "Let not propositions and 'ideas' be the rules of your Being [Sein]. The Führer alone *is* the present and future German reality and its law. Learn to know ever more deeply: from now on every single thing demands decision, and every action responsibility. Heil Hitler!"[33] Of course, the second sentence does not follow logically from the first one. Other existentialists could just as easily substitute Stalin, Mao, or anyone or anything else for the Führer. However, by rejecting propositional truth, Heidegger clears traditional forms of morality out of the way, opening the path for accepting new movements or moral innovations—including (but not limited to) Nazism.

Despite solemnly adjuring the students in Freiburg to take responsibility for their decisions, however, Heidegger was peculiarly loath to taking responsibility for his own misguided decision to jump on Hitler's bandwagon. After the war he never apologized for his role in aiding and abetting the Nazi regime. Philosophy professor John Caputo writes that when Heidegger's friend and colleague Rudolf Bultmann, the famous theologian, suggested after the war that he should write up a recantation, "Heidegger's face froze over and he left Bultmann without saying a word."[34] Even more problematically, recent historical scholarship has demonstrated conclusively that after the collapse of the Third Reich he consistently misrepresented his own decisions made during the Nazi regime.[35] So much for taking responsibility for one's decisions. Indeed, though he distinguishes between Heidegger's earlier and later writings, the philosopher Tom Rockmore argues that the later "Heidegger's rejection of the idea of responsibility other than through the commitment to Being is incompatible with the assumption of personal moral accountability." This is why, Rockmore explains, Heidegger failed to condemn Nazi atrocities, even long after Nazism was dead.[36]

Even more disturbing is the fact that Heidegger accepted some of the dehumanizing tendencies inherent in Nazi ideology, even though he rejected their biological determinism. In December 1933 he wrote to a colleague, "The individual, wherever he may stand, is worth nothing. The destiny of our people (*Volk*) in its state is worth everything."[37] This reflects the same attitude as Hitler, who stated, "The individual must and will as always perish; only the Volk must remain."[38] Heidegger's contempt for the individual and his dismissal of each person's value fly in the face of the Judeo-Christian tradition, in which each individual has value because he or she is created in the image of God. Heidegger was so intensely anti-Christian that he blocked appointments of philosophers if they were Christians, because, he said, Christianity and philosophy are contradictory. When the Catholic scholar Theodor Haecker published a book defending the Judeo-Christian view that humans are created in the image of God, Heidegger launched a counterattack in his 1935 university lectures.[39] Further, in the early days of the Nazi regime, Heidegger suggested that euthanasia should be seriously contemplated in order to preserve the health of the state.[40] Apparently Heidegger—like many German physicians and leading Nazis—believed that it was morally justified to kill people who are disabled, especially if it contributed to the health and well-being of the community. He did not believe that humans were intrinsically and equally valuable.

Heidegger never recanted anything he said or wrote during the Nazi period, though he did try to cover up his worst offenses. He also never condemned any Nazi atrocities. Worse yet, he showed astounding insensitivity to the suffering of Nazi victims. In a 1949 speech, he told an audience in Bremen, "Agriculture is now a mechanized food industry, the same thing in its essence as the production of corpses in the gas chambers and the extermination camps, the same thing as blockades and the reduction of countries to famine, the same thing as the manufacture of hydrogen bombs."[41] This comment was purged from the published version of the speech, so it only resurfaced after his death, creating a scandal. Heidegger was a vitriolic opponent of many forms of modern technology, which he believed contributed to alienation and malaise. However, even if he was trying to display concern for modern farmers, it seems bizarre to claim that industrial-style farming is the same as the Nazis' mass extermination or the Soviet blockade of Berlin or nuclear weapons. To compare the use of agricultural technology—which produces food to give life to multitudes—to death-bringing technologies, trivializes the death of millions. In an essay trying to defend Heidegger against the accusation that he had no concern for others in his philosophy, Robert John Sheffler Manning nevertheless notes that Heidegger's agriculture remark is still "a towering testament to insensitivity," demonstrating that Heidegger only had concern for some others, not for all others.[42]

Sartre displayed the same kind of insensitivity toward the victims of his political allies, the communists. Ironically, his radical political commitments evinced concern for the downtrodden and underprivileged—but only those oppressed by "bourgeois" Western societies, especially the United States. He publicly castigated the United States and its allies for fighting the Vietnam War, insisting that they were committing genocide there.[43] However, he joined the French Communist Party in 1952, while Stalin was still in power in the Soviet Union. He knew about Stalinist terror, but instead of condemning it, he exulted in it and argued that the ends justify the means.[44] In 1954, after Stalin's death, he visited the Soviet Union, proclaiming that there was complete freedom there. In a 1975 interview he admitted that he had lied in 1954, "saying nice things about the U.S.S.R. that I did not believe."[45] Though his blend of Marxism and existentialism was unorthodox and provoked criticism from many Marxists, Sartre remained committed to Marxism even after withdrawing from the Communist Party in 1956. When asked in 1975 what contemporaries he respected, he replied that Mao had his full respect. He did express some misgivings about Mao's Cultural Revolution, because he did not understand it, but he added: "Not that I'm in the least opposed to it."[46] Victims of communism found little sympathy from him.

As with Nietzsche and Heidegger, Sartre's political commitments were not logically rigorous deductions from his philosophy (not that existentialists cared much about logic, anyway, since they opposed rationalism). However, his appalling lack of concern for multitudes of his fellow humans was rooted in his worldview. Sartre is well-known for portraying life as absurd, both in his philosophical work and his literary productions. For him, "Existentialism is nothing else than an attempt to draw all the consequences of a coherent atheistic position."[47] Without God there is nothing to provide life with meaning or significance, so we should just face up to reality and learn to live without any transcendent purpose. Sartre saw this as liberating, opening up a magnificent opportunity for us to create our own purpose in an ultimately meaningless world. He posed the important question, "Meaning has to be created by each of us, but since we are meaningless, how can we create meaning?"[48] Sartre fashioned his meaning through activism, all the while acknowledging that his deeds had no objective meaning in an absurd world: "My activism gave me a sense of purpose, true. But my depression, caused by my awareness that my existence, like all of ours, was totally absurd, made me realize that I, we, are doomed to nauseating insignificance.... I was not, and never would be, significant, nor would anyone else."[49] Tragically, Sartre denied that human life—including his own—had any importance or meaning. His activism might have been exhilarating, but it was ultimately pointless. As the book of Ecclesiastes says, "Vanity of vanities! All is vanity."

On the other hand, Sartre was hoping that his philosophy would rescue humans from the indignity of being mere machines in a materialistic universe. No, he countered, humans are radically free to shape their own lives, and this sets them apart from inert nature. In human affairs there is no determinism, because "man is free."[50] He never explained how, in an impersonal universe without a deity, humans could have escaped the sway of natural laws to make free decisions, but it was an article of faith with him nonetheless. Human freedom was central to his worldview, allowing him to escape the bonds of materialism and rescue humanity from being regarded as a mere object.[51] Humans are undefinable, because they only come to be as they define themselves by making decisions. As Sartre put it, "Man is nothing else but that which he makes of himself. That is the first principle of existentialism." He continued, "Man is, indeed, a project which possesses a subjective life," but "Before that projection of the self, nothing exists;...man will only attain existence when he is what he purposes to be."[52] Sartre does not say what implications this has for infants or those with mental disabilities, but it seems that his definition would exclude them from being fully human.

I am still perplexed, however, about the answer this apostle of free choice gave when asked in an interview: "Why did you choose writing instead of being a gangster?" Knowing his philosophy, I suspected he would insist that his choice of being a writer was an unconstrained, personal decision. To my amazement, however, Sartre actually replied: "Upbringing. Family. Class. Education."[53] This seems like an environmental determinist explanation for his behavior, which runs contrary to his own insistence on freedom and choosing our own essence. Maybe this was his Marxist side overwhelming his existentialist commitment.

But maybe it does not matter if Sartre is consistent. Nietzsche reveled in his many inconsistencies, which was likely a deliberate ploy to evade and trounce Western rationalism. Like Nietzsche, Sartre insisted that objective truth is non-existent. Truth is a matter of subjectivity; it is created, not discovered. However, Sartre faced two insuperable problems. First, he took individual subjectivity to be objectively true, which is a self-contradiction. Sartre asserted that his point of departure was individual subjectivity, "because we seek to base our teaching upon the truth."[54] The truth, then, is that there is no truth. Second, as a writer trying to communicate with others Sartre understood his own pronouncements to have some kind of truth value. He once explained that he had no other power over anyone "other than the power of the truths

I tell."[55] It is possible, of course, that Sartre was being ironic here, not intending this to mean that he was communicating objective truths. However, later in the same interview he explained why he was so zealous about writing: "To tell the truth about existence and to strip the pretenses from bourgeois lies was one and the same thing, and that was what I had to do in order to fulfill my destiny as a man, because I had been created in order to write."[56] Somehow he recognized that some statements are true and some are lies, and that truth is preferable to deception. Sartre's intense passion for writing derived from his desire to tell people what the cosmos and their human existence was really like. He wanted to be on the side of truth (or dare I say, Truth?). Further, Sartre's indication in this passage that he was fulfilling some destiny he had been created for is remarkably inconsistent with his claim that life is absurd, without any purpose or meaning.

On another occasion Sartre divulged that he wanted to strip others of their delusions about the world, implying that some ways of seeing the world are true and others are false. He said, "But don't forget that the absurd is an objective description of reality, and who lives accordingly?" One cannot choose whether or not life is absurd, he pontificated. It is a brute fact that confronts everyone, whether we accept it or not. Indeed, Sartre admitted that many do not accept this reality, since "subjectively, each of us refuses to live according to the absurd. The majority will deny that it is absurd, just like the majority want to believe in a god who will satisfy all."[57] Sartre did not think that anyone's subjective denial of the absurdity of existence changed the objective reality that life is absurd. Subjectivity and free choice apparently did not extend that far. All in all, Sartre seemed to think that his philosophy was conveying some objective truths, not just his own perspective on things.

However, when he discussed morality, he usually tried to be ruthlessly (but, alas, truthlessly) consistent: since God does not exist, there cannot be anything intrinsically good or evil. He stated, "Dostoevsky once wrote 'If God did not exist, everything would be permitted'; and that, for existentialism, is the starting point. Everything is indeed permitted if God does not exist, and man is in consequence forlorn, for he cannot find anything

to depend upon either within or outside himself."[58] Sartre faced considerable opposition from those uncomfortable with his claim that we as
humans must create our own morality. Sartre confronted these critics
head-on who claimed that "'values aren't serious, since you choose them.'
My answer to this," Sartre wrote, "is that I'm quite vexed that that's the
way it is; but if I've discarded God the Father, there has to be someone to
invent values. You've got to take things as they are. Moreover, to say that
we invent values means nothing else but this: life has no meaning *a priori*.
Before you come alive, life is nothing; it's up to you to give it a meaning,
and value is nothing else but the meaning that you choose."[59]

Trying to be rigorously consistent, Sartre maintained that even if
other people adopted values that he found repugnant, they would be true
for those accepting them. He offered the example of fascism, which he
despised, asserting, "Tomorrow, after my death, some men may decide
to set up Fascism, and the others may be cowardly and muddled enough
to let them do it. Fascism will then be the human reality, [and] so much
the worse for us."[60] At first it might seem that Sartre is hewing true to
his philosophy by admitting that fascism would be true for those who
believe it to be true. However, Sartre's statement contains two value
judgments that fly in the face of his view that life is absurd and anything
is permitted. First, by claiming that fascism would be "worse for us," he
implied that it would be morally retrograde. But why? If anything is
permitted, then why not fascism? Why is his act of choosing communism
superior to Heidegger's decision for Nazism? Second, he called those who
embrace fascism cowardly, a common term of derision he slung at those
who behave in "bad faith" and not in complete freedom. However, this
is a problem for Sartre, for, as Peter Singer notes, "if all choice is arbitrary, how can one choose one alternative over another? Even a preference for authenticity over bad faith needs some kind of justification."[61]
Sartre never explained why in an absurd world where everything is
permitted, bravely making "authentic" decisions was better than cowardly making choices in "bad faith." Why is the former not as meaningless as the latter?

Several times Sartre attempted to write up his reflections on ethics, but he was never able to pull it off. As a convinced anarchist, he thought that "there can never be an ethical code of action unless there's total freedom first."[62] That is perhaps why he once stated, "Any ethic which does not explicitly consider itself to be impossible *today* contributes to the alienation and the mystification of man."[63] Late in life he was asked if he was still working on his ethics, and he replied, "It's hard. I keep trying. It's very hard."[64] Some scholars suggest that Sartre's task was not merely hard, but Sisyphean. The intellectual historian Tony Judt remarks, "A Sartrean ethics would have been intrinsically inconceivable."[65] It would have been a contradiction of his whole project.

In advancing his ethic of freedom and anarchism, Sartre explicitly justified the killing of innocent people. In an interview he was asked about the radical leftist German terrorist group, the Baader-Meinhof Gang, also known as the Red Army Faction. By 1972 this organization had killed thirty-four innocent people, as well as burned down buildings, robbed banks, and bombed military installations. According to Sartre, "In context, they were totally justified." What was the context that justified murder, arson, and theft? In 1967 Benno Ohnesorg, a leftist demonstrator, had been shot dead by a German policeman, and the following year another leftist, Rudi Dutschke, was shot in an assassination attempt. (Neither Sartre nor his contemporaries knew that Ohnesorg had actually been shot by an East German secret police agent who had infiltrated the West German police force.) According to Sartre, faced with such opposition from the West German regime, the Red Army Faction's actions were understandable and even right. He stated, "From a moral and revolutionary point of view, the group's rampage and murders of German industrialists are absolutely justified. But...you see my problem—all ethics depends on circumstances."[66] Sartre's contextual ethics sanctioned murder (but only in contexts where leftists were fighting against bourgeois society). While Sartre thought Andreas Baader's murderous campaign was morally justified, he protested against the prison conditions imposed on Baader after his capture. He showed his solidarity with Baader by

getting permission to visit him in his cell.[67] Apparently the alleged mistreatment of Baader in prison was a moral travesty, while Baader's murders were fine and dandy.

Not only did Sartre manifest absolutely no sympathy for the murder
victims of the Red Army Faction, but he did not even show much concern
about the death of close relatives and friends. He professed fondness for
his grandmother, but "when she died I was totally neutral." For Sartre,
death was just as meaningless and absurd as life, so he refused to mourn
about it. He was sharply criticized in 1966 for his lack of grief over the
death of Evelyne Lanzmann, who had been his mistress for thirteen
years. She committed suicide shortly after Sartre broke up with her.
Sartre explained in an interview why he was not concerned about her
death: "When I was told she had killed herself, I had a short asthma
attack, but then nothing. Since I am absolutely certain that after one's
death there's nothing, I cannot grieve. Now, is that because I have identified my survival with my literature, even though intellectually I know
that's all meaningless? Let the shrinks debate that. For me, it's simple:
death is nothingness, hence not part of life, so I do not think of death."[68]

Instead of sympathizing with suicide victims, Sartre then criticized
Lanzmann and others who commit suicide. Sartre lamented that they were
unwilling to face the reality that "Life is a fact. It has no value in itself. It's
not even a question of accepting or not accepting it. It is, period."[69] Instead
of taking responsibility for his own actions, which precipitated her suicide,
Sartre placed all the blame on her. Sartre's message to those facing suicide
was simple: life has no purpose or value; get over it and make the "best"
of it (knowing all the while that "best" is a non-existent category). Sartre
never explained satisfactorily, however, why choosing to continue living a
meaningless and valueless life is superior to committing suicide. After all,
his mentor Nietzsche had voted in favor of suicide.

One of the most famous philosophers of the late twentieth century,
Michel Foucault, not only agreed with Nietzsche's theoretical stance on

suicide, but he even attempted suicide in 1948 and several times thereafter. He was so obsessed with death and suicide that his biographer James Miller states, "Foucault, by contrast, had long placed death—and the preparation for suicide—at the heart of his concerns."[70] One of Foucault's first publications was a 1954 introduction to the German psychiatrist Ludwig Binswanger's essay, "Dream and Existence," which discussed a patient who fantasized about suicide.[71] In that essay Foucault put a positive spin on suicide, asserting, "To commit suicide is the ultimate mode of imagining; to try to characterize suicide in the realistic terms of suppression is to doom oneself to misunderstanding it. Only an anthropology of the imagination can ground psychology and an ethics of suicide."[72] Foucault not only wanted to permit suicide, but hoped to formulate an "ethics of suicide"!

Indeed, iconoclast that he was, Foucault apparently wanted to elevate suicide to a praiseworthy endeavor, rescuing it from the opprobrium of the bourgeois society that he hated. Toward the end of his life he stated that we must "teach people that there is not a piece of conduct more beautiful or, consequently, more worthy of careful thought than suicide. One should work on one's suicide throughout one's life."[73] It is unlikely that Foucault deliberately contracted AIDS to bring about his early demise, since he often expressed skepticism about the existence of AIDS. (He found out to his chagrin that it was not just a socially constructed disease. At first he dismissed the emerging knowledge about AIDS as the bogey of a prudish, anti-homosexual society, as a ruse to oppress homosexuals.) Thus, despite his admonition to others, it does not seem that he worked on his own suicide. However, in 1983—after knowledge about the dangers of AIDS was circulating—he was warned by a colleague to practice "safe sex" in the San Francisco gay bathhouses that he frequented. He replied that he was not afraid to die, and then recounted that he had once had a brush with death in 1978 when he was struck by a car. It was an exhilarating, euphoric experience, as he sensed himself leaving his body briefly before regaining consciousness. Foucault apparently thought death would be a glorious and pleasurable experience. He then told his colleague, "To die for the love of boys. What could be more beautiful?"[74] Another time he wrote, "Sex is worth dying for."[75] Worth it or not, he did die because of it.

Foucault not only contemplated his own suicide, but he was fascinated by the suicides of others. He wrote an entire book on the French writer Raymond Roussel, who died of an apparent suicide after weeks in a drug-induced stupor.[76] Foucault idealized Roussel's allegedly euphoric suicide, expressing the hope that he could somehow reach a state of such intense pleasure that it would literally kill him. In a 1983 interview, he explained, "I would like and I hope I'll die of an overdose of pleasure of any kind.... I think that the kind of pleasure I would consider as *the* real pleasure would be so deep, so intense, so overwhelming that I couldn't survive it. I would die."[77] His own death of AIDS in 1984 in a Paris hospital was much more prosaic, though it was the consequence of his pleasure-seeking.

Foucault also fantasized about helping other people kill themselves. While discussing social security in an interview in 1983, Foucault broached "the question of what life is worth" and how to die. There should be, he asserted, "a recognized right for everybody to kill himself when he wishes in decent conditions." He then promised hypothetically, "If I won a few billion francs in the national lottery, I'd set up an institute where people who wanted to die could come and spend a weekend, a week or a month, enjoying themselves as far as possible, perhaps with the help of drugs, and then disappear, as if by obliteration." When the interviewer asked if this meant a "right to suicide," Foucault responded affirmatively.[78]

But wait a minute. How can Foucault talk about a "right" to suicide? For that matter, how can he talk about a "right" for anything? Though Foucault is deliberately slippery, altering his views from one work to the next, he is well-known for his rejection of all universals, of all objective "truths," of all conventional morality. Foucault admitted in a 1979 lecture, "I start from the theoretical and methodological decision that consists in saying: Let's suppose that universals do not exist."[79] Foucault held that truth is something to be created, not discovered. Present knowledge, he maintained, is decided by whomever is dominant in society and has the power to impose their definitions and concepts on the rest of society. He confessed that he was a follower of Nietzsche's view that knowledge is a product of the will. The original French title of his first volume of *The History of Sexuality* was "The Will to Knowledge," a nod to Nietzsche. Once he admitted, "What I do is a kind of historical fiction. In a sense I know very well that what I say is not true." He immediately denied that he was lying, because he hoped that his "books become true after they have been written—not before."[80] He wanted to create "truth."

He was especially insistent in denying any universal or objective morality. In a 1971 debate with Noam Chomsky, Foucault took a position so amoral that he shocked Chomsky, who later remarked, "I felt like I was talking to someone who didn't inhabit the same moral universe."[81] In that exchange Foucault and Chomsky agreed about the need for the proletariat to resist the power of contemporary society. Foucault insisted that present society, including not only the government, but other institutions, such as the family, the educational system, and even medicine, was a class dictatorship. Foucault's hatred for his father (a physician) and for bourgeois society permeated this discussion, as they do many of his works.[82] Chomsky agreed with Foucault that injustices needed to be redressed, if necessary, by revolution. However, he and Foucault butted heads when Chomsky insisted that the purpose of fighting against bourgeois society has to be the restoration of justice. Foucault objected strenuously, arguing that justice is non-existent. Rather, Foucault asserted that the proletariat is fighting against the ruling class not because they want justice, but because they want power. "One makes war to win, not because it is just," Foucault stated. He then exulted in the revolutionary violence that would be unleashed in this class struggle, stating, "When the proletariat takes power, it may be quite possible that the proletariat will exert towards the classes over which it has just triumphed, a violent, dictatorial, and even bloody power. I can't see what objection one could make to this."[83] Contra Foucault, I can think of many objections to the exercise of dictatorial violence and bloodshed. Given the history of the dictatorship of the proletariat in the twentieth century, and since

Foucault had been anti-communist since the 1950s, this support for the violent dictatorship of the proletariat is rather astonishing. It certainly shows that Foucault had no respect for human life.

This was not just a slip of the tongue or a momentary lapse in Foucault's intellectual trajectory. He expressed his penchant for violence against the powers-that-be at other times, too. In the early 1970s, he debated some Maoists who wanted to set up revolutionary tribunals to bring bourgeois oppressors to justice. Foucault objected to revolutionary tribunals, not because he thought this Maoist proposal was too radical, but because it was not radical enough! Foucault claimed that courts should be abolished altogether, because there can never be a neutral party dispensing justice. Rather Foucault suggested unleashing "popular justice," and ominously he gave as his example French Revolutionaries lynching their enemies. Foucault saw nothing wrong with revolutionary violence, and he did not want any kind of court—even a revolutionary tribunal—to restrain the violence of the mob. In Foucault's view, the proletariat is fighting for power, not for justice. It can and should use violence to crush its class enemies, because justice and morality are only bourgeois notions used to oppress the proletariat.[84]

However, as with so many other secularists, at times Foucault smuggled universal moral standards into his discourse. Just like Marx, who exerted considerable influence on Foucault, he used morally loaded terminology, such as "oppression," suggesting that there really is something wrong with the way that modern bourgeois society treats workers. Foucault zealously campaigned for penal reform to alleviate the suffering of prisoners, who were allegedly being mistreated by society. In 1981 Foucault issued a statement on human rights, in which he stated, "There exists an international citizenship that has its rights and its duties, and that obliges one to speak out against every abuse of power, whoever its author, whoever its victims. After all, we are all members of the community of the governed, and thereby obliged to show mutual solidarity."[85] What could Foucault possibly mean by "rights," "duties," or the verb "obliges," all of which imply some kind of moral standards applicable to everyone? What could he mean by "abuse of power" and "victims"? These are morally loaded terms that suggest he really did recognize some transcendent moral standards, despite his asseverations to the contrary.

Foucault again forgot about his amoral stance when criticizing the French (socialist) regime for its lackluster response to the communist coup in Warsaw in 1981, which resulted in the suppression of the Solidarity Trade Union. Foucault signed a declaration that stated, "We remind it [Mitterand's regime] of its promise to assert the obligations of international moral standards against the obligations of *Realpolitik*."[86] This is a strange statement coming from someone who denied the existence of any moral standards whatsoever. According to James Bernauer and Michael Mahon, Foucault rejected any universal norms. They explain, "In opposition to any universal system of ethics founded on humanism or a monolithic conception of rationality, Foucault boldly proclaims that the quest for a morality to which everyone must submit would be 'catastrophic.'" Later in the same essay, they inform us that Foucault was committed to human rights.[87] How can Foucault fight for rights that, according to his philosophy, do not exist? Ironically, they do not have to exist, because he can just make them up (and then impose them on everyone else, if he is able).

The key to understanding Foucault, I think, is that he was motivated more by hatred for bourgeois society than by love for the oppressed. Gary Gutting, editor of *The Cambridge Companion to Foucault*, notes that his hatred for bourgeois society "gives power and intensity to Foucault's prose," but also leads him to serious misunderstandings about its institutions.[88] Foucault hated his father, whom he viewed as a disciplinarian and a bully.[89] Since his father was a physician, Foucault's attack on the medical profession, which he depicted as an integral part of his oppressive society, reflected his personal experiences. When Foucault attempted suicide, his father took him to a psychiatrist. This, together with the fact that psychiatry before his time generally viewed homosexuality and suicidal tendencies as mental illnesses, brought Foucault into opposition to the psychiatric community. His homosexuality brought him into conflict with the dominant sexual mores of the mid-twentieth century.

Rejecting morality as an instrument of bourgeois oppression thus served the purpose of trying to find freedom from the society that he hated.

So how did Foucault try to find fulfillment in this amoral world? Through the pursuit of pleasure. Not just any pleasures, but very intense ones. Foucault admitted that he was not very interested in moderate pleasures, such as fine food. Rather, he sought euphoria. From the time of his youth, the Marquis de Sade was one of his favorite writers, and Foucault was a faithful disciple his entire life, practicing sado-masochistic sex as a means to attain higher levels of pleasure. He also indulged frequently in mind-altering drugs, especially pot, hashish, and opium, but also LSD and cocaine, in search of what he named a "limit-experience." He called his experience with LSD at Death Valley in 1975 the greatest experience of his life.[90] In 1983 he explained, "Some drugs are really important for me because they are the mediation to those incredibly intense joys that I am looking for."[91] However, while pursuing pleasure, Foucault was skeptical of the utilitarian claim that pleasure could bring happiness. In a 1967 interview he countered the humanistic attempt to create human happiness, stating, "Now, I do not think that the notion of happiness is truly thinkable. *Happiness does not exist—and the happiness of men exists still less.*" After quoting this, his biographer remarks that happiness may not be thinkable in Foucault's "Sado-Nietzschean view of the world."[92]

Not only did Foucault think that happiness is elusive, but his anti-humanistic worldview also led him to proclaim the "death of man." In an unpublished 1961 thesis Foucault wrote that the Nietzschean death of God—which he enthusiastically endorsed—should be understood also as the death of humanity. He wrote:

> The Nietzschean undertaking might be understood as finally putting an end to the proliferation of questioning about mankind. Was not the death of God, in fact, revealed in a doubly murderous act that, at the same time that it put an end to the absolute, assassinated man himself? Because man, in his

finitude, is inseparable from the infinite, which he both negates and heralds. The death of God is accomplished through the death of man.[93]

This theme reverberates through other of Foucault's works, too. In his 1966 work, *The Order of Things,* he concludes the book by explaining that his Nietzschean stance means the death of humanity. Philosophers and poets in the nineteenth century had wrestled with the death of God. "In our day and once again," he explained, "Nietzsche indicated the turning-point from a long way off, it is not so much the absence or the death of God that is affirmed as the end of man." Foucault exults in the end or disappearance of humanity, and his closing sentence of *The Order of Things* expressed his desire and/or prediction "that man would be erased, like a face drawn in sand at the edge of the sea."[94] My mentor in European intellectual history, Allan Megill, has called Foucault one of the "prophets of extremity" (along with Nietzsche, Heidegger, and Derrida). It would also be apt to call Foucault—along with Nietzsche and other of Nietzsche's disciples—a prophet of the death of humanity.

Indeed, in his biography of Foucault, James Miller is sympathetic with Foucault's Nietzschean bent, but he is remarkably candid about the horrific consequences of such a worldview. Miller admits,

> I am someone who holds the not entirely happy conviction that there is no Aristotelean mean, no Platonic idea of the good, no moral compass implicit in our ability to reason, and no regulative ideal of consensus that could help us to smooth away the rough edges of competing forms of life and enable us to reconcile their incommensurable claims. Therefore, Nietzsche's philosophy has always been for me a puzzle and a provocation, if only because, in terms of its inner logic, which I have yet to see refuted, I can find no easy way to rule out the sort of cruel and murderous practices embraced by some of his followers.[95]

I do not know if Miller had Mussolini and Hitler in mind here, but Miller obviously thinks that Nietzsche's rejection of morality provides no bulwark against human cruelty, violence, and even murder. It provided no moral fulcrum to keep Heidegger from embracing Nazism, Sartre from accepting communism and lauding Stalin, or Foucault from supporting revolutionary violence—including Khomeini's revolution against the shah of Iran.

While most academics are aghast at Heidegger's fascism, Sartre's Stalinism, and Foucault's enthusiastic support for Khomeni (before the Iranian revolution), they have nonetheless exalted them as brilliant philosophers. Miller thinks that Foucault's elevation to a "kind of patron saint" by liberal intellectuals in the U.S. is based on a misunderstanding. Miller explains that many of these liberal intellectuals are "high-minded democrats" committed to a society that lives in

> compassionate harmony—an appealing if difficult goal, with deep roots in the Judeo-Christian tradition. Unfortunately, Foucault's lifework, as I have come to understand it, is far more unconventional—and far more discomfiting—than some of his "progressive" admirers seem ready to admit. Unless I am badly mistaken, Foucault issued a brave and basic challenge to nearly everything that passes for "right" in Western culture—including nearly everything that passes for "right" among a great many of America's left-wing academics.[96]

I am convinced that Miller is right. Many Western intellectuals who admire Foucault (and Heidegger and Nietzsche) still retain some of the vestiges of the Judeo-Christian morality that they claim to spurn. Despite their asseverations from the podium and in their publications, they would not want to live in an amoral, loveless society where everyone is engaged in a raw pursuit of power. Many of them still love their spouses and their children and give money to help the disadvantaged—noble goals taught in the Jewish and Christian scriptures (but not by Nietzsche or Foucault). They still regularly invoke "values" and "social justice," and they express consternation and dismay if someone opposes their "values." They do not really believe that "anything goes," and they certainly do not teach their children that way. While loudly proclaiming the non-existence of any objective morality and the freedom for everyone to create and live according to their own "values," they deny that right to Christian evangelicals, Muslim fundamentalists, traditionally-minded Catholics, Republicans, pro-life activists, climate-deniers, or _____ (fill in the blank with any of their bêtes noires). Just push the right button on many ostensible Nietzscheans (or other moral relativists) and rivers of objective morality gush forth with tremendous ire directed at those with differing moral beliefs.

In the Nietzschean cosmos, however, ultimately human life has no significance, value, or purpose. The universe is amoral, so everything is permitted, including oppression, violence, and murder. Not only are these permitted, they are encouraged, for Nietzsche exulted in oppression and death. Thus, even though Nietzsche's philosophy resists the dehumanizing mechanistic vision of humanity purveyed by materialists and positivists, his worldview still promotes and hastens the death of humanity.

SEVEN

A Matter of Life and Death

Suicide, Euthanasia, Infanticide, and Abortion

I n September 2013, a year after undergoing a sex-change operation, forty-four-year-old Nathan Verhelst (formerly Nancy Verhelst) was given a lethal injection by the Belgian physician Wim Distelmans. Verhelst was not suffering from a terminal illness nor was she experiencing any physical pain. From the time of her birth, her mother and her family despised her for being a girl, so in 2009 she began hormone therapy to become male. After the sex-change operation in 2012, Verhelst was horrified with the results and requested euthanasia based on psychological distress. Distelmans, a leading proponent and practitioner of euthanasia in Belgium, was delighted to comply with Verhelst's suicidal desires, and he even allowed Belgian television to film and broadcast the killing. In this tragic case, a woman rejected by her family and in need of love, compassion, and acceptance was instead destroyed by medical professionals with the full blessing of the Belgian government and society, who allow physician-assisted suicide for nearly any reason.[1] This is a poignant confirmation of Jesus' prophecy that the "the love of many will grow cold."[2]

In another shocking case in Belgium in early 2013, a forty-four-year-old woman with anorexia who was sexually abused by a psychiatrist decided to seek euthanasia. Another psychiatrist signed off on her request. Instead of providing her with the compassion and healing she needed, these members of the psychiatric community added to her already fragile mental problems and signed her death warrant.[3] Indeed, since Belgium legalized physician-assisted suicide in 2002, those applying for euthanasia have been steadily increasing. In 2012 there were 1,432 recorded cases of euthanasia in Belgium, accounting for about 2 percent of the total deaths there. Further, in many cases physicians are killing disabled people unrequested, despite the fact that this is still technically illegal. The Belgian Society for Intensive Care Medicine recently asked the government to legalize involuntary euthanasia, requesting that physicians be the sole decision-makers, not the individuals being killed nor their families.[4]

The beginning of the life cycle has also been the subject of considerable controversy. The medical ethicists Alberto Giubilini and Francesca Minerva provoked a firestorm in 2012 by publishing an article in the *Journal of Medical Ethics* on "after-birth abortion." Giubilini and Minerva argue that it is morally permissible to kill infants after they are born but hope that charged verbiage—such as "infanticide"—can be eliminated from the discussion. Since multitudes in Western societies believe that abortion is allowable, why not simply think of killing newborns as "after-birth abortions" to qualm our queasy consciences? In their article Giubilini and Minerva claim that newborn infants are not persons in a morally relevant sense, so they can be killed for any reason. They state, "Therefore, we claim that killing a newborn could be ethically permissible in all the circumstances where abortion would be. Such circumstances include cases where the newborn has the potential to have an (at least) acceptable life, but the well-being of the family is at risk." They specifically mention that if a perfectly healthy child would be a financial hardship on the family—no problem—"after-birth abortion" to the rescue. Just put the economic burden out of its misery. Except the baby is not really in misery, so the directive would actually be: just put the economic burden in the trash bin, so you can continue your own selfish existence.

Shortly after this article appeared, many commentators protested against this cavalier dismissal of a newborn's right to life, and two congressmen denounced the article from the floor of the U.S. House of Representatives. The editor of the *Journal of Medical Ethics* expressed astonishment at the public reaction, because he noted that some prominent ethicists have been making similar arguments for many years. In intellectual circles advocacy for infanticide and involuntary euthanasia is not all that uncommon, though the general public is still shocked by such sentiments.[5] Let us examine some of the prominent arguments by these end-of-life advocates, starting with those pertaining to suicide.

❋

Until the eighteenth-century Enlightenment, Western societies were so imbued with the Judeo-Christian sanctity-of-life ethic that there was no significant debate over the propriety of suicide. Christian doctrine solidly opposed suicide, not only because of the biblical prohibition against murder and because a Christian's body is supposed to belong to God, but also because Christians interpreted suffering as having—at least in many cases—a redemptive purpose.[6] While Christian theology recognized that suffering was a natural evil that came into the world as a result of sin and would be forever removed for the redeemed in the afterlife, it also praised those who endured suffering in this life. In addition to religious penalties for suicide, such as not being buried in hallowed ground, medieval and early modern European legal codes forbade suicide and even tried to restrain it by threatening confiscation of property from the heirs of those guilty of taking their own lives.[7] The Protestant Reformation only stiffened attitudes against suicide in the sixteenth and early seventeenth centuries.[8]

Beginning in the eighteenth century some prominent Enlightenment thinkers, especially those with a materialistic worldview (but also some deists), began defending the permissibility of suicide. Voltaire, Montesquieu, Holbach, and numerous other Enlightenment figures either stated or implied that they considered suicide in some cases a rational alternative to suffering. They no longer regarded human life as sacred and having eternal significance. According to historian Lester Crocker, "For these humanists [who defended suicide], life has no meaning other than what man cares to give to it, no importance except for himself."[9] Especially for the materialists, but even for some deists, human life was merely an arrangement of particles in the cosmos that had no higher significance than other particle configurations.

Few expressed the pro-suicide position as forcefully as the Piedmontese Count Alberto Radicati, who was arrested in England for publishing his shocking *Philosophical Dissertation upon Death* in 1732 in London. Under the influence of Epicureanism and Spinoza's deterministic pantheism, Radicati argued that human life is simply a bundle of matter in motion that is neither more valuable nor more important than other combinations of matter. He rejected objective morality, and since he denied free will, he held that humans were not responsible in any meaningful sense for their actions, anyway. He dismissed as nonsensical the Judeo-Christian teaching that humans are created in the image of God. It is completely foolish, he complained, for humans to consider their own species superior to others, as they are wont to do. Nature, Radicati proclaimed, has given people the right to commit suicide if they no longer get pleasure out of their life.[10]

Radicati's pro-suicide treatise created a sensation at the time, in part because shortly after his book appeared, a London bookbinder and his wife, Richard and Bridget Smith, shot their toddler in the head and then committed suicide. They felt trapped in poverty and misery, to be sure, but their motivation for killing their child and themselves was more complex. They left behind a suicide note that set forth rationalist arguments similar to Radicati's to justify their murder-suicide. Predictably, the Smiths' murder-suicide created a media sensation in London. On the whole, the British public was horrified by this wanton display of the radical consequences of such irreligious philosophies.[11]

The Smiths were not the only ones to find inspiration from the rising tide of secularization and draw what they considered the logical conclusion by killing themselves. Studies of suicide in early modern England indicate that secularized attitudes toward human life prompted a growing tide of suicides at the end of the seventeenth century that continued to increase during the first half of the eighteenth century. By the 1750s the suicide rate was double what it had been forty years earlier, and many of these suicidal individuals were influenced by the rising tide of Enlightenment rationalism. For many of those imbibing Enlightenment philosophy, Epicurean concerns about their personal pleasure trumped religious imperatives, and they no longer gave credence to threats of divine retribution. Further, many agreed with Radicati that human life did not have any objective value, meaning, or significance, thus erasing a strong barrier against suicide.[12] Eighteenth-century literature, such as Goethe's *Sufferings of Young Werther*, reflected this newly emerging approval of suicide by glorifying self-murder, and inspired further suicides.[13]

The most famous defense of the moral propriety of suicide to come out of the Enlightenment was David Hume's essay, "On Suicide." Hume was the quintessential empiricist skeptic who considered math and science the only true path to knowledge. His faith in the inviolability of the laws of nature caused him to reject all miracles. In the closing paragraph of his *Enquiry concerning Human Understanding*, he enjoined his readers to ask two questions about any books making truth claims: "*Does it contain any abstract reasoning concerning quantity or number?*" and "*Does it contain any experimental reasoning concerning matter of fact and existence?*" If not, he wrote, "Commit it then to the flames: for it can contain nothing but sophistry and illusion."[14] Essentially, Hume was saying that if truth claims are not statements of mathematics or empirically verifiable, then they can be safely ignored. Unfortunately for Hume, this is a self-refuting statement, because it does not contain any empirical or mathematical reasoning. Hume was inadvertently condemning much of his own work as "nothing but sophistry and illusion." Ultimately Hume's empiricist philosophy is not empirically verifiable.

Hume wrote his essay on suicide in the mid-1750s, but it was too controversial to publish during his lifetime, so it only appeared publicly in an English edition posthumously in 1777.[15] Suicide was not merely a theoretical issue for Hume, since ten years before he wrote this essay he had discovered a man bleeding from self-inflicted wounds. Hume called a physician and the man survived for twenty-four hours, during which time Hume conversed with him about his suicidal action and his beliefs. Hume reported to his brother, "Never a man exprest a more steady Contempt of Life nor more determined philosophical Principles, suitable to his Exit."[16] Based on this experience, Hume knew very well that his theoretical reflections would encourage some to take the irrevocable step of taking their own lives.

In his essay Hume insisted that God does not intervene in nature, so there is no divinely-ordained method of dying. Humans, however, do have the power to intervene in nature, and we make use of that power all the time. He then asked why we should not use the God-given ability we have to end our lives. Perspicaciously he answered that the only reason we should not commit suicide would be if human life were so important that it would be presumptuous for us to dispose of it. As much as I disagree with Hume's philosophy overall, I concede the logic of this last point. However, Hume goes badly astray in the following sentence, "But the life of a man is of no greater importance to the universe than that of an oyster." By rejecting a personal God, Hume consequently reduced the importance of humanity, which has little or no value or significance in an impersonal universe.[17]

Once one reduces the value of human life, it is hard to stop at suicide. Indeed some of the positions Hume advanced in his essay could just as easily justify the killing of others. Hume confused the issue by comparing suicidal behavior to other, life-giving interventions in nature, such as building houses (as though people opposing suicide were opposed to every kind of interference with natural events). It is not criminal, he reminded his readers, to divert the Nile or the Danube. So, he asked, "Where then is the crime of turning a few ounces of blood from their natural channel?"[18] If one takes Hume's reasoning here seriously, this would justify murder as much as suicide.[19]

Further, later in the essay Hume claimed that suicide can be a positive benefit for society: "But suppose that it is no longer in my power to promote the interest of society; suppose that I am a burden to it; suppose that my life hinders some person from being much more useful to society. In such cases my resignation of life must not only be innocent but laudable." Hume thus encouraged those who see themselves as useless or a burden to step aside so others can get on with their lives unhindered. Hume thereby crossed the line from presenting suicide as morally permissible to portraying it as morally praiseworthy. He claimed that "both prudence and courage should engage us to rid ourselves at once of existence, when it becomes a burthen [burden]." In some cases, Hume thought, suicide is a moral duty rather than a regrettable action.[20]

As secularist philosophies have gained ground since the eighteenth century, acceptance of suicide has grown in tandem. Hume's position on suicide seems to resonate with many secularists. After a hiatus in the early nineteenth century, by the late nineteenth century and into the twentieth many secular thinkers and activists began promoting the "right to suicide." This right was enshrined in the Humanist Manifesto II in 1973, which was signed by a host of secularist intellectuals, including Isaac Asimov, Francis Crick, Alan Guttmacher, Andre Sakharov, B. F. Skinner, Alfred Ayer, Joseph Fletcher, Julian Huxley, and Jacques Monod, among others. The "right to suicide" (and euthanasia and abortion) does indeed seem consistent with the general philosophy of the Humanist Manifesto II, which declares that "we can discover no divine purpose or providence for the human species. While there is much that we do not know, humans are responsible for what we are or will become."[21] The prevailing wind among secularists seems to be in favor of suicide.

However, in her recent book, *Stay: A History of Suicide and the Philosophies against It* (2013), Jennifer Michael Hecht tries to reverse this general trend. Troubled by the suicides of two friends in 2007 and

2009, she set out to find completely secular reasons for opposing suicide. She reminds us that some secular philosophers have opposed suicide, even though she recognizes that the general trend in secular circles has been in the opposite direction. I applaud Hecht for her compassion and zeal in trying to convince others not to commit suicide, and I wish her every success in that endeavor. However, ultimately her attempt at refuting Hume and other secularists who support suicide is a spectacular failure, because the reasons she advances for opposing suicide only make sense if one accepts some hidden presuppositions that are not part of her secular worldview. She smuggles ideas into her argument that are fundamentally incompatible with her philosophy. Likely these presuppositions will resonate with many people, who might overlook the fact that they are ultimately at odds with her secular perspective.

Her first argument is that when one commits suicide, this encourages others to commit suicide. Thus by taking one's life, one is contributing to the death of others. As Hecht explains, "If suicide has a pernicious influence on others, then staying alive has the opposite influence: it helps keep people alive. By staying alive, we are contributing something precious to the world."[22] Precious? Where did that come from? As far as I can tell, Hecht has no resources in her secular outlook to exalt human life as precious. Nonetheless, by fiat she simply declares that no one "need wonder whether his or her life is worth living. It is worth living."[23] To be sure, I am happy that Hecht regards human life as precious and worth living, but she never explains what gives human life value in a God-forsaken world without meaning or purpose. She never tells us how her claim that life is worth living could possibly be consistent with her secularist outlook. I doubt it is.

Also, the notion that what is wrong about committing suicide is that is encourages others to commit suicide is a circular argument, because it assumes that when others commit suicide, that is a bad thing. But why? Because they will cause yet others to commit suicide? Hecht is assuming what she is supposed to be proving. Consider it this way: if by playing chess I encourage other people to play chess (as is inevitable, if I play with other people), this would only be immoral if playing chess is immoral.

Interestingly, because Hume was pro-suicide, he claimed that by committing suicide, one is setting a positive example, so Hume saw the copycat effect as an argument in favor of suicide, rather than an argument against it, as Hecht thinks.[24]

Hecht's second reason is even more problematic: "that the suicidal person owes something to his or her future self."[25] Unless Hecht believes in an afterlife—and I am pretty confident she does not—then this makes no sense at all. How can anyone owe something to an entity that does not and never will exist? According to Hecht's own perspective, the "future self" of a person who commits suicide is as non-existent as the tooth fairy, so it seems odd that anyone would have an obligation toward a figment of their imagination.

Hecht's third reason makes a lot more sense, but even so, I suspect she is coopting values that are not consistent with her worldview. She claims that "we owe it to society at large, and especially to our personal communities, to stay alive."[26] Now, I happen to agree with Hecht that this is a good reason to oppose suicide. "Love your neighbor as yourself" makes a lot of sense to me. However, I cannot figure out how Hecht conjures up this obligation to the community—or any moral obligation at all—from her worldview. She never explains why we have such obligations, but must hope we will simply agree with her and move on. But why should her fellow secularists—who seem to be the main audience for the book—agree with this claim? If we are simply the products of chance events in an impersonal cosmos, then how would this give us any objective obligations to anyone? Some might say that we simply have moral feelings, perhaps put upon us by the evolutionary process, so the obligation is really just a feeling that we act upon. However, in this case, why should a suicidal individual consider these moral feelings superior to his or her feelings of despair? Such moral feelings are merely illusory, anyway, as Michael Ruse and E. O. Wilson have admitted, so why follow illusions? If Hecht thinks that morality has some existence beyond our feelings, intuitions, or arbitrary choices, she never explains whence this morality arises. Thus, while I tend to agree with her that we have moral obligations toward our community and toward ourselves that make suicide immoral, I suspect she is borrowing these moral resources from worldviews incompatible with her own.

❉

If serious discussion about suicide began in earnest in the eighteenth century, the debate over assisted suicide or euthanasia only surfaced in the late nineteenth century. Before the late nineteenth century the term "euthanasia" had simply meant providing comfort and pain relief to dying patients, inasmuch as that was possible. Assisted suicide was uniformly illegal in Western societies before the late twentieth century, and until the late nineteenth century the immorality of physicians helping patients commit suicide was undisputed. (Thomas More's fictional Utopian society practices euthanasia, but it is a pre-Christian society, and some scholars think his portrayal may not have been intended as serious advocacy.) As the assisted suicide debate emerged, however, the term "euthanasia" was increasingly used to mean not only physician-assisted suicide, but also killing those with congenital illnesses, especially mental illnesses. This latter form of euthanasia is often called involuntary euthanasia to distinguish it from assisted suicide, which is at least in theory voluntary.

The year 1870 was pivotal in the history of euthanasia, since the first serious advocacy of assisted suicide and killing the disabled appeared then. Ernst Haeckel, a leading German Darwinian biologist, discussed killing the disabled in the second edition of his popular book on evolutionary theory, *The Natural History of Creation*. He worried that some of the effects of modern medicine and humanitarianism would allow the weak and sick to reproduce and thus lead to biological degeneration and decline rather than evolutionary progress. In order to offset these allegedly deleterious developments, he promoted eugenics. One such eugenics policy that he suggested was infanticide. He wrote,

> If someone would dare to make the suggestion, according to
> the example of the Spartans and Redskins, to kill immediately

after birth the miserable and infirm children, to whom can be prophesied with assurance a sickly life, instead of preserving them to their own harm and the detriment of the whole community, our whole so-called "humane civilization" would erupt in a cry of indignation.[27]

Though some claim that Haeckel was not hereby endorsing infanticide for the disabled, in 1904 Haeckel made his support for killing the disabled—and this time he included disabled adults—crystal clear. He also admitted that his passage from 1870 was indeed intended to promote infanticide for babies with disabilities.[28]

In Britain the debate over euthanasia also began in 1870 with the publication of an essay on "Euthanasia" by Samuel D. Williams in *Essays of the Birmingham Speculative Club*. Despite the small circulation of this journal, Williams's essay attracted attention and was discussed in other British journals in the 1870s. Williams, like Haeckel, intended to replace the Judeo-Christian sanctity-of-life ethic with a secular ethic. Both men also stressed the beneficent role of death in the evolutionary struggle for existence, which eliminated the biologically weak and sick. Williams pointed out that the struggle in nature results in "the continuous crushing out of the weak, and the consequent maintenance of what is called 'the vigour of the race.'" Since death for the sickly was inevitable—and indeed beneficial to society—he thought that "Man should ensure that the weak went to the wall in the most comfortable fashion."[29] Williams's position was too radical for most Britons, and the medical profession remained adamantly and uniformly opposed to euthanasia. Only in 1901 did the first British physician publicly support assisted suicide and involuntary euthanasia for the disabled.[30]

However, the growing tide of secularism, together with the increasing acceptance of Darwinism, contributed to a climate that made euthanasia more acceptable. In an 1894 essay the British philosopher F. H. Bradley claimed that Christian ethics had been superseded by Darwinian theory. In his essay Bradley argued forthrightly against the idea that human life is sacred, that individuals have inherent rights, and that humans are equal. He stated, "But when justice (as it must be) is dethroned, and when Darwinism (as it will be) is listened to, there will be a favorable hearing for the claims of ethical surgery." By "ethical surgery" and other synonyms—"social surgery," "moral surgery," and "social amputation"—Bradley meant getting rid of those deemed unfit. He insisted this was based squarely on Darwinian science, which "urged on us that a condition of welfare is the selection of the more fit, and it added emphatically that selection means the rejection of worse varieties." He continued, "The removal of diseased growths, of worse varieties, Darwinism insisted was obligatory." Bradley clearly invoked Darwinian sanction for killing those he deemed unfit, those whom he judged a "noxious lunatic," "dangerous specimens," and those whose lives are a "useless burden."[31]

The debate over euthanasia did not emerge in the United States until the 1890s. One of the most prominent early advocates of euthanasia in America was Robert Ingersoll, a flamboyant freethinking lawyer who campaigned ardently against Christianity. In 1894 he favored permitting assisted suicide for those with terminal illnesses. Six years later the physician William Duncan McKim argued in his book *Heredity and Human Progress* that science militated against the "unreasonable dogma that *all* human life is intrinsically sacred." The novelist Jack London was another prominent American lending his support to euthanasia about this time.[32]

What brought about this shift in thinking about suicide, assisted suicide, and killing the disabled in the late nineteenth and early twentieth centuries (albeit among a minority)? Ian Dowbiggin and Nick Kemp in their fine studies of the history of the euthanasia movement in the United States and Britain, respectively, both emphasize the role of secularization in general and Darwinian theory in particular in mediating this transformation. Dowbiggin states, "Trends such as eugenics, positivism, social Darwinism, and scientific naturalism had the effect of convincing a small yet articulate group in the early twentieth century that traditional ethics no longer applied to decisions about death and dying." He also argues, "The most pivotal turning point in the early history of the euthanasia movement was the coming of Darwinism to America."[33] Kemp strongly supports Dowbiggin's position, emphasizing the role of secularization and Darwinism on the budding euthanasia movement. He writes, "While we should be wary of depicting Darwin as the man responsible for ushering in a secular age we should be similarly cautious of underestimating the importance of evolutionary thought in relation to the questioning of the sanctity of human life."[34]

Scholars studying the German euthanasia debates largely agree with Dowbiggin and Kemp. One of the leading experts on the pre–World War I euthanasia debates in Germany, Hans-Walter Schmuhl, explains, "By giving up the conception of the divine image of humans under the influence of the Darwinian theory, human life became a piece of property, which—in contrast to the idea of a natural right to life—could be weighed against other pieces of property."[35] Another leading scholar of the German euthanasia movement, Udo Benzenhöfer, spends an entire chapter in his book on the history of euthanasia discussing the impact of social Darwinism and eugenics on the budding euthanasia movement in the late nineteenth century.[36]

Concern and controversy about euthanasia and infanticide erupted in the United States in late 1915 when the Chicago physician Harry Haiselden publicized the case of the Bollinger baby, who was born severely deformed. Haiselden convinced the parents not to request life-saving surgery, so the baby died in five days. Haiselden then took his case for passive euthanasia to the American public by starring in *The Black Stork*, a film he co-wrote. When the controversy first erupted in 1915, Haiselden insisted that he only supported passive measures (such as not operating or withholding treatment), not actively killing infants. However, later he gave a lethal dose of medication to a microcephalic infant and increasingly supported active infanticide.[37]

Haiselden claimed that his actions were protecting society from "lives of no value." He warned that society was being overrun with "horrid semi-humans": "Our streets are infested with an Army of the unfit—a dangerous, vicious army of death and dread." Though Haiselden proclaimed that he was exalting science above sentimentality, his dim view of people with disabilities apparently owed a great deal to his childhood prejudices. In his autobiography he related that as a boy he and some comrades beat up a helpless girl who had a mental disability. Not only did he not express any remorse for his youthful transgression, but he claimed that this aggression was justifiable, because it was directed against "the menace in these wretched beings." Being assaulted by "normal" people such as himself was, in Haiselden's view, "only part of the price that the inferior forms of human life must pay if they wish to live among their more fortunate brothers."[38] It seems Haiselden never grew up—even in adulthood continuing to exult in his childhood bullying of a hapless girl with a disability.

Haiselden's utter contempt for people with disabilities and his inegalitarian philosophy were, unfortunately, not uncommon in American society at the time. Clarence Darrow, the infamous trial lawyer of the early twentieth century mentioned earlier, agreed with Haiselden's position about infanticide, stating, "Chloroform unfit children. Show them the same mercy that is shown beasts that are no longer fit to live." Even Helen Keller, whom one would think should know better, weighed in, supporting Haiselden, claiming the Bollinger baby was just a "hopeless being spared from a life of misery. No one cares about that pitiful, useless lump of flesh." But perhaps someone did care. Anna Bollinger, the mother, never recovered from grief about her baby and died two years later.[39]

In the first half of the twentieth century the euthanasia movement continued to gain adherents, culminating in the formation of the Voluntary Euthanasia Legalisation Society in Britain in 1935 and the Euthanasia Society of America in 1938. Most of the members of these two organizations were secular progressives, such as H. G. Wells, George Bernard Shaw, Julian Huxley, and Margaret Sanger, though some were Unitarian or liberal Protestants, such as Harry Emerson Fosdick. Havelock Ellis, a prominent British physician and sexologist who joined the Voluntary Euthanasia Legalisation Society, reflected a common attitude among euthanasia proponents when he asserted that the prohibition against infanticide was "one of the unfortunate results of Christianity." He hoped to sweep away these allegedly benighted restrictions on killing the weak, since, he stated, "there is a place in humanity for murder, that is to say by killing the unfit."[40] Margaret Sanger, the founder of Planned Parenthood, claimed that her zeal for birth control and support for euthanasia were similar, "one being to bring entrance into life under control of reason, and the other to bring the exit of life under that control."[41] Though both organizations officially campaigned for assisted suicide, many of their members also supported involuntary euthanasia for people with disabilities.

More ominously, in Germany a regime took power in 1933 under Hitler that was committed to a radical, racialized version of social Darwinism. Not only did Hitler hope to rid the world of so-called inferior races, but he was equally hostile toward Germans deemed to be biologically inferior. The German psychiatrist Alfred Hoche and the law professor Karl Binding popularized the term "life unworthy of life" in their provocative and controversial 1920 book advocating the destruction of such "inferior" people.[42] Hitler and the Nazis imbibed this mentality. In a major speech at the Nuremberg Party Congress in August 1929, Hitler strongly implied that he supported infanticide for people with disabilities. In that speech he declared,

> If annually Germany would produce a million children and dispose of 700,000 to 800,000 of the weakest, then in the end the result would possibly even be an increase in strength. The dangerous thing is, that we ourselves interrupt the process of natural selection and thereby slowly deprive ourselves of the possibility to increase our population.

Hitler then praised Sparta—which he and his contemporaries understood to practice infanticide—as the "clearest racial state in history."[43] Hitler was not likely serious about wanting to kill 70–80 percent of German infants, but this suggestion indicates the radical nature of his philosophy of destruction.[44]

When Hitler authorized "mercy killing" of the disabled in 1939, which resulted in the murder of about two hundred thousand disabled

Germans by 1945, he did not have to twist the arms of German physicians. Karl Brandt, Hitler's personal physician who was put in charge of the Nazi euthanasia operation, was a fanatical supporter of killing people with disabilities.[45] Other Nazi physicians zealously supported this program, as well as conducting gruesome human experiments in concentration camps. They also participated directly in the mass murder of the Jews, Sinti, and Roma (also known as Gypsies). Their zeal for killing people with disabilities was so intense that in one case, the psychiatrist in charge of a German asylum continued killing inmates even after being liberated by the American army.[46] The physicians and staff at Hadamar were so enthusiastic about their mass murder of people with disabilities that they threw a party celebrating the death of their ten thousandth victim.

In the wake of Nazi atrocities, euthanasia became a harder sell in Western societies in the late 1940s and 1950s. Nonetheless, Joseph Fletcher, one of the founding figures in the nascent discipline of bioethics (and an early member of the Euthanasia Society of America), developed new justifications for euthanasia.[47] Since Fletcher was an Episcopal priest and taught at an Episcopal seminary for many years, some might assume that Fletcher's bioethics reflected some kind of Christian perspective. However, this assumption would be a mistake. In his autobiographical reflections, Fletcher explained that as a young man he was radicalized by reading George Bernard Shaw, H. L. Mencken, and other intellectual fare by skeptics and leftists. He joined the Episcopal priesthood, not because he was convinced of the truths of Christianity, but because he wanted an outlet for his social activism.

Fletcher's ideology in the 1930s and 1940s was a blend of John Dewey's pragmatism, Marxism, and Christianity. Pragmatism ultimately won out, and he eventually abandoned both Marxism and Christianity. In any case, Fletcher himself claimed that his bioethics was not grounded in Christianity but in pragmatism. He stated, "My own ethics, as I tackled value problems and the right-wrong issues posed by medicine and biological innovations, was essentially humanist—humanist in the sense of nontheist. Like Protagoras I saw man as the measure of things, the determiner of value and truth, not God or a revelation of any kind." He also admitted that his "situation ethics as a theory of moral action is, of course, utterly independent of Christian presuppositions or beliefs."[48] Despite his priestly status, Fletcher's outlook was essentially secular.

In his book, *Morals and Medicine* (1954), Fletcher promoted voluntary euthanasia by articulating a kind of personhood theory. Fletcher's personhood theory was simply a more sophisticated philosophical defense of human inequality than the cruder versions circulating before his time, such as those in the eugenics movement. At the beginning of the book he noted that birth and death are decisive events for us, "nor is anything more precious than the health of mind and body which makes our passage between these two crises one of beauty and joy rather than of ugliness and crippled being."[49] By exalting health to the highest ideal and by denigrating "ugliness and crippled being," Fletcher was perpetuating the dehumanizing ideology so common in the eugenics movement.

In the chapter on euthanasia in *Morals and Medicine*, Fletcher asserted that humans have a right to commit suicide. He offered two arguments to support this contention. First, he reminded us that martyrs and heroes often give up their lives, and they are honored for it, not condemned. Here Fletcher ignored the huge difference between heroes giving up their lives to save other lives (in which case they are dying to preserve the sanctity of life, not to controvert it) or martyrs being killed by others for their beliefs, and those who take their own lives for their own purposes. Second, Fletcher takes up Hume's argument that we should be able to exert control over the end of our life, because if God has the sole right to decide when our lives should end, "then it follows with equal force that it is immoral to lengthen life." This is a weak argument, because it caricatures the position of those arguing that we as humans do not have the right to end another person's life. Those accepting a divine prohibition on killing any innocent human being also generally believe in a divine imperative to help others stay alive. They are not so stupid as to believe that any interaction with others that helps them stay alive is impermissible as an interference with divine activity. Fletcher was aiming at a non-existent target.[50]

To be sure, in *Morals and Medicine* Fletcher only promoted voluntary euthanasia as "merciful release from incurable suffering" for those with "fatal and demoralizing illnesses." However, I suspect that his focus on voluntary euthanasia was a tactical ploy to gain greater traction for his ideas in a culture that largely disapproved of any form of assisted suicide. The personhood theory he developed to defend voluntary euthanasia would certainly have profound implications for people who no longer enjoyed the status of "persons." This is especially the case, because the U.S. Constitution guarantees to "persons" the right not to be "deprived of life, liberty, or property, without due process of law." Fletcher tried to do an end run around these constitutional safeguards by redefining the commonly accepted meaning of "person."

As Fletcher explained, "In the personalistic view of man and morals, asserted throughout these pages, personality is supreme over mere life. To prolong life uselessly, while the personal qualities of freedom, knowledge, self-possession and control, and responsibility are sacrificed is to attack the moral status of a person." He dismissed the idea that simply having a human body makes one a person. Rather to be a person one must have certain qualities, such as the ability to make moral decisions, self-awareness, self-consciousness, and self-determination.[51] In later works Fletcher drew up even longer lists of what it takes to be a "person." In a 1979 book he listed fifteen traits:

1. minimal intelligence
2. self-awareness
3. self-control
4. sense of time
5. sense of futurity
6. sense of the past
7. capability to relate to others
8. concern for others
9. communication
10. control of existence
11. curiosity

12. change and changeability
13. balance of rationality and feeling
14. idiosyncrasy
15. neocortical function.[52]

Any human who lacks these characteristics, Fletcher asserted, has no moral significance. He stated, "Humans without some minimum of intelligence or mental capacity are not persons, no matter how many of their organs are active, no matter how spontaneous their living processes are.... A human vegetable is not a person, not truly a human being." He then suggested that an IQ score of 20 would approximate the lowest level of personhood. He also made explicit what was implied in his earlier formulation of his personhood theory: fetuses, infants, and those with some disabilities would no longer be considered persons and thus would no longer be considered part of our moral community.[53]

Fletcher's personhood theory suffers from several major problems:

1. the characteristics used to gauge personhood are not self-evident and undisputable—it's a list that Fletcher unilaterally came up with
2. these are characteristics—most of them cognitive functions and therefore unmeasurable—that are present in individuals in varying degrees, and are not traits that one either does or doesn't have
3. in many instances we have no way of knowing when or if specific individuals have these cognitive functions
4. since some humans have more or less of these traits than other humans, the dividing line between the "person" and "non-person" is ultimately arbitrary

Let us examine each of these points briefly.

While Fletcher defines persons to include those with rationality, self-awareness, and moral freedom, he never provides cogent reasons for privileging these particular traits. Presumably all these are traits that

Fletcher himself possessed, so he made sure he was a "person." What if we instead privilege other characteristics, such as the capacity to love people? Indeed Fletcher seemed to include this in his list of fifteen traits ("concern for others"), but what happens when someone has one or two of the fifteen traits, but not the other ones? Or what if someone has fourteen out of fifteen traits? Is he or she still a "person"? What if we put greater stress on features Fletcher ignores, such as creativity in music, fine arts, or crafts? Choosing which traits to use to define a "person" is an intractable problem.

An even greater problem, however, is that none of the traits Fletcher selected are something one either has or does not have. People have these traits in varying quantities. Thus personhood theory implies that some people—those possessing these characteristics in higher measure—are more valuable than others. Not coincidentally, this is precisely the conclusion that many leaders in the eugenics movement had been promoting long before Fletcher, and he was simply enshrining this inegalitarian theory into his philosophy. The problem for Fletcher is that he wants to assert that "persons" have equal value and rights, but those rights are based on traits that people have in differing amounts. Some people are more intelligent than others, but most of us understand that this does not give people with Ph.D.s or an IQ of 130 a greater right to life or greater value than the multitude of people with an IQ of 100 or even less. Further, some highly intelligent people have little or no regard for other people. Would this make a genius any less of a "person"?

Third, we have no way of knowing for sure when particular individuals have these characteristics. Some severely autistic individuals seem to be uncommunicative and unable to relate to others, two of Fletcher's fifteen attributes of what it is to be a person. Because of the difficulty— or sometimes impossibility—of communicating with them, we may wrongly conclude that they are devoid of intelligence, self-awareness, self-control, and other features that Fletcher thinks necessary to display personhood. However, since the advent of computers, some autistic individuals have been able to communicate by typing their thoughts into computers. This has led to the amazing discovery that some of them are highly intelligent, caring individuals with a sophisticated understanding of their condition. In other cases, some individuals with severe mental disabilities have shown remarkable musical ability. Further, people in unconscious states, who could be defined as non-persons if one takes Fletcher literally, sometimes understand everything going on around them, even though they cannot communicate at the moment. After recovering their physical ability to communicate, they can sometimes remember visitors and conversations that occurred in their presence, even though they were unresponsive at the time. In the case of fetuses, it is impossible to know when they attain any particular level of rationality or self-awareness.

Finally, in order to overcome the objection that these qualities differ from one individual to the next, Fletcher assumes that there is some threshold level of these characteristics. Those under the threshold are non-persons. However, the threshold is completely arbitrary. When he actually tried to pinpoint a dividing line, Fletcher indicated that an IQ of twenty would be the minimal intelligence necessary to be deemed a "person." Aside from the hotly debated issue of whether we are even able to measure intelligence accurately, such a dividing line is inherently subjective. Why not make the dividing line between person and non-person an IQ of 50 or even 70, rather than 20? And how is one to objectively measure concern for others or self-awareness or other indicators of personhood?[54]

In his discussion of infanticide in 1979, Fletcher took a position even more radical than his personhood theory. First he called infanticide a form of euthanasia, and then equated it with abortion: "It is reasonable, indeed, to describe infanticide as postnatal abortion."[55] However, then Fletcher threw his own personhood theory to the wind by claiming that the real question was not whether an infant was a person at all, but rather, "'Can a person's life ever be ended ethically?' It all turns on the issue of whether the value of a human life is absolute or relative." Of course, Fletcher, who popularized the term "situation ethics" in the 1960s, took the relativistic position that moral questions can only be determined by weighing the consequences of one's actions, not by relying on divine edicts or abstract ideas about human rights or responsibilities. He then stated, "We could accept Kluge's thesis that fetuses are persons, and still justify both abortion and infanticide in some cases, because, in a given case, to prolong life would be to engender more evil than good." Based on his relativistic position, Fletcher thought that some people "might properly be sacrificed on the principle of proportionate good." Fletcher summarized his view thus: "And this chapter's answer is, plainly and confidently, that human happiness and well-being is the highest good or *summum bonum*, and that therefore any ends or purposes which that standard or ideal validates are just, right, good." In Fletcher's view utilitarianism—the greatest happiness of the greatest number—trumped the sanctity of life.[56]

It is hard to see why anyone taking Fletcher's utilitarian call to sacrifice some humans for the well-being of others would have to halt with abortion, infanticide, and voluntary euthanasia. Indeed his way of thinking seems remarkably similar to the dehumanizing tendencies we have already seen in other utopian social projects, such as communism and fascism. Communists persecuted the bourgeoisie, and Nazis massacred multitudes of those belonging to allegedly inferior races. Thus they were not targeting the same groups as Fletcher and some other modern bioethicists. However, the idea that killing some people is beneficial because it will promote greater happiness for those remaining is common to them all. They all eviscerated the sanctity-of-life ethic, because they wanted freedom to kill those they defined as sub-human. They thought that sweeping away the detritus of "sub-humans" would lead to greater human happiness and historical progress.

Peter Singer, whom we met in the introduction, is one of the most notorious adherents of Fletcher's personhood theory. In many books on bioethics Singer has fulminated against the "speciesist" prejudice that all humans are equal and have a right to life. On the contrary, he continually asserts, being a human has no moral significance at all. Rather, only a "person," whom he defines as "a rational and self-conscious being," has the right to life. He not only denies that a human fetus is a "person," but he does not think that newborn infants make the grade either, because they allegedly lack self-consciousness and rationality. He asserts, "If the fetus does not have the same claim to life as a person, it appears that the newborn baby does not either, and the life of a new born baby is of less value than the life of a pig, a dog, or a chimpanzee." On this basis, Singer thinks that we should alter present homicide legislation to make it legal for parents to kill their infants up to one month old.[57]

According to Singer, once the Judeo-Christian sanctity-of-life doctrine is abandoned, euthanasia is a logical consequence. He rejects involuntary euthanasia for those capable of objecting to their demise, but he clearly thinks that family members should have the right to terminate the lives of those unable to communicate their desires, if their lives are deemed miserable. He especially emphasizes the worthlessness of those whose lives are filled with pain and suffering. He states, "A life of physical suffering, unredeemed by any form of pleasure or by a minimal level of self-consciousness, is not worth living."[58] In Singer's view, it is better to end such a life than to endure suffering. Singer's reasoning leads to a fateful conclusion: if killing a "defective" infant will lead to the birth of an infant with better prospects for happiness, then "the total amount of happiness will be greater if the defective infant is killed. The loss of happy life for the first infant is outweighed by the gain of a happier life for the second."[59] Though Singer would likely deny it, this kind of consequentialist reasoning opens the floodgate to many forms of killing, depending on what one construes as the best way of contributing to human happiness.

Singer's views are so radical that even some of his supporters find them disquieting. In an interview with Johann Hari, Singer remarks that it is just a small step from abortion to infanticide. Pro-life activists have been preaching this for decades, but they draw the conclusion directly opposite to Singer's. Singer thinks abortion is perfectly acceptable, so he proposes that we expand the killing to include babies already safely out of the womb. At the close of this interview, Hari enthuses that "Singer is pure, disembodied rationality—the Enlightenment made flesh." Despite his sympathy with Singer's position, however, Hari experienced some queasiness with Singer's rationality. He concludes: "I agree with

most of his arguments. Give me Singer over the Vatican-style superstitions he is trying to dispel any day; and yet, as I leave the interview, I
can't shake off a strange—Singer might say sentimental—anxiety."
Fortunately, Hari has not yet figured out how to shake off his humanity
and become "disembodied," as Singer apparently can. Even though he
mentally agrees with Singer, he knows deep down inside that something
is fundamentally wrong with Singer's dehumanizing philosophy.[60]

While Fletcher, Singer, and others were promoting euthanasia in
intellectual circles, the journalist Derek Humphry took the cause to the
general public. Humphry was not an ivory-tower theoretician, but an
activist who participated in multiple suicides of family members. A few
years after assisting his first wife to commit suicide in the UK in 1975,
he co-authored (with his second wife, Ann Wickett) *Jean's Way* (1979),
a sanitized version of the events and emotions surrounding the assisted
suicide. After moving to Los Angeles, he and his wife founded the Hemlock Society in 1980 to promote assisted suicide for those with terminal
illnesses. In addition to lobbying for pro-euthanasia legislation, Humphry
published suicide manuals to provide practical tips on how to painlessly
end one's life. When Ann was diagnosed with breast cancer in 1989,
Derek, who had not been faithful to her even before that time, deserted
her, and Derek turned the leaders of the Hemlock Society against her,
too. Abandoned by her erstwhile husband, friends, and co-militants in
the euthanasia movement, in desperation she sought out the advice and
friendship of a former ideological foe, Rita Marker, director of the International Anti-Euthanasia Task Force. Derek continued to malign and
badger Ann, until finally she committed suicide in 1991. In her suicide
note she accused him of having "done everything conceivable to pre-
cipitate my death."[61]

Derek Humphry (and Ann before he abandoned her) campaigned
vigorously against the Judeo-Christian sanctity-of-life ethic, preferring
some kind of secular ethic instead. He did not really specify what kind
of ethics he espoused, preferring instead to tell emotional stories about
people suffering. However, he often criticized Christianity, especially the
Catholic Church, for its moral stance, and he exulted in the rationalist

approach to suicide that emerged in the Enlightenment. Once he asked rhetorically, "Do we live in a society whose laws must still be governed by the dogmas of the Judeo-Christian religions, or should secular, commonsense, and humanitarian politics help us to frame our laws?"[62] Though he insisted that the Hemlock Society had many Christians in it, his own statistics suggest that it was largely secular. Over 50 percent of the members were atheists or agnostics, and less than one-third had some kind of religious affiliation with Christian churches. Only about 15 percent actually attended church regularly.[63]

Though Humphry posed as a compassionate humanitarian, his philosophy contributed to the dehumanization of those suffering pain. In his 1986 book co-authored with Ann, he stated, "A life wasted by persistent and unrelenting pain was not worthy; it was a useless life, often demanding a merciful release. In short, a man living such a life was no longer a man."[64] As we have seen so many times in history, defining some of our fellow humans as non-human is a fateful step, opening a Pandora's box. Indeed in a co-authored book, *Freedom to Die* (1998), Humphry shows the direction that his hedonistic philosophy can take. Though he continues to insist that he is advocating only voluntary euthanasia, he broaches an issue that most dare not discuss: the relationship of euthanasia to the spiraling cost of healthcare. Indeed Humphry hopes that this economic factor will become the highest consideration motivating us to legalize assisted suicide. If we want to know why the right-to-die movement should succeed in our day, he explained, "one must look at the realities of the increasing cost of health care in an aging society, because in the final analysis, economics, not the quest for broadened individual liberties or increased autonomy, will drive assisted suicide to the plateau of acceptable practice."[65] This is quite a stunning admission, but perhaps we should not be too surprised that those adopting a hedonistic philosophy are gripped by the "love of money [which] is the root of all kinds of evil."[66]

Indeed, in the midst of explaining the unsustainability of rising end-of-life healthcare costs, Humphry asks, "Is there, in fact, a duty to die—a responsibility within the family unit—that should remain voluntary but

expected nonetheless?"[67] Once again, the right to die morphs into the duty
to die. Also, what will "voluntary" mean if we as a society decide that the
morally proper thing is to commit suicide, so we do not have to put up with
you any longer? In such a situation, the pressure will be intense to choose
suicide. Despite the asseverations of much pro-euthanasia propaganda, this
kind of assisted suicide will not be a clear-headed, non-emotional, rational
choice based solely on the interests of the person committing suicide.

The most controversial euthanasia activist of the 1990s was Jack
Kevorkian, who gained instant infamy by devising a "suicide machine"
in 1989. Kevorkian's parents had escaped the Armenian genocide, and
as a boy Kevorkian abandoned Christianity, because he could not fathom
how a loving God could allow genocide to happen. He did not believe in
any kind of afterlife, but rather thought that nothingness awaited us after
our death. According to his sympathetic biographers, Neal Nicol and
Harry Wylie, "It also infuriated him when doctors began using religious
arguments on the sanctity of life as a basis for denying him his license
[to assist in suicide]." Even as a resident physician, he was so fascinated
with death and dying that nurses nicknamed him "Dr. Death." His
paintings reveal the allure that death exercised on his psyche.[68]

After an article in *Newsweek* brought him publicity, people began
contacting him to help them commit suicide. His first victim was Janet
Adkins, a fifty-four-year-old woman with Alzheimer's, who died on June
4, 1990. Despite the public outcry against him, Michigan did not have
a law forbidding assisted suicide, and Kevorkian was twice acquitted.
He continued with his grisly project, even expressing the grandiose hope
that he would win a Nobel Prize for his efforts. After the Michigan
legislature responded to Kevorkian by banning assisted suicide in 1993,
he flouted the law. In late 1998 he allowed *60 Minutes* to broadcast a
videotape of the suicide of Thomas Youk, which resulted in his arraign-
ment on murder charges. The following year he was convicted of second-
degree murder and was sentenced to ten to twenty-five years in prison.
His hope for a Supreme Court case overturning the ban on assisted
suicide never materialized.[69]

In 1997 the U.S. Supreme Court ruled that assisted suicide is not a fundamental constitutional right, though two U.S. district courts had already ruled otherwise. The Supreme Court, however, did not ban assisted suicide, either, so states had the authority to regulate it one way or the other. Oregon became the first U.S. state to legalize physician-assisted suicide. Its 1994 law was held up by legal challenges, but a 1997 referendum went into effect immediately. Since then, three other states have adopted similar legislation: Washington in 2008, Vermont in 2013, and California in 2015. Aside from these four states, the Montana Supreme Court legalized physician-assisted suicide in 2009. Other states have rejected referenda and other efforts to legalize it.

Euthanasia made even greater strides in the Netherlands, Belgium, and Switzerland. In the Netherlands attitudes opposing active euthanasia softened in the 1970s. In 1981 the Dutch Justice Ministry signaled that it would no longer prosecute cases of physician-assisted suicide, even though Dutch law clearly forbade such a practice. The Dutch Supreme Court recognized this agreement not to prosecute in 1984. By 1990 about 2 percent of all deaths in the Netherlands were physician-induced, and more than one-third of these were involuntary euthanasia, not assisted suicide. Even though involuntary euthanasia was technically illegal, none of these cases were prosecuted. Interestingly, physical pain was only a factor in about 40 percent of the patients put to death. After the Netherlands passed legislation in 1993 to confirm the legality of voluntary euthanasia, both physician-assisted suicide and involuntary euthanasia increased.[70]

In Switzerland assisted suicide has been legal since 1942, but until recently this had little practical effect. However, more recently, right-to-die organizations have begun to run suicide clinics in Switzerland. Tourism has long been an important part of the Swiss economy, as sightseers, mountaineers, and skiers have flocked to the breathtaking Alps, the beautiful lakes, and the exciting slopes. Now Swiss tourism has another attraction for those wanting to escape the problems and ugliness of this life. Instead of a relaxing time enjoying the incredibly beautiful scenery, you can now come to Switzerland to die, no matter what your reason for seeking death. Dignitas, a Swiss organization, will assist you in ending your life. In 2014 a retired British art teacher availed herself of its services, not because she had a physical problem, but because, she explained, she just could not adapt to modern society.[71] An elderly Italian woman was disturbed by the effects of aging on her physical beauty, so she killed herself at a Swiss clinic without even informing her family. They were shocked to receive her ashes in the mail. Couples have committed suicide together, because neither wanted to live apart from the other. The Swiss Supreme Court has upheld the right for people with mental illnesses to commit suicide, too. The floodgates for suicide are open wide in Switzerland. However, make sure you do not flush a live goldfish down the toilet or decapitate a flower, for goldfish and plants enjoy rights under Swiss law.[72]

❧

As we have already seen in the case of Fletcher and Singer, philosophical justifications for abortion have often followed a similar trajectory as those for euthanasia. Unsurprisingly, many of the most ardent proponents for legalizing abortion have been secularists who have jettisoned the Judeo-Christian sanctity-of-life ethic. They often hurled ridicule at Christian churches, especially the Catholic Church, for its moral stance opposing abortion. The staunchest advocates for granting the unborn the right to life have been those who believe that all humans are equally and intrinsically valuable and have an inherent and inviolable right to life. Nonetheless, the abortion issue has played out historically quite differently from euthanasia, since abortion was legalized in the U.S. and most European countries by the 1970s, while assisted suicide is still illegal in most states and nations.

Before the nineteenth century a major problem in figuring out the ethical and legal status of the unborn was that no one knew when his or her life began. The first empirical evidence of life was when the mother felt it moving and kicking within her. This event, which was known as quickening, usually occurs in the fourth or fifth month of pregnancy.

For centuries, many people wrongly assumed that before quickening, the fetus was not alive. In any case, they could not be sure he or she was alive yet. Thus, until the nineteenth century Anglo-American common law forbade abortions, but only after the time of quickening. The law protected unborn humans as soon as people knew that they were indeed living human beings.

By the mid-nineteenth century, biological and medical knowledge had advanced, consigning quickening to the same status as geo-centrism and other outmoded theories. Biologists learned that from the moment of conception embryos and fetuses are living organisms. Whether a woman could feel her infant inside her or not had no bearing on its status as a living being. This new knowledge, together with the still-prevailing Judeo-Christian sanctity-of-life ethic, convinced legislators throughout the U.S. and Europe to forge tougher anti-abortion statutes in the nineteenth century. One did not have to believe in anything distinctively Christian to embrace the new anti-abortion laws (and indeed some non-Christian nations, such as Japan, forbade abortions, too). One only had to understand the latest scientific knowledge about embryology and accept that all humans have natural rights, including the right to life. In 1803 the UK banned pre-quickening abortion, though it still carried a lesser penalty than post-quickening abortion. The UK abandoned the quickening distinction altogether in its Offences against the Person Act of 1861. Likewise most U.S. states forsook the quickening doctrine in a flurry of anti-abortion legislation in the period between 1860–1880. By 1900 abortion at any period of pregnancy was illegal throughout the U.S. and in most European states.[73]

Even while legislators throughout the U.S. and Europe were banning abortion at any stage of pregnancy, secularization was beginning to undermine the Judeo-Christian sanctity-of-life ethic and natural rights philosophy that underpinned these anti-abortion statutes. The German biologist Ernst Haeckel, for instance, admitted that human life begins at conception, and he even celebrated his birthday nine months early one year to underscore this fact. However, he believed that as human embryos developed, they traversed the stages of evolutionary development of their ancestors. Thus he thought the embryo was still at the level of animals. He stated in 1904 "that the developing embryo, just as the newborn child, is completely devoid of consciousness, is a pure 'reflex machine,' just like a lower vertebrate."[74] (Note that he also saw the newborn infant as not fully human.) Abortion, in Haeckel's view, is thus no different from killing an animal.

Other Germans apparently agreed with Haeckel, for Germany became the first country with a significant movement for the legalization of abortion. One of the leading women activists pressing for legalization of abortion in early twentieth-century Germany was Helene Stöcker, who helped found the League for the Protection of Mothers in 1905. In her early teens, Stöcker rejected the Christian faith of her parents and later became enamored of Nietzsche's anti-Christian philosophy. She campaigned stridently against Christian morality, advocating a new ethic that included sexual liberation, abortion, and eugenics. Stöcker argued that abortion should be permissible in just about any case, including for eugenic reasons and if the mother would suffer adverse mental and emotional distress by having a child. She claimed that the life of the mother was superior to that of the fetus, so it is not reasonable "to 'protect' the undeveloped embryo at the expense of *unspeakable misery* of adult, developed humans."[75]

Many of the early twentieth-century feminists in Germany who joined Stöcker in her campaign to legalize abortion, such as Lily Braun, were ardent Nietzscheans who rejected Christian and humanitarian ethics. Braun was drawn to socialism for a time and even joined the Social Democratic Party, a Marxist political party. However, she later bolted from the party, in part because she rejected its emphasis on human equality. Nature, she explained, demonstrates the inequality of biological organisms, including humans. Thus she scoffed at every "Hans Fool" ("Hans Narr") who called himself a brother of Goethe.[76] As Braun illustrates, while fighting for women's rights, the movement to legalize abortion in Germany often minimized the rights of other people.

Like Fletcher and Braun, many of the early proponents of legalization of abortion were political radicals, but unlike Fletcher, most of them were intensely anti-religious. The notorious early twentieth-century American anarchist Emma Goldman supported free sex and birth control. She worked as a midwife, and though she did not perform abortions, she rejected the idea that unborn babies had a right to life. She wrote about her unwillingness to perform abortions, "It was not any moral consideration for the sanctity of life; a life unwanted and forced into abject poverty did not seem sacred to me."[77] Nor did the Soviet communist regime have any regard for the sanctity of life. The Soviet Union became the first European country to legalize abortion when Lenin's regime repealed its anti-abortion statute in 1920. Stalin recriminalized abortion in 1936, but clearly not because he considered anyone's life sacred. Probably he was hoping the abortion ban would promote greater population growth. In 1955 the post-Stalinist Soviet regime again legalized abortion, as did most of its Eastern European satellites in the ensuing years.[78] When public controversy erupted in Germany in 1931 about legalization of abortion, the leading pro-abortion forces were the communists and other leftists.[79] I am not implying that support for abortion is necessarily hinged to political radicalism, but at least in the early twentieth century they were companion ideas, because both tended to reject Christianity and its ethical doctrines, including its stress on the sanctity of human life.

Overt pro-abortion activism was considered radical in the early twentieth century. However, many women in the United States and Europe silently defied the laws forbidding abortion. Some were married and already had as many children as they wanted, while others were unmarried and wanted to avoid disgrace. In most major cities of the United States, abortionists—sometimes professional physicians and sometimes amateurs—plied their trade with little or no interference from the authorities. By the 1950s this tension between the law and practice would create greater sympathy for legal reform.

Aside from Fletcher, whom I have already discussed, Glanville Williams was one of the most outspoken intellectuals in the 1950s campaigning for abortion legalization (as well as legalization of infanticide and voluntary euthanasia). In 1956 Williams, a British law professor who later taught at Cambridge University, gave some prestigious endowed lectures at Columbia University in New York. These lectures were expanded into his book, *The Sanctity of Life and the Criminal Law* (1957). In his book Williams attacked the Christian teaching on the sanctity of life, which he perceived as the foundation for Anglo-American legislation against abortion, infanticide, and euthanasia. His critique was directed almost exclusively against Catholic moral theology, especially against doctrines he (and most fellow secularists) found objectionable, such as the Catholic teaching that humans—and preborn infants at some point—have immortal souls. He wrongly claimed that the real reason Christians opposed abortion was because it destroyed infants before they could be baptized, thus consigning their souls to hell.[80]

Williams admitted that Catholics (and many other Christians and some secularists, as well) have another argument against abortion, namely that humans have natural rights. However, curiously, he only mentioned this in passing, and he never overtly refuted this far more powerful argument against his position. Clearly Williams rejected natural rights philosophy, but unfortunately, he never provided any philosophical justification for his preference for a more pragmatic, utilitarian philosophy of law. In his preface he laid out the guiding principles of his legal philosophy (though he did not defend them): "Much of the law of murder rests upon the pragmatic considerations of the most obvious kind. Law has been called the cement of society, and certainly society would fall to pieces if men could murder with impunity." He then noted that prohibitions against some kinds of killing, such as infanticide, abortion, and suicide, are "rather the expression of a philosophical attitude than the outcome of social necessity.... The prohibition of killing imposed by these three crimes does not rest upon considerations of public security. If it can be justified at all, this must be either on ethico-religious or on racial grounds."[81] Thus Williams believed that what is wrong about killing is not that it harms the individual being killed, as natural rights philosophy teaches, but that it damages society or breaches "public security." If killing someone would not damage society, he considered it permissible. He asserted that "the killing of babies who are not old enough to experience fear is different from the murder of adults." As he made abundantly clear in the section of his book on infanticide, some people have no right to life. Indeed he used the dehumanizing term, "monsters," to refer to disabled infants who, he asserted, had no claim to legal protection.[82]

In two long chapters on abortion, Williams argued that prohibitions against abortion were unenforceable. However, his primary argument for its legalization was that opposition to abortion was a theological construct, an imposition of "theocratic morality" on society. Strangely, though, Williams did not provide any sustained argument about why he thought the unborn should not have the same rights as those who are born (though implicitly he rejected natural rights philosophy altogether, so perhaps this was a moot point). The closest he came was when he quoted another author's assertion that "abortion with the consent of the woman wrongs no one," because the fetus is not conscious and is not an independent entity.

In most cases Williams simply assumed that right-thinking secular intellectuals would agree with him that the unborn do not have the same value as those already born. For instance, at one point he correctly formulated a syllogism of his opponents: "Killing human beings is wrong. The unborn child is a human being. Therefore killing the unborn child is wrong." Williams then mentioned that the second premise was problematic because it assumes that conception is the dividing line giving one human status. If Williams had a knockdown argument against the unborn being human, this was his opportunity to unleash it. However, instead he merely asked why the "moral theologian" (note the loaded term for those embracing natural rights philosophy) draws the line at impregnation? He continued, "If the line is to be drawn by reference to social considerations and human happiness, then pretty obviously the time of impregnation is the wrong one to take." But why should we draw the line based on "social considerations and human happiness," rather than the intrinsic rights and value of the unborn infant? And why wouldn't "social considerations and human happiness" include consideration of the unborn and their happiness? I rather doubt that the legalization of abortion has made our society a better, happier society, anyway; but even if it has, killing some people to benefit others is not a morally acceptable way to promote happiness and social welfare.[83]

Some scholars, unwilling to throw human rights completely overboard, as Williams did, have constructed a different argument to support abortion rights. Judith Jarvis Thomson pioneered the bodily rights argument for abortion in her widely-touted 1971 article, "A Defense of Abortion." She clearly did not think a fetus is a person, but for the sake of argument she set aside the personhood debate, providing instead a rationale for abortion even if the fetus is a person from the moment of conception. Essentially, she argued that even if the fetus has a right to life, the woman's right to her own body trumps the fetus's right to life. Sadly, Thomson portrayed the unborn baby as an intruder assaulting its mother, and the pregnant woman as the baby's victim. She argued that a pregnant woman is free to defend herself against this intrusion. In her most famous illustration, she compared pregnancy to being kidnapped and medically hooked up to a famous violinist, who needs the use of your kidneys for nine months (she then quickly altered this to nine years and then to a lifetime to garner even more sympathy for the fictitious victim). Later in the essay, she also compared the fetus to a burglar invading a woman's home.[84]

Thomson's argument has several glaring problems. It compared pregnancy to being kidnapped or burgled, when in untold millions of examples women (and men) eagerly anticipate and joyfully announce pregnancies. Many women love being pregnant. They do not feel like they are being assaulted, kidnapped, or burgled. Even when pregnancy is not intended, the notion that the unborn child is attacking or molesting its mother does not do justice to their relationship. The unborn is an innocent being that has been procreated through the activity of two others (hopefully consensually). It is not attacking its mother any more than a newborn is assaulting and stealing from its mother when breastfeeding.

Further, Thomson assumed that the fetus does not have any right to inhabit the mother's body, unless the woman deliberately grants it. If it dwells in its mother's body without her permission, it is violating her right of bodily integrity. Thomson provided several examples to try to show that we do not have universal moral obligations to provide for others (such as the violinist). However, these analogies fall short, because mothers have obligations to their offspring that they do not have to other children. Also, if we apply this line of reasoning to fathers, we find that it makes no sense. If a deadbeat dad tells the judge, "Your honor, I had sex with this woman, but we used contraception, and I never intended to beget a child. I even offered to pay for an abortion, but she refused. Thus I have no moral obligation to provide child support for the next eighteen years, which is a burden far beyond what I should bear." What judge would accept this line of reasoning? No, he would say: You knew that sexual intercourse is designed to procreate and no contraception is foolproof. Even though you used contraceptives to try to avoid this natural consequence, you still need to take responsibility for the consequences of your actions, unintended or not.[85]

While Thomson was hammering out her philosophical justifications for abortion, feminists in the National Organization for Women (NOW) were helping lead the political struggle for the legalization of abortion. Mallory Millett, a sister of Kate Millett, one of the leading women activists in NOW, recently described the goals animating her sister and like-minded Marxist-feminist activists in the late 1960s. In a consciousness raising group in 1969, Kate and her compatriots chanted that they wanted to introduce a Cultural Revolution to destroy the American family and monogamy "by promoting promiscuity, eroticism, prostitution and homosexuality!" Their hatred for the monogamous family and their desire to pursue a professional career filled them with disdain for having children. Pregnancy was not an option, so if that hated event ever transpired, they insisted they should be free to kill their progeny in utero. No man should be able to tell them otherwise. Mallory was taken aback by their attitudes and came to recognize the damage done to women by these anti-family ideologies. At the close of her article, she laments the real-life consequences of her sister's pernicious philosophy, "And so, mass destruction, the inevitable outcome of all socialist/communist experiments, leaves behind its signature trail of wreckage. So much grace, femininity and beauty lost. So many ruined lives."[86] As so often happens in history, Kate Millett's utopian vision backfired. Despite the lofty ideals, females ended up more rather than less oppressed, and millions ended up dead, if they happened to be in the wrong uterus.

In the permissive and promiscuous Sixties, pressure for abortion reform reached a critical threshold, culminating in the British parliament legalizing abortion in 1967, followed by the landmark *Roe v. Wade* decision of the United States Supreme Court in 1973. Most Western countries had legalized abortion, at least in the early stages of pregnancy, by the end of the 1970s. In *Roe v. Wade*, the majority opinion by Justice Blackmun argued that women have a "right to privacy" that guarantees them the right to get abortions without government interference. Blackmun claimed that in light of disagreements among scholars, the court "need not resolve the difficult question of when life begins." Of course, the "question of when life begins" is not really the issue, because everyone knows the fetus is alive. The real question is: When does a developing human life begin to possess human rights? I assume this is what Blackmun really meant. However, even here the Justices could not avoid answering the question, despite their claim to the contrary.

The court did indeed provide an answer as to "when life begins." Blackmun stated—relying almost entirely on the faulty scholarship of a single legal scholar—that based on the legal history of abortion in the nineteenth century, he was convinced "that the word 'person,' as used in the Fourteenth Amendment, does not include the unborn."[87] Thus, the Supreme Court denied any unborn humans the constitutional and legal rights shared by all other human beings. Essentially the beginning of "life"—for the purposes of obtaining rights—was birth. However, later Blackmun asserted that states could protect "potential life" by proscribing abortion in the final trimester, since by then the fetus had reached viability, i.e., the ability to live outside the mother's womb. But he also insisted that if states banned third trimester abortions, they must allow exceptions for the preservation of the mother's life and health. The "mother's health" was interpreted so broadly in *Doe v. Bolton* that the

Supreme Court effectively made abortion on demand at any stage of pregnancy the law of the land. [88]

The Supreme Court's decision to relegate the unborn to the status of non-persons has remained the law of the land in the United States, though it remains controversial. Since that time, well over fifty million unborn humans have been aborted in the United States alone, and hundreds of millions of abortions have occurred elsewhere in the world. The voices of these babies will never be heard. We need to speak up for them, just as Horton did for the "Whos" he encountered. In Dr. Seuss's whimsical children's book, *Horton Hears a Who*, an elephant named Horton hears some ultra-tiny creatures called Whos on a speck of dust. He saves them by putting them on a soft clover, declaring, "A person's a person, no matter how small." The other animals think Horton is deranged and don't believe any persons could possibly be so small, so they try to destroy the clover with the persons on it. Finally, just in the nick of time, the tiny creatures make enough noise to convince Horton's comrades that they really do exist. Horton smiled, saying, "They've proved they ARE persons, no matter how small."

Dr. Seuss's book probably had nothing to do with abortion, since it was written in the 1950s (and later his widow supported Planned Parenthood and sued a pro-life organization for using Dr. Seuss's famous quotation). Nonetheless, many pro-life advocates have noticed that the book reads like an anti-abortion tale depicting the culture wars of the late twentieth and early twenty-first centuries. Horton recognizes the value of the tiniest persons and does everything he can to protect them, but everyone in his society thinks he is crazy and tries to destroy the small persons, claiming they do not exist. Horton's zeal to defend the right to life of the smallest and weakest members of society has never been as needed as in our day, when "personhood theory" has robbed some people of their right to life, when assisted suicide is becoming more popular, and when abortion and infanticide are rampant. Some bioethicists no longer want us to believe that "a person's a person, no matter how small."

EIGHT

The Future of Humanity

Utopias, Dystopias, and Transhumanism

"I the miserable, and the abandoned, am an abortion, to be spurned at, and kicked, and trampled on. Even now my blood boils at the recollection of this injustice."[1] No, these are not the words of some fictionalized fetus in a pro-life tract. They are the lamentations the nameless monster directed toward his creator Victor Frankenstein in Mary Shelley's immortal novel that warns against scientific hubris. The monster was incensed that Frankenstein, the brilliant scientist who had conquered the secret of reanimating a dead body, was devoid of sympathy and love for his creation. Of course, Shelley was not intending to make a pronouncement about today's abortion debate. However, her cautionary tale of a scientific experiment run amok has profound implications for today's debate over the appropriate uses of biotechnology. Should we yield to the siren song of biotechnological progress and its utopian promises, or should we fear unintended consequences?

Victor Frankenstein, of course, had the best of intentions. He foresaw nothing but happiness and bliss once he had mastered the technique of infusing life into inanimate bodies. While he was diligently working on his experiment, he exulted, "Life and death appeared to me ideal bounds, which I should first break through, and pour a torrent of light into our dark world. A new species would bless me as its creator and source; many happy and excellent natures would owe their being to me." His utopian vision evaporated, however, once his creature came to life. He quickly recognized his tragic mistake, admitting, "now that I had finished, the beauty of the dream vanished, and breathless horror and disgust filled my heart." After the monster began its campaign of murderous revenge on its maker, Frankenstein cried, "Alas! I had turned loose into the world a depraved wretch whose delight was in carnage and misery." Because the creature was stronger than its creator, at one point the monster remonstrated with Frankenstein, saying, "You are my creator, but I am your master; —Obey!" Frankenstein refused, so his creation murdered him and others dear to him.[2]

Another theme woven throughout Shelley's novel is the need for human love and companionship. The monster insists that when he was created, he was kindly and benevolent. However, no one reciprocated his love, not even his own creator, who spurned him. Only the mistreatment he received from people who rejected him and injured him drove him to malfeasance. At one point, the monster berated Frankenstein for his unloving behavior, saying, "I was benevolent and good; misery made me a fiend. Make me happy, and I shall again be virtuous." After receiving this scolding, Frankenstein confessed, "For the first time, also, I felt what the duties of a creator towards his creature were." This is an astounding revelation. It suggests that in his zeal to contribute to scientific progress, Frankenstein had not even thought about his moral obligations, either before or even after creating this being. Shelley seems to be reminding us that raw scientific pursuit, carried on without love and without considering our moral responsibilities, may come back to haunt us—or even destroy us.[3] This lesson still resonates today, contributing to the popularity of her novel, which still sells over fifty thousand copies a year in the U.S.[4]

Shelley dedicated her novel to her father, William Godwin, who was already famous for his utopian treatise on political philosophy, *Enquiry concerning Political Justice* (1793). As so many other Enlightenment intellectuals, Godwin believed that human reason was paramount. He was more radical than most, however—embracing atheism and determinism.[5] He based his anarchist political theory on the principle of justice, which he defined as the "impartial treatment of every man in matters that relate to his happiness." As a utilitarian, Godwin considered happiness the highest good—indeed the only good—and pain the only evil. If humans would only begin acting rationally, they would promote the general happiness of the entire human community.[6]

According to Godwin, justice entailed impartiality toward everyone, to such an extent that it was impermissible even to favor one's own family in any of our decisions. "What magic is there in the pronoun 'my,' that should justify us in overturning the decisions of impartial truth?" he asked. Individuality trumped social relationships, so much so that Godwin pronounced cooperation as evil and denounced such cooperative activities as sharing a common domicile (as families usually do), cooperative labor, and shared meals, because these allegedly infringed on each individual's prerogatives. He did not think that humans could entirely avoid society, but he hoped they could cut their ties to the greatest extent possible. He stated, "We ought to be able to do without one another. He is the most perfect man, to whom society is not a necessary of life, but a luxury."[7]

While embracing individual liberty, justice, and voluntary economic leveling, Godwin was conflicted about human equality. In one chapter, "On the Equality of Mankind," he insisted that all humans were morally equal, although he qualified this considerably by noting an exception: "There is indeed one species of moral inequality, parallel to the physical inequality that has been already described. The treatment to which men are entitled, is to be measured by their merits and their virtues."[8] This is a gigantic exception, not just a minor loophole, which becomes even clearer when Godwin discussed the value of human life elsewhere in his book.

Indeed, in the preceding chapter Godwin had argued forcefully that some humans had greater worth than others. He began this discussion by quoting Jesus' command to love your neighbor as yourself. He then asserted that this command has "considerable merit as a popular principle, [but] is not modeled with the strictness of philosophical accuracy. In a loose and general view I and my neighbor are both of us men; and of consequence entitled to equal attention. But, in reality, it is probable that one of us, is a being of more worth and importance than the other." He then explained that the reason humans have more value than animals is because they have higher faculties. Within humanity, he thought, the same was true, and he provided a concrete example to illustrate this point: the archbishop Fénelon had greater worth than his valet, so if in an emergency only one of their lives could be saved, one should save Fénelon. A second reason that Fénelon's life had greater value than his valet's, according to Godwin, was because Fénelon contributed more to the happiness of mankind than his valet did.[9]

Godwin's philosophy seems to be radically inegalitarian, while masquerading as radically egalitarian. This manifests itself elsewhere when Godwin discussed ways to circumvent the population problem. Thomas Robert Malthus wrote his famous *Essay on the Principle of Population* in 1798 as a refutation of Godwin's political philosophy. According to Malthus, the human population tends to increase faster than the food supply, so misery and poverty are inescapable. In an 1800 essay responding to Malthus, Godwin acknowledged that Malthus may be right about the biological propensity of human reproduction to outstrip the food supply. However, he disputed Malthus's conclusion that poverty and misery are inevitable. He reminded his readers that, repulsive as such practices might seem to Europeans, some societies practice infanticide, which can restrain population growth. Indeed, in this discussion Godwin exhibited the dehumanizing tendencies of his philosophy. He mentioned that "nothing [is] more illustrious and excellent than man. But it is not man, such as I frequently see him, that excites much of my veneration," because many people are corrupt and degraded. Apparently only some people were valuable to Godwin.[10]

Aside from devaluing the lives of those he considered degraded, Godwin also had no respect for the life of infants. He remarked,

> Neither do I regard a new-born child with any superstitious reverence. If the alternative were complete, I had rather such a child perish in the first hour of its existence, than that a man should spend seventy years of life in a state of misery and vice. I know that the globe of earth affords room for only a certain number of human beings to be trained to any degree of perfection; and I had rather witness the existence of a thousand such beings, than a million of millions of creatures, burdensome to themselves, and contemptible to each other.[11]

In the context of this passage Godwin specifically mentioned the practice of infanticide as a way to keep the population under control, so his solution to misery and poverty was killing babies.

Perhaps this should not have surprised anyone who had read his 1793 book, in which he explicitly denied that people have a right to life. Godwin believed that under normal circumstances, every person should preserve their life and health, because usually that will benefit the entire human community. However, he asserted, "If the extraordinary case should occur, in which I can promote the general good by my death more than by my life, justice requires that I should be content to die." This implies that one should be willing to commit suicide for the good of humanity. Ominously, Godwin apparently did not always think that this human sacrifice should be voluntary. He specifically disputed that people have a right to life, and then proclaimed, "He [i.e., any person] has no right to life, when his duty calls him to resign it. Other men are bound...to deprive him of life or liberty, if that should appear in any case to be indispensably necessary to prevent a greater evil."[12] This ends-justifies-the-means defense of killing would be the hallmark of the Great Terror of the French Revolution, which broke out just months after Godwin completed his manuscript. It also became the excuse for mass killings by fascist and communist regimes in the twentieth century, who promised utopia if the "wrong" people could be eliminated. Undoubtedly they considered these deaths "indispensably necessary to prevent a greater evil," to use Godwin's pernicious phraseology.

In the wake of the Jacobin Terror and the horrors of the Napoleonic Wars, utopianism went into decline, but many Europeans in the nineteenth century continued to put their faith in human progress, especially as science made gigantic strides forward. The famous novelist H. G. Wells studied biology in the 1880s (partly under the famous evolutionist T. H. Huxley) and started his career as a biology teacher in the 1890s. Though later he became famous for his utopian writings, his earliest novel, *The Time Machine*, warned of the degenerative effects of modern society. On the one hand, his novel exuded optimism about the possibilities of scientific advance. By the year 802,701, humans had eliminated gnats, weeds, fungi, and disease, so at first the time traveler thought he had entered the Garden of Eden. Later he learned the grim truth: the laboring class, who had been relegated to the underworld, had evolved into a grotesque, separate species, known as Morlocks. The physically weak and unintelligent descendants of the capitalists—the Eloi—lived in apparent ease on the surface, but in reality they were merely the cattle of the Morlocks, who feasted on their flesh.[13]

Despite this dystopian novel, Wells was more optimistic than pessimistic about the future of humanity. Some of his later writings, such as *A Modern Utopia* (1905), reflected his belief in human progress through science and rational planning. Wells later called *A Modern Utopia* "one of the most vital and successful of my books."[14] In the utopian society he sketched, humans themselves must come under the control of science. Wells claimed that earlier utopias had erred, because they "ignored that reproductive competition among individualities which is the substance of life." Wells suggested that we as humans should streamline the evolutionary process by eliminating society's "congenital invalids, its idiots and madmen, its drunkards and men of vicious mind, its cruel and furtive souls, its stupid people, too stupid to be of use to the community, its lumpish, unteachable and unimaginative people." Though Wells was a socialist lampooning his society's socio-economic inequality, he was convinced that biological inequality made some people more valuable than others. Those less valuable should eliminated. He was not convinced that some races are superior to others, but he urged us to apply cold, emotionless rationality to all human affairs, including race relations. "Suppose, then, for a moment," he conjectured, "that there is an all-around inferior race; a Modern Utopia is under the hard logic of life, and it would have to exterminate such a race as quickly as it could." Lest we accuse Wells of openly preaching murder, we need to understand that the method of elimination and extermination that he favored was not direct killing. He insisted, "There would be no killing, no lethal chambers." Rather these inferior specimens would be eliminated by curtailing their reproduction. Eugenics was one of the keys to Wells's utopia.[15]

In his later novel *Men Like Gods*, Wells described a utopia where "Nearly all the greater evils of human life had been conquered; war, pestilence and malaise, famine and poverty had been swept out of human experience." Eugenics and population control were both crucial to the creation of this utopia. According to one of the Utopians (Wells's name for the inhabitants of this parallel world) their "Last Age of Confusion" was similar to today's world. During that age they had experienced rapid scientific advance, but real progress was hindered by overpopulation, which was "the fundamental evil out of which all the others that afflicted the race arose." In order to attain their utopian society, they had reduced their population from two billion to two hundred fifty million (presumably by restricting reproduction, though this was not clear).[16] In an introduction to the birth-control advocate Margaret Sanger's *Pivot of Civilization*, Wells wrote that the new society that he favored needs to keep from being "swamped by an indiscriminate torrent of progeny." He expressed contempt for the "ill-bred, ill-trained swarms of inferior citizens" currently being "inflict[ed] upon us."[17]

The Utopians in *Men Like Gods* had also created a "nobler humanity" through eugenics measures: "For centuries now Utopian science has been able to discriminate among births.... There are few dull and no really defective people in Utopia; the idle strains, the people of lethargic dispositions or weak imaginations, have mostly died out." The Utopians' (and presumably Wells's) attitude toward death manifested little regard for the value of human life. They never mourned the dead, and even considered mourning a sign of a "racial taint." When a woman's husband and two children died, for Utopians "it seemed rather an occasion for gladness than sorrow that her man and her children had met death fearlessly. They were dead; a brave stark death; the waters still glittered and the sun still shone." Death had little significance in a universe that was "very carelessly put together," as the protagonist philosophized.[18] One of the Utopians—reflecting Wells's own anti-humanistic philosophy—explained that "Mother Nature" is "purposeless and blind. She is not awful, she is horrible.... She made us by accident; all her children are bastards—undesired; she will cherish or expose them, pet or starve or torment without rhyme or reason. She does not heed, she does not care."[19] Death and life are thus all the same in a cosmos that is impersonal and unloving. However, Wells's own concern for human thriving suggests that he did find some meaning or purpose in life, but I cannot see how he derived it from his own bleak worldview. I suspect he borrowed it from a more hopeful worldview that unfortunately is incompatible with his own.

Wells had a powerful influence on early twentieth-century British intellectuals, but some, such as Aldous Huxley and C. S. Lewis, feared that Wells's utopian aspirations would turn sour—or even horrific—if anyone seriously tried to implement them.[20] In Aldous Huxley's *Brave New World* (1946), set about six hundred years in the future, almost all the people are biologically mass-produced, psychologically manipulated, and drowned in pleasure or drug-induced "happiness." The citizens of this world are programmed to accept their lot in life and to be happy. If anything upsets their equilibrium, the police forces spray them with soma, a drug that makes everyone happy and compliant. Collectivism reigns in this dystopia, where the proverb, "every one belongs to every one else," is imprinted in their brains early in life by constant repetition while they are asleep. Individuals are of no account, and their deaths are not mourned, because "the social body persists although the component cells may change." A high-ranking official once remarks that "no offence is so heinous as unorthodoxy of behavior. Murder kills only the individual—and, after all, what is an individual?" In this brave new world the death of individuals is trivial; only society matters. Thus, children are conditioned not to mourn the death of anyone, but rather to accept people's death as a ho-hum event with no significance.[21]

The protagonist of *Brave New World*, Bernard Marx, however, shows a spark of individuality that marks him as an oddball and eventually gets him into trouble with the authorities. When Bernard asks Lenina, another main character, if she wants to be free, she is completely clueless, replying, "I don't know what you mean. I am free. Free to have the most wonderful time. Everybody's happy nowadays." She, like everyone in this society, lives solely for pleasure, including sexual pleasure, and there is plenty of pleasure to be found—either directly, or through a media called the "feelies," or through drugs. This brave new world should be a utilitarian's dream-come-true, but of course, Huxley ultimately exposed the many dehumanizing aspects of this pleasure-saturated society. Bernard, after indulging in sex with Lenina, derisively thinks that she "doesn't mind being meat." Indeed the people in this new world are treated as nothing more than conglomerations of matter—blobs of chemicals manufactured by technicians.[22]

When Bernard visits an Indian reservation in New Mexico, he gets permission to return to England with a "Savage" named John, who has not undergone the biological selection and psychological conditioning of everyone else. Bernard admires John's individualism, but most inhabitants of the brave new world view John as a fascinating, but uncouth, curiosity. John the Savage contrasts markedly with the denizens of the brave new world because he values human relationships, love, beauty, truth, religion, and self-control, all of which have been systematically eliminated from this futuristic world. He once remarks, "I'd rather be unhappy than have the sort of false, lying happiness you were having here." After John creates a public disturbance, he, Bernard, and a friend of Bernard are arrested and meet with the World Controller in charge of their part of the world. The Controller explains that they will have to go into exile, because their individualism will disrupt social stability. He tells them that his society has sacrificed the fine arts and beauty for the sake of happiness and stability. The Controller admits that "truth's a menace, science is a public danger." The humanities—and even true science—have no part in this anti-human society. When John tells the Controller that he wants religion, poetry, and freedom more than comfort, the Controller replies that he would then be choosing the right to be unhappy, which was against their way of life.[23] Huxley's work profoundly and soberly laid bare the dehumanizing potential of worldviews that see humans as products to manipulate or as utilitarian pleasure-seeking machines.

In an earlier philosophical work, *Ends and Means: An Inquiry into the Nature of Ideals and into the Methods Employed for Their Realization* (1937), Aldous Huxley explained why he reacted so strongly against these dehumanizing philosophies. We all wonder if the universe as a whole has any meaning or value, he admitted, but

> This is a question which, a few years ago, I should not even have posed. For, like so many of my contemporaries, I took it for granted that there was no meaning. This was partly due to the fact that I shared the common belief that the scientific picture of an abstraction from reality was a true picture of reality as a whole; partly also to other, non-intellectual reasons. I had motives for not wanting the world to have a meaning; consequently assumed that it had none, and was able without difficulty to find satisfying reasons for this assumption.[24]

Huxley exposed this "philosophy of meaninglessness" to be an intellectual façade.

While this is already a stunning revelation, Huxley dropped another bombshell by explaining what some of the motives were that impelled him and so many of his contemporaries to embrace such a worldview. He wrote,

For myself as, no doubt, for most of my contemporaries, the philosophy of meaninglessness was essentially an instrument of liberation. The liberation we desired was simultaneously liberation from a certain political and economic system and liberation from a certain system of morality. We objected to the morality because it interfered with our sexual freedom; we objected to the political and economic system because it was unjust.[25]

Remarkably, Huxley confessed that he and his contemporaries were driven by their political concerns and their sexual immorality to embrace the view that life is meaningless.

Huxley was convinced that the desire for sexual freedom had induced La Mettrie and Sade to embrace materialism in the eighteenth century. According to Huxley, "De Sade's philosophy was the philosophy of meaninglessness carried to its logical conclusion. Life was without significance. Values were illusory." Sade dismissed any notion of love and concern for other people, because pleasure was the only value worth pursuing. Morality was meaningless, in Sade's view, and he believed that "For those who found rape and murder amusing, rape and murder were fully legitimate activities." Though Huxley had earlier embraced Sade's general outlook, by 1937 he was horrified by this amoral philosophy.[26] He had come to conclude that life does indeed have purpose and meaning, that morality, love, and beauty are not illusory, and that art and religion can help us gain access to knowledge outside the bailiwick of science. He also blamed the "philosophy of meaninglessness" for having spawned sinister counter-movements, including a renewed interest in nationalism, fascism, or communism, all of which appeal to people craving for meaning in life.[27]

Another British intellectual who discovered the poverty of materialist explanations for human reality, C. S. Lewis, embraced Christianity as the true antidote for the dehumanizing mentality that pervaded the British intelligentsia in his day. Lewis emerged as one of the most influential Christian apologists of the twentieth century, widely renowned for his defense of Christianity in *Mere Christianity*, but also famous for his children's fantasy novels, the *Chronicles of Narnia*. As a professor of literature at Oxford and later at Cambridge, Lewis knew the pulse of British intellectual life. His most powerful broadsides against the tendencies in British academe to reduce humanity to automatons were his novel, *That Hideous Strength*, and his brief book, *The Abolition of Man*.

That Hideous Strength is a complex tale about a nefarious plot by the National Institute of Co-ordinated Experiments to subjugate all humanity. N.I.C.E., the ironic acronym for the agency, was anything but nice to Mark Studdock, a sociologist whom they manage to flatter, cajole, threaten, and manipulate to join their ranks at their institute. Studdock, a convinced materialist at first, does not see any problem with N.I.C.E.'s approach to humanity, until their attempts to psychologically manipulate him arouse rebellion in his heart. An official at the institute initially recruits Studdock by telling him that the purpose of the institute is "to take control of our own destiny. If Science is really given a free hand it can now take over the human race and re-condition it: make man a really efficient animal. If it doesn't—well, we're done." He then admits to Studdock that the program of controlling people really means that some people will be controlling the rest, so those who get on board first will be the controllers rather than the controlled. The program would begin with "sterilization of the unfit, liquidation of backward races (we don't want any dead weights), selective breeding." Then it would proceed to psychological and biochemical conditioning, and finally move to "direct manipulation of the brain." For N.I.C.E humanity is simply a product of nature that can be manipulated at will—that is, at the will of those in charge of the "experiment."[28]

When one of the leading opponents of N.I.C.E.—known as "the Director"—found out that they were making strides in reanimating dead people, he remarks that their search for immortality would ultimately lead to creating a new species. "They will call it," he suspects, "the next step in evolution. And henceforward, all the creatures that you and I call human are mere candidates for admission to the new species or else its slaves—perhaps its food." N.I.C.E.'s contempt for the masses of humanity was laid bare when one official tells Studdock that wars are beneficial because they cut down on overpopulation. In fact, he also reveals that they are planning over a dozen more wars in the twentieth century to get rid of the riff-raff of humanity, while making sure they spare the intelligentsia. That same official tells Studdock that human emotions are nothing but chemical reactions. Even "Friendship is a chemical phenomenon; so is hatred." Since they view humans as nothing more than conglomerations of chemicals, the scientists at N.I.C.E. hope to conduct experiments on humans. Prisoners would be kept in their care until they were "cured," not for fixed sentences, as in the old-fashioned penal system. Even intellectuals they recruited to join their institute were targets of their experimental mania, as they manipulated them via various means, including torture.[29]

Lewis's novel—which he called a fairy tale for adults—is in many ways fanciful, filled with clairvoyant dreams and tame bears. However, in *The Abolition of Man* Lewis explained how dehumanizing ideas, similar to those he portrayed in *That Hideous Strength*, had insidiously crept into the British educational system. In an English textbook, authors told impressionable students that when they call a waterfall sublime, they are not making a statement about the waterfall, but rather about their own feelings. Lewis pointed out that this exercise would lead students to the following two conclusions: 1) all sentences about values are about the emotions of the speaker; and 2) these statements are ultimately unimportant. Many intellectuals make the same point about moral values, interpreting them as merely expressions of an individual's preferences.[30]

Lewis had two counterpoints to this denial of objective truth about morality or aesthetics. First, he pointed out that in the vast majority of cases, skepticism about values is selective. It is used to dismiss (often with contempt) the "traditional" values that one opposes, but it leaves untouched one's own "progressive" values, which remain unstated, but assumed. Lewis asserted, "A great many of those who 'debunk' traditional or (as they would say) 'sentimental' values have in the background values of their own which they believe to be immune from the debunking process." Lewis understood the hypocrisy behind this kind of debunking.

Second, he argued that if we are not rational beings in a world with objective values, then we are "mere nature to be kneaded and cut into new shapes for the pleasures of masters who must, by hypothesis, have no motive but their own 'natural' impulses."³¹ Thus Lewis recognized that controllers, who claim to be taking the destiny of humanity into their own hands, have no control over themselves.

If everyone's behavior is determined, then ultimately no one can choose to control others. We are all controlled. The claims by the intelligentsia that they have superior knowledge or wisdom in order to manipulate the rest of humanity is then a vacuous claim, because the intelligentsia's statements are just as much the product of random, material processes as the ideas and behavior of the masses. Their beliefs or plans have no special claim to be true, or good, or beautiful, since none of these categories exist. So, why do they get so worked up in proclaiming the superiority of their policies and aspirations? Why do they get so indignant at those who— through no fault of their own (since "fault" is non-existent, according to their worldview)—continue to embrace values that they oppose? Perhaps they would respond—if they want to be consistent with their own deterministic philosophy—that they cannot help themselves. But I find it more likely that at some level they think their beliefs are actually superior to those they criticize. Perhaps their indignation also indicates that they really do think that others have some kind of choice about their beliefs and values.

Though animated by similar concerns as Huxley's and Lewis's about totalitarian government control over its citizens, the atheist Ayn Rand crafted dystopian novels that brought her fame as a guru of radical individualism and laissez-faire capitalism. Rand, who was a twelve-year-old Russian Jew when the Bolsheviks overthrew the government in 1917, experienced firsthand the destructiveness of the Soviet experiment. She came to despise the communist regime for expropriating her father's chemistry shop. As a youth Rand embraced atheism and became entranced with Nietzsche's philosophy. Though she later rejected Nietzsche's irrationalism, she consistently agreed with his radical individualism and his exaltation of the creative individual above the masses of humanity.³²

After relocating to the United States in the mid-1920s, she moved to Hollywood to write movie scripts. While there, she wrote a movie script based on a news story. As her biographer Jennifer Burns explains, "When the tabloids filled with the sensational case of William Hickman, a teen murderer who mutilated his victim and boasted maniacally of his deed when caught, Rand was sympathetic rather than horrified." She admired Hickman, stating, "It is the amazing picture of a man with no regard whatever for all that society holds sacred, and with a consciousness all his own. A man who really stands alone, in action and in soul." She described her protagonist—who was modeled on Hickman—as one who "does not understand, *because he has no organ for understanding,* the necessity, meaning or importance of other people."[33] Rand was more interested in individual self-assertion than in the victim's right to life, at least in this episode. Later in life, she moved away from her uncritical fascination with Nietzsche and asserted every individual's right to life, but she still admired the creative individual who could snub society and have no care or concern about what others think or feel.

In her most famous novel, *Atlas Shrugged,* set in a future United States, the protagonist John Galt recognizes the evils of altruism that has given rise to a collectivist society. Galt, a brilliant inventor, is horrified that the creative, talented, and productive individuals—who are primarily capitalists and inventors—are exploited by the dimwitted, non-productive elements of a collectivist society. Galt calls on industrialists, inventors, and other creative people to withdraw from this corrupt society and form their own alternative society, where everyone is free to pursue his or her own selfish interests without any government interference. Galt recruits many talented people to join his strike, which throws the economy into a tailspin, because the masses of people who remain to run the country are inept and bungling. They have always depended on the creative individuals to do everything for them.

Toward the end of the novel, Galt hijacks the airwaves and delivers a radio address that expresses Rand's individualistic philosophy. Galt remonstrates against the past conceptions of morality that told people to live primarily for God or for others. Rather, one should live entirely for oneself. Galt claims this individualistic morality of living for oneself is dictated entirely by reason and logic. It is founded solely upon the human need to survive, which necessitates the free use of human reason. Galt claims that the human right to life, liberty, and the pursuit of happiness is based entirely upon human nature, not upon God or society. He states, "*Rights* are conditions of existence required by man's nature for his proper survival. If man is to live on earth, it is *right* for him to use his mind, it is *right* to act on his own free judgment, it is *right* to work for his values and to keep the product of his work."[34] Galt insists that this morality means that no individual has the right to initiate violence against others, and the only right of government is to protect individuals from violence.

Rand claimed, like so many others appropriating the moniker "humanist," that her individualistic philosophy was exalting humans and rescuing them from the mediocrity of collectivism. In the 1968 preface to her earlier novel, *The Fountainhead* (1943), she explained, "The man-worshippers, in my sense of the term, are those who see man's highest potential and strive to actualize it." These man-worshippers were "those dedicated to the *exaltation* of man's self-esteem and *sacred-ness* of his happiness on earth."[35] The hero of that novel, Howard Roark, who Rand admitted was her ideal man, is a radical individualist and loner who has nothing but contempt for his fellow travelers on this earth. Before being ejected from architectural school for rejecting all traditional forms of architecture, he "had not made or sought a single friend on the campus."[36] Roark was brilliant and creative, but a man of cold, hard logic who "had no sense of people." By his own admission, he is not kind. His creations are more important to him than people, so when someone alters his construction designs of a housing project for the indigent, he blows up the housing project. At his trial he defends his action in a long speech to the jury that sums up Rand's philosophy of selfishness. In his oration he admits that he has no concern for the destitute, whose housing he has destroyed, because "a man's creative work is of greater importance than any charitable endeavor."[37] Rand's ideal is a man with no care or concern for anyone but his own brilliant creations. Other people are inconsequential.

In *The Virtue of Selfishness* (1964), Rand reiterated her philosophy, which had already been explained by her fictional characters in her novels. She summed up her moral philosophy thus:

> The basic *social* principle of the Objectivist ethics is that just as life is an end in itself, so every living human being is an end in himself, not the means to the ends or the welfare of others—and, therefore, that man must live for his own sake, neither sacrificing himself to others nor sacrificing others to himself. To live for his own sake means that *the achievement of his own happiness is man's highest moral purpose.*[38]

As she explained so often, everyone should be free to pursue his or her own interests, and one should never become dependent on others.

Despite writing *Atlas Shrugged* and *Anthem*, two dystopian novels decrying the evils of altruism and collectivism, Rand had utopian aspirations. She hoped for a rational society where humans would be untrammeled to exercise their talents and abilities to the fullest. She insisted that such a society of selfish individuals would be free from violence and coercion, because the rational interests of individuals could be fulfilled through trade, as each individual recognizes the rights of others to life and liberty. Rand claimed that her system of ethics "holds that the *rational* interests of men do not clash," so if we would only embrace her rationalist ethics, human violence would cease.

Rand's philosophy contributes to dehumanization in many ways. While it exalts the creative individual, the masses of humanity are treated with scorn and ridicule. After the industrial elites withdraw from society in *Atlas Shrugged*, the remaining people are so incompetent that no one else is capable of running the factories and railroads. The masses are ignorant and dependent. In *The Fountainhead* the hero Roark says that anyone "who attempts to live for others is a dependent. He is a parasite in motive and makes parasites of those he serves."[39] Since Rand came from a Jewish family, it is ironic that this novel was written at the same time the Nazis were annihilating Jews for allegedly being parasites. Clearly Rand had contempt for most people, since most people think that living for others is noble, not degrading, as she seems to think (making most of us "parasites"). As far as I know, Rand never spelled out the implications of her philosophy for children (she had none herself) and people with disabilities, but since she bashed everyone who is dependent on anyone else, this does not bode well for them. Indeed, she vociferously rejected the right to life for the most dependent humans, i.e., babies in their mothers' wombs.[40]

Further, even though Rand claims that she is committed to non-violence, this is not always clear. In a controversial passage in *The Fountainhead*, the hero Roark rapes a woman "as an act of scorn. Not as love, but as defilement."[41] Roark is the individualist par excellence, but he still has the desire to dominate this woman. Rand's assertion that if we just follow her rational ethics, there will be no violence and no one will dominate others any longer, is naive in the extreme.

More importantly, Rand's promotion of self-centeredness means that humans only have value to other humans inasmuch as they grant them meaning. She understands that people can have friends and lovers, but only based on their free choice, not a need, which would make them dependent on others. Further, she claimed that these friends should be chosen based on their virtues that resonate with us. The hero of *Anthem* states, "I ask none to live for me, nor do I live for any others," and then explains that he will only love those who deserve it.[42]

In Rand's vision of humanity, love is a selfish value. She explained, "Concern for the welfare of those one loves is a rational part of one's selfish interests; if a man spends money to save his wife's life, he does it not for her, but for his own selfish interests, because she is important to him and he values her." The flip side of this is that we have no real duties toward strangers, because they have little or no meaning or value to us.[43] Galt manifests this callous attitude toward strangers when he explains that sacrificing for the sake of others is not good, but evil. He then states, "If you give money to help a friend, it is *not* a sacrifice; if you give it to a worthless stranger, it *is*."[44] Thus, for Rand other people really have no value to each other, unless they choose to give value to another person.

Here Rand is caught in a conundrum. If from the standpoint of one individual, other people are not intrinsically valuable, then why should any individual refrain from dominating, controlling, or perpetrating violence against another individual, if this will bring the former more happiness and fulfillment? Rand asserted that harming others is not consistent with our rational self-interest, but this is far from obvious. Certainly throughout history many people have perpetrated violence in order to increase their wealth and prosperity. Ultimately, if the individual is the final determiner of moral values, why should the individual care if others perish? Even if humans were able to live the rational, non-violent lifestyles that Rand proposed, this loveless, forlorn existence is radically deficient, resulting in a life that is far below the dignity of humanity.

Some intellectuals in the late twentieth and early twenty-first centuries have thrown Aldous Huxley's and C. S. Lewis's warnings about the perils of technocracy to the wind. The transhumanist movement, in particular, hopes to re-engineer humans to a higher evolutionary level, where we will move beyond humanity (as the name "transhumanism" suggests). Nick Bostrom, a philosophy professor at Oxford University and cofounder with David Pearse of the World Transhumanist Society in 1998, rightly sees transhumanism as an intellectual movement rooted in Enlightenment rationalism. Bostrom is clearly a fan of the Radical Enlightenment, acknowledging the Enlightenment materialist La Mettrie as his forerunner. Bostrom embraces La Mettrie's materialistic vision of humanity, which inspires Bostrom to take scientific control of the future of the human race. He states, "If human beings are constituted of matter obeying the same laws of physics that operate outside us, then it should in principle be possible to learn to manipulate human nature in the same way that we manipulate external objects." Many leaders in the transhumanist movement advocate using pharmaceuticals and genetic engineering to transform humanity and to bring about a blissful future for the super-humans they manage to produce.[45]

Julian Savulescu, professor of philosophy at Oxford University and editor of the *Journal of Medical Ethics*, is a prominent figure in the transhumanist movement. He is a prolific author of articles in leading bioethics journals, many of them co-authored with other bioethicists, who share his views.[46] He provocatively argues in a popular 2012 article in *Reader's Digest* that "It's Our Duty to Have Designer Babies."[47] Interestingly, however, he is not a strong proponent of cognitive genetic enhancement, which many parents wanting a designer baby would probably favor. Indeed, Savulescu thinks cognitive enhancement might make us humans even more dangerous to each other, given our technological prowess at building weapons of mass destruction and our propensity to pollute our environment. He regularly invokes the fear of humans destroying themselves; one talk he gave was entitled "Unfit for Life: Genetically Enhance Humanity or Face Extinction."[48] The solution that Savulescu proposes to keep us humans from killing each other off is what he calls moral enhancement, which comes in two forms: genetic engineering and hormone therapy, both designed to make us more cooperative and altruistic. Savulescu's goal in advocating for designer babies, then, is to transform human nature, to rid us of our selfish tendencies, and to help us to love one another. Who could argue with such a noble goal?

As a historian, however, I am acutely aware that dehumanizing ideologies sometimes accompany noble goals. My book, *Hitler's Ethic*, demonstrates that Hitler hoped to elevate the human race morally by building a "People's Community" among the allegedly more moral Aryans and getting rid of those deemed immoral (such as the allegedly greedy Jews). Other historical examples come to mind, such as Marxism, which also tried to transform human nature and make people less selfish and more cooperative. I am not implying that Savulescu is a Hitler, but I do find it interesting that his project of improving human morality has some similarities to Hitler's, since both advocated biological selection of those deemed to have a greater biological propensity for altruism. Of course, there are many differences as well, since Savulescu rejects Hitler's insistence that some races have higher levels of morality than others.

It seems to me that Savulescu's project of moral enhancement is fraught with several major philosophical problems:

1. the genetic determinism on which it is based is shaky scientifically and philosophically
2. "moral enhancement" implies a moral goal, which is fundamentally in conflict with Savulescu's view that morality is the product of mindless evolutionary processes
3. Savulescu has no objective grounds for choosing which specific behaviors to favor
4. if humans are so morally deficient that they need moral enhancement, how can these morally deficient individuals make wise choices that will foster moral enhancement?
5. the method Savulsecu proposes for bringing about genetic moral enhancement—embryo or fetus selection, i.e., killing those embryos and fetuses not considered up to snuff—is itself ethically problematic.

Most of these problems are not restricted to Savulescu, but plague the transhumanist project as a whole.

Savulescu is a devotee of evolutionary psychology, arguing forcefully that our behavior is shaped largely by our genetic constitution. In a 2009 lecture he stated, "Differences in behavior, even differences in ability to stay in a long-term relationship, have a biological basis. They differ between different individuals, and we will be able at some point to influence that biology to achieve whatever goal we choose to achieve."[49] These genetic tendencies were allegedly produced through eons of natural selection operating on the human species. One example of genetic determinism that Savulescu likes to point out is the different mating behavior of two species of voles. The monogamous voles have more receptors for oxytocin and vasopressin than the polygamous voles. Scientists have genetically engineered the polygamous species to become monogamous, thereby demonstrating that oxytocin and vasopressin are involved in bonding. Human experiments using oxytocin demonstrate that it can induce more trusting behavior that could increase human cooperation. Interestingly, however, some studies suggest that it only helps increase bonding within groups, and in some scenarios it can actually increase out-group hostility—thus it could inadvertently increase xenophobia, racism, and warfare. Tampering with hormone levels may not be as smart as Savulescu and other transhumanists think.[50]

Building on his view that behavior is largely chemically induced, Savulescu is vigorously promoting moral enhancement to increase our ability to live together in harmony. In one specific case Savulescu suggests that we should genetically engineer humans to promote monogamy, since many sociological studies have shown that monogamy is beneficial to children. He also recommends developing "love drugs," such as oxytocin, that could be given to wedded couples to keep spouses faithful to each other. But why is our genetic makeup deficient with respect to monogamy (or any other behavior)? Savulescu argues that our biological constitution is one hundred fifty thousand years behind our cultural developments. He claims that millennia ago a human's average life span was so short that spouses would usually not be married for more than fifteen years or so. Thus, according to Savulescu, "it seems unlikely that natural selection equipped us to keep relationships lasting much more than a decade."[51] Increased life spans in the modern world have left us "unfit" for life-long monogamy, thus resulting in widespread divorce.

There are a number of problems with Savulescu's biological account. First, comparing voles to humans is problematic. Monogamous voles are always monogamous, and polygamous ones are always polygamous. Humans, however, show much more plasticity in their mating behaviors. Some human societies are monogamous, some are polygamous, and in some—such as ours today—the institution of marriage is no longer as important as it once was. Even within societies that are dominantly monogamous, some individuals rebel against the prevailing sexual mores.

Humans seem to have—dare I say it—greater free will to alter their mating and marriage behavior.

The historical changes in divorce rates make Savulescu's evolutionary account of divorce especially problematic. Explaining divorce as the consequence of evolved genetic traits ignores the fact that in many societies monogamy has been far more successful than it is today. Has Savulsecu never heard about the Sexual Revolution of the 1960s? In the U.S. and Europe in the 1950s, the divorce rate was considerably lower than it was two decades later. Marriages lasted much longer. So how can we blame the high divorce rate in modern societies on our hard-wired psyche inherited from our Pleistocene ancestors, when divorce was relatively rare in many intervening epochs? It seems clear that the institution of marriage has changed radically over the course of one or two generations, thus dramatically calling into question biological determinist explanations for marriage behavior. Why resort to genetic manipulation and love potions to biologically engineer us to become more committed to monogamy—neither of which is even technologically feasible at this time (and may never be)—when we could choose to be monogamous, if we wanted to be (as many societies and individuals have)?

The second problem with Savulescu's project of moral enhancement is that he never defines its goal. Enhancement implies getting better, and indeed he often uses vague terminology implying moral progress, such as "better," or "human welfare," or "human well-being," or "benefit," etc. However, he rarely indicates what any of these terms might mean. In one article he states, "Yet from our human perspective, happiness and flourishing are primary goals." But what constitutes happiness and flourishing? What does human welfare or human well-being mean? In several venues he tries to deflect this objection by arguing that moral enhancement is congruent with a variety of ethical philosophies, including utilitarianism, desire fulfillment theories, and deontological ethics.[52]

I must admit that I am still left scratching my head. According to his account, morality is the product of biological evolution, and he seems to agree with most biologists and evolutionary psychologists that these are mindless, purposeless processes.[53] If a non-teleological process produced human morality, then how can we find a measuring rod for morality outside of nature that allows us to prefer so-called moral behaviors to so-called immoral behaviors? Savulescu insists that we can "liberate ourselves from evolution," but it is unclear to me where we can acquire the moral fulcrum to do that.[54]

This problem of lacking a coherent goal leads to the third major problem: Savulescu has no objective grounds for choosing which specific behaviors to favor. Like many evolutionary psychologists, he discusses the evolutionary advantages of various altruistic behaviors, but he rarely mentions that selfish behavior, wars, racism, atrocities, rape, and many other kinds of immorality are also a natural part of human history. Indeed various evolutionists have provided evolutionary explanations for these kinds of behavior, too. If both selfishness and altruism have evolved simultaneously, and both have benefitted individuals in the struggle for existence, why should we think that one is superior to the other? Indeed, some biologists have insisted that selfishness is every bit as important as altruism in advancing the well-being of individuals or species.

What if these biologists are right, that selfishness contributes to human well-being and welfare, however defined? What if making our children more selfish would help them in the struggle for existence and thus assist them in flourishing, providing them a healthier, happier life? In that case, according to Savulescu's own teaching about designer babies, we would have strong moral reasons to genetically engineer our children to be more selfish. This is not an outlandish scenario. Indeed one of the most famous geneticists of the twentieth century, James Watson, once advised students to be selfish in their pursuit of scientific glory. I for one am happy that Savulescu thinks that increased cooperation is preferable to selfishness, but I do not understand where he conjures up the rationale for it, since he seems committed to a naturalistic understanding of the origin of morality.

If we examine other moral characteristics, we run into the same problem: what grounds do we have for preferring one over the other? For instance, in one article Savulescu notes that compared to men, women have a lower tendency to harm other people. Because of this, he suggests that "we could make men more moral by biomedical methods by making them more like women."[55] Even if this sexist version of evolutionary psychology proves to be accurate, why should we prefer female empathy to male aggression? Why assume that empathy will lead to greater human thriving and welfare than aggression? I assume that here Savulescu will invoke the fear of weapons of mass destruction, as he frequently does. However, some people like me have an even greater fear of the *Brave New World* that Savulescu's bioengineering program could spawn.

The fourth problem is that if humans are so morally deficient that they need moral enhancement, how can these morally deficient individuals make wise choices that will foster moral enhancement? Savulescu recognizes this problem, but I am not sure he takes it seriously enough. What would motivate people to genetically engineer their children to be morally enhanced? Savulescu regularly appeals to the fear of humans annihilating each other with weapons of mass destruction or through environmental degradation. However, what about other human motivations that could lead parents not to want to morally enhance their children? Based on their desire for their children to have the best possible life, some parents might want their children to be assertive and aggressive, so they will rise to become leaders (especially if the rest of the population is becoming cooperative and docile through moral enhancement). Considering the importance of sports in our society, undoubtedly some parents will value athletic prowess, and thus prefer a competitive spirit to a more cooperative ethos. Other parents of designer babies will likely value beauty, musical ability, intellectual acuity, or other traits, rather than empathy and cooperativeness.

In some venues, Savulescu stresses that he does not want to use coercive measures to implement moral enhancement. If this is the case, I have no confidence that masses of parents will choose moral enhancement for their children (even if it were possible). However, at times Savulescu suggests that some forms of moral enhancement should be compulsory. In one article he states, "If safe moral enhancements are ever developed, there are strong reasons to believe that their use should be obligatory, like education or fluoride in the water, since those who should take them are least likely to be inclined to use them. That is, safe, effective moral enhancement would be compulsory."[56] This stress on compulsion is all the more troubling, because Savulescu is often critical of liberal democracies. However, while in some regards sympathetic to authoritarian regimes for their ability to rule in the best interests of the people (he praises China for its one-child policy, for instance), he understands that ruling elites in authoritarian regimes usually rule in ways that benefit themselves, not all the people. Thus, Savlescu (seemingly reluctantly) favors liberal democracy, but only if we can overcome its problems by introducing moral enhancement.[57] Here we once again confront the circular problem: Why would a non-morally enhanced liberal democracy make the altruistic decision to introduce moral enhancement, especially since moral enhancement will likely be extremely expensive (a point Savulescu does not seem to consider)?

Another problem with morally deficient humans being in charge of moral enhancement is that Savulescu regularly bases many of his moral arguments on various common-sense moral views. For example, when defending his view that human life has value, the only explanation he provides is this: "We shall however proceed on the assumption that human life is normally better than non-existence, since we believe that this is the view that most of us would take."[58] This is not an isolated example. In one essay Savulescu states, "...common sense morality seems committed to favouring selection of children who are more advantaged," and that "our moral intuitions about timing of conception recognize reasons to select future children."[59] It is remarkable how often Savulescu appeals to our common moral intuitions to persuade us of his position (though in cases where most people's moral intuitions collide with his own he calls on us to dispense with our allegedly irrational moral intuitions). The problem is this: How can he appeal to our present moral intuitions, if we are so morally flawed that we need a drastic moral overhaul? This undermines the foundation of many of his arguments.

The fifth problem is that moral enhancement is not yet even technologically feasible, and some of the methods Savulescu suggests as possible methods in the future are morally objectionable. Savulescu's desire to engineer designer babies with greater genetic propensities for altruism is still science fiction, though he optimistically opines that in five years we might have the capability to screen for genes affecting every physical and mental trait.[60] Currently there are no genetic tests available to determine how cooperative or moral a person will be.

Even if we could screen for genetic moral traits, presently the primary ways to produce designer babies are embryo selection and selective abortion, both of which Savulescu favors. He argues that since we already allow embryo selection and selective abortions to eliminate embryos and fetuses with diseases, there should be nothing objectionable about using these methods to choose other genetic traits, such as intelligence or empathy. For those who embrace the pro-life position, as I do, Savulescu's suggestion that we should make the world more moral by killing off those who are allegedly less moral is grotesque. As an alternative, I suggest that Savulescu and other transhumanists consider the possibility of bioengineering people to stop killing their unborn progeny. I have no doubt that they would balk at this, but why? Why should we bioengineer people to meet the moral specifications of transhumanists, when not everyone agrees with this moral vision—indeed when many people are revolted by it?

What will the future hold for humanity: a blissful utopia or a horrific brave new world? Frankenstein's monster or Wells's *Men Like Gods*? If we continue in scientific hubris to regard humanity as an engineering project, then the future will probably be bleak. Judging from the two most radical political experiments at engineering humanity thus far— Nazism and communism—the track record does not look all that promising. However, what if we abandon the misguided notion that humanity is an object to be manipulated, a purely physical entity that we can engineer? What if we treat humans as the personal moral agents that they are, as individuals needing love, joy, and peace? It makes a profound difference whether we see each other as mere cosmic accidents spewed forth by an impersonal cosmos, or as immortal souls created in the image of a loving God. The future of humanity is at stake.

Conclusion

Humans on display in zoos. Comparing farm animals in captivity to Holocaust victims. "After-birth abortion." Physicians killing patients, sometimes even when they are not sick or in pain. Accusing fetuses of assaulting their mothers, just because they are living peaceably in utero. Promoting "love drugs" to make us more moral. Granting computer programs moral status.[1] These are just a few examples that powerfully illustrate how sick our society is. As many intellectuals have abandoned the Judeo-Christian sanctity-of-life ethic in favor of secular philosophies, we have descended into a quagmire of inhumanity. Some today view humans as nothing more than sophisticated machines or just another type of animal. For them, humans are nothing special—just another random arrangement of particles in an impersonal cosmos.

Noted twentieth-century Christian journalist and intellectual Malcolm Muggeridge recognized the connection between abandoning God and discarding humanity. He wrote, "If there was no God, nor any transcendental purpose in the experience of living in this world, then a human being's life [would be] no more intrinsically sacred than is that of a broiler-house chicken, which, if it stops laying eggs, or is otherwise incapacitated, no longer rates its allowance of chicken feed and has its neck wrung."[2] Unfortunately, some secularists agree with Muggeridge, but draw the exact opposite conclusion. They confirm Muggeridge's fear by biting the bullet and degrading humans, equating them with chickens (as PETA does).

This is not just a theoretical issue of interest only to philosophers, for real people are being put to death as a result of these dehumanizing philosophies. We have already witnessed many grotesque horrors, such as the Stalinist and Maoist communist atrocities against class enemies, or the Nazi Holocaust against racial groups. In most Western societies, we have opted for more democratic forms of killing, such as abortion, infanticide, and euthanasia. On a smaller scale, some mass killers in Western societies, such as the Columbine perpetrators, have been influenced by secular philosophies to despise humanity and scorn prohibitions against murder. Why not kill people, they reason, if we are all just meaningless blobs of protein, and it will give them a thrill?

If you think my warnings are overblown, consider Sue Blackmore's brief 2006 article in *The Guardian*, "Survival of the Selfish." Blackmore, an atheist psychologist and writer, is convinced that the human population is several times larger than the carrying capacity of the earth, so she warns that we are headed for catastrophe, unless we reduce the "current plague of humans," as she calls us. She exhorts us to make the difficult choice between four stark alternatives:

1. selfishly save ourselves (meaning fellow Britons) and watch billions perish elsewhere in the world
2. unselfishly try to save all humanity, which will backfire by leading to conflict and devastation, resulting in the demise of the vast bulk of humanity anyway

3. accept that we humans are a "pathogen" of the earth and try to save the earth by radically reducing our population
4. try to save civilization by deciding which kinds of people— scientists, artists, musicians, etc.—we want to save in a "drastically reduced population"

Blackmore does not say explicitly which of these four she prefers, though she clearly thinks the unselfish approach is untenable. The only remaining alternatives, she thinks, are for us to consciously decide which humans we should eliminate. This is eerily kin to the "Values Clarification" exercise I discussed in the introduction.[3]

I suspect that Blackmore is not really being consistent with her own atheistic outlook. On the one hand, she denies that the universe has any purpose. In an interview, she said, "It seems to me that, as far as I can tell, the universe has no ultimate purpose—it's pointless. We are here just because it so happens the laws of physics are the way they are and evolution is inevitable given the way it is."[4] But if the universe is pointless, then we should be completely indifferent about which of these four scenarios transpires. Why would it make any difference whether humans survive, or whether we are selfish, or whether our civilization survives—or even if our planet survives? If life is meaningless and morality is non-existent, then all our choices are meaningless as well, so why should these be such excruciating choices? Blackmore, however, apparently thinks it does make a difference, so she must recognize in her heart that there is a purpose and meaning to human life. Whether she will admit that publicly— or even to herself—is another matter.

If Blackmore's pseudo-scientific approach to ridding the world of most of humanity is not enough to make you queasy, consider the inhumane attitude of the French postmodernist philosopher Jean Baudrillard. While some secularists rightly condemned the 9-11 tragedy as a case of religious fanaticism run amok and then unfairly extrapolated that blame to all forms of religion, Baudrillard took a different approach. In 2002 he published two essays that are paeans of praise to the Islamic terrorists

who killed nearly three thousand people. Baudrillard's hatred for humanity was so intense that he approved of the vicious attacks and even
claimed that the massacre was the fulfillment of his prior wishes. Even
though he admitted that terrorism is immoral, he exulted in that immorality. He wrote, "Terrorism is immoral. The World Trade Center event,
that symbolic challenge, is immoral, and it is a response to globalization
which is itself immoral. So, let us be immoral; and if we want to have
some understanding of all this, let us go and take a little look beyond
Good and Evil." While most of the world was revolted by the carnage,
as a Nietzschean, Baudrillard reveled in the evil. He also claimed implau-
sibly that the "horror of living and working" in the Trade Center towers
was every bit as horrific as the catastrophe and mass death on 9-11.
Baudrillard was thus elated that the towers came down and people perished. Human life—and death—has no meaning to this progressive
intellectual.[5]

Fortunately, most secularists are not as ruthlessly consistent as Baudrillard, whose consistency comes at the price of being gleeful about
terrorism and mass killing. As I have shown throughout this book, many
of those loudly preaching the purposelessness of human life, the meaninglessness of existence, and the non-existence of objective morality and
human rights often only mean the non-existence of certain values they
despise. They do not really mean that slavery, genocide, oppressing workers, and destroying our environment are morally acceptable. Push the
right button and often you will find them just as absolutist in their morality as the staunchest Christian or Muslim fundamentalist. Some of them,
while proclaiming the cosmic insignificance of humanity, have a deep
concern for other people.

Part of the reason for this is that many people who critique the
Christian sanctity-of-life ethic grew up in a society that taught them to
respect human life. Kurt Bayertz, a philosopher who organized a conference in Germany in 1992 to examine the twin concepts of the sanctity
of life and human dignity, stated in the resulting anthology that both
terms carry enormous moral weight. He called them debate stoppers,

because "hardly anybody doubts that human life is worthy of protection or human dignity of respect."[6] That may be less true today than it was in 1992, especially since some of the conference contributors tried to chip away at the moral power of the sanctity-of-life ethic.

In any case, some secularists, even as they discard some elements of their Christian upbringing, still live with deeply entrenched Christian values that they import into their worldview whenever they need to mitigate the harsher features of their philosophy. If they do not like the logical consequences of their own position, they can fall back on the moral resources they imbibed one way or another from a society and culture deeply influenced by Christian morality. This accounts for some of the cognitive dissonance I have exposed in this book. Also, many of those trying to escape from religious influences still have consciences, even though they may be partially deadened. They cannot fully escape their own humanity. Thus, even while they proclaim the death of humanity, they might be the most kindly, saintly individuals in their personal lives—giving to the poor, volunteering for community service, and speaking up for the oppressed. These activities make perfect sense in a Christian worldview, but secularism gives us no reason to privilege acts of charity over behavior that oppresses the poor or to prefer altruistic deeds to selfishness. Secularists may insist philosophically that life is meaningless and absurd, but they are outraged if someone tries to live his or her life in accord with that insight in ways that are mean-spirited or violent. They know deep down that "anything goes"—or as Dostoevsky put it, "everything is permitted"—just does not correspond to reality. Some things are impermissible, so morality is not simply illusory or subjective.

Thus, it seems clear to me that most people—and I suspect all people—understand at some level that human life has meaning, that it is not devoid of purpose. We all know deep down that human life is valuable, and killing innocent people is objectively wrong. We may disagree on some points about what is morally good, but often lying behind these disagreements are common moral goals, such as helping people live and thrive. Very few people are radically consistent with their

philosophy of meaninglessness, and for this I am thankful. More frightening are those who are ruthlessly consistent with their amorality and
purposelessness, for they have no reason to respect human life.

I suggest that Christianity can help us make sense of our intuitions
that human life is meaningful and that morality is objective, while secular philosophies cannot. The Christian understanding of humans as
created in the image of God gives real value to human life that is absent
in secular worldviews. Christians have good reason to believe in human
equality and human rights, but these values are not explicable from a
secular standpoint. Secularism cannot explain why slavery or genocide
is wrong, but Christianity can. Thus it is bizarre that many secularists
accuse Christianity of justifying or even promoting slavery and genocide.
Why should secularists even care about slavery or genocide? If secularism
is true, then slavery and genocide are just facts of nature, and thus nothing to get worked up about. If secularism is true, then human life has no
value. If Christianity is true, then loving God and loving one's neighbor
are the highest moral commands. If Christianity is true, then human life
has value.

This does not mean, of course, that people calling themselves Christians have always lived in harmony with the precepts and insights of
Christianity. No, there have been spectacular moral failures among those
claiming to follow Jesus. They have not always valued human life, but
have all too often killed in the name of their religion, as happened during
the Crusades and the Inquisition. Interestingly, the apostle Peter prophesied as early as the first century that false Christians would give Christianity a bad reputation. He wrote that "there will be false teachers
among you...and many will follow their destructive ways, because of
whom the way of truth will be blasphemed."[7]

When people calling themselves Christians lost sight of Jesus' teaching in the Sermon on the Mount to love our enemies, they distorted
Christianity. When these same Christians held political power, they
perpetrated atrocities against non-Christians by forcing them to accept
Christianity. (Forcing someone to become a Christian is actually

impossible, because every individual has to make a free decision to follow Jesus, so forced Christianity is not really Christianity at all.) Sadly, Christianity, which is a religion of love and compassion, became in the eyes of many a religion of violence and oppression. Secularism gained traction in the modern world by pointing out the brutality and intolerance of the Christian churches. Ironically, however, secularism sawed off the branch it was sitting on, because its concern about oppression and intolerance was nurtured by Christian ethics. Secular philosophies undermined the moral injunctions against oppression and intolerance. Thus, secular philosophies have bred their own brutality, which has often exponentially exceeded the atrocities committed by the churches.

Other religions besides Christianity might be able to make sense of our valuing of human life, too. I recognize there are other options besides secularism and Christianity. However, I am convinced that there are sound philosophical, historical, scientific, emotional, and spiritual reasons to prefer monotheism and specifically Christianity to other religions.[8] Our intuition that human life has value, purpose, and meaning is just one of many reasons I find Christianity superior to a wide variety of secular worldviews. Thus I consider Christianity the proper antidote for the death of humanity. Jesus told his disciples, "The thief does not come except to steal, and to kill, and to destroy. I have come that they may have life, and that they may have it more abundantly."[9]

Acknowledgments

Thanks to Jeremy Anderson for inviting me to give a talk to Chi Alpha Christian Fellowship at California State University, Stanislaus, and at the University of California, Merced, in November 2011. Though I had already intended to write something about the history of the devaluing of human life at some time, giving these presentations clarified my ideas and motivated me to write the book in this format. I also thank Darren Rodrigues for inviting me to present some of the material of this book to the Central Valley Chapter of Reasonable Faith; this helped me fine-tune some of my arguments.

I also want to express my appreciation to all those who have taught me modern European intellectual history, both in the classroom (especially Allan Megill and Mitchell Ash) and through their writings. They may not agree with my religious and philosophical perspectives, and since I cover such immense territory of intellectual history in this work, they will undoubtedly discover weaknesses in some of my portrayals. Nonetheless I owe a great debt to them.

A special thanks to those scholars who read and commented on all or part of the manuscript: Charles Bellinger, J. Budziszewski, Paul Copan, Mike Egnor, Mike Flannery, Douglas Groothuis, Jennifer Lahl, Paul Nesselroade, and Russell DiSilvestro. They helped me improve it considerably, and also helped me avoid some mistakes; any mistakes that remain are my responsibility. I also thank my agent, Steve Laube, and my editor, Bob DeMoss, for believing in the value of this book and for bringing it to publication.

Finally, I thank my precious wife of thirty-two years, Lisa, and my seven dear children: Joy, John, Joseph, Miriam, Christine, Hannah, and Sarah. They contribute immensely to my life, and I hope and pray that they will contribute just as powerfully to our whole society by shaping a culture of life, love, and joy.

Notes

INTRODUCTION

1. Proverbs 26:27.
2. Probably not coincidentally, "Values Clarification" was developed at the same time that some environmentalists were cautioning the earth was exceeding its carrying capacity, meaning that we had no choice but to reduce the human population or face dire consequences. See Wesley Smith, *The War on Humans* (Seattle: Discovery Institute Press, 2014), for a discussion of the desire by radical environmentalists to eliminate billions of humans from the globe.
3. "Excerpts from Students Evaluations—Spring 1998," www.zo.utexas.edu/courses/bio357/357evaluations.html, accessed April 3, 2006.
4. Eric Pianka, "The Vanishing Book of Life on Earth," p. 3, www.zo.utexas.edu/courses/bio373/Vanishing.Book.pdf; accessed December 18, 2012.
5. "Bill Nye Weighs in on the Universe's Finite Lifespan Theory," *HuffPost Live*, February 22, 2013, http://www.huffingtonpost.

com/2013/02/22/bill-nye-higgs-boson_n_2745010.html; accessed May 2, 2013.

6.   "Arthur Rosenbaum Dies," http://blogs.laweekly.com/informer/2010/07/arthur_rosenbaum_dies.php, accessed June 29, 2012.

7.   Jeffrey Dahmer interview with Stone Phillips, MSNBC, 1994, http://www.youtube.com/watch?v=u9uQMx-ztkI; accessed June 26, 2012.

8.   Eric Harris, "Journal," at: http://acolumbinesite.com/eric/writing/journal.html, accessed June 29, 2012. In quotations I have retained Harris's grammatical and spelling errors, but I have deleted expletives.

9.   "Pekka-Eric Auvinen Manifesto," http://oddculture.com/weird-news-stories/the-pekka-eric-auvinen-manifesto/, accessed June 29, 2012.

10. Ibid.

11. E-mail from Gil Dodgen to author, July 12, 2012.

12. A good defense of the slippery slope argument in relation to euthanasia is John Keown, *Euthanasia, Ethics, and Public Policy: An Argument against Legalisation* (Cambridge: Cambridge University Press, 2002), 71–78.

13. Joachim C. Fest, *The Face of the Third Reich: Portraits of the Nazi Leadership,* trans. Michael Bullock (New York: Pantheon, 1970), 115.

14. Hugo Ribbert, *Heredity, Disease and Human Evolution,* trans. Eden and Cedar Paul (New York: Critic and Guide, 1918 [originally published in German in 1912]), 57.

15. Viktor E. Frankl, *The Doctor and the Soul: From Psychotherapy to Logotherapy* (New York: Vintage Books, 1986), xxvii.

16. I discuss these issues in great detail in *Hitler's Ethic: The Nazi Pursuit of Evolutionary Progress* (New York: Palgrave Macmillan, 2009).

17. James W. Von Brunn, *"Kill the Best Gentiles": The Racialist Guide for the Preservation and Nurture of the White Gene Pool* (Easton, MD: Holy Western Empire, 2002), 14–15.

18. Martin Luther King Jr., *Letter from the Birmingham Jail* (San Francisco: HarperSanFrancisco, 1994), 11–12.

19. Ibid., 28.

20. Matt. 23:12.

21. Konrad Lorenz, *On Aggression,* trans. Marjorie Kerr Wilson (New York: Harcourt, Brace and World, 1966), ch. 12.

22. George Gaylord Simpson, *The Meaning of Evolution: A Study of the History of Life and of Its Significance for Man* (New Haven: Yale University Press, 1950), 344, 292, 285.

23. See also Christian Smith, "Does Naturalism Warrant a Moral Belief in Universal Benevolence and Human Rights," in *Believing Primate: Scientific, Philosophical, and Theological Reflections on the Origin of Religion*, ed. Jeffrey Schloss et al. (Oxford: Oxford University Press, 2009), 292–317.

24. Some of my favorites are C. S. Lewis, *Mere Christianity*; Douglas Groothuis, *Christian Apologetics*; William Lane Craig, *Reasonable Faith*; Nancy Pearcey, *Finding Truth*, and various works by J. P. Moreland and Francis Schaeffer.

25. Matt. 7:7.

ONE: MAN THE MACHINE

1. Joni Eareckson Tada, lecture at Central California Disability Summit, Fresno, CA, October 25, 2014.

2. In addition to La Mettrie's own writings, cited below, my discussion draws from Kathleen Wellman, *La Mettrie: Medicine, Philosophy, and Enlightenment* (Durham, NC: Duke University Press, 1992); Jonathan Israel, *Enlightenment Contested: Philosophy, Modernity, and the Emancipation of Man 1670–1752* (Oxford: Oxford University Press, 2006), 794, 802, 812–13; Ann Thomson, *Materialism and Society in the Mid-Eighteenth Century: La Mettrie's* Discours Préliminaire (Geneva: Librairie Droz, 1981); and Ann Thomson, *Bodies of Thought: Science, Religion, and the Soul in the Early Enlightenment* (Oxford: Oxford University Press, 2008), ch. 6.

3. Julien Offray de La Mettrie, *Man a Machine* (La Salle, IL: Open Court, 1912), 135.

4. Ibid., 119, 109.

5. Ibid., 93–94.

6. Julien Offray de La Mettrie, *The System of Epicurus*, in *Machine Man and Other Writings*, ed. Ann Thomson (Cambridge: Cambridge University Press, 1996), 103.

7. La Mettrie, *Man a Machine*, 114.

8. Ibid., 146.

9. Alan Charles Kors, *D'Holbach's Coterie: An Enlightenment in Paris* (Princeton: Princeton University Press, 1976); see also Jonathan I. Israel, *Radical Enlightenment: Philosophy and the Making of Modernity 1650–1750* (Oxford: Oxford University Press, 2001), 709–11.

10. M. Helvétius, *A Treatise on Man, His Intellectual Faculties and His Education*, trans. W. Hooper, vol. 1 (London: B. Law and G. Robinson, 1777), 4, 146.

11. Lester G. Crocker, *An Age of Crisis: Man and World in Eighteenth Century French Thought* (Baltimore: Johns Hopkins Press, 1959), 12.

12. Mary Pickering, *Auguste Comte: An Intellectual Biography* (Cambridge: Cambridge University Press, 2009), 2:101.

13. Ibid., 2:116.

14. Auguste Comte, *The Essential Comte: Selected from Cours de Philosophie Positive*, ed. Stanislaw Andreski, trans. Margaret Clarke (London: Croom Helm, 1974), 22–23.

15. Pickering, *Auguste Comte*, 1:599.

16. Ibid., 2:402.

17. Ibid., 2:14.

18. Ibid., 1:113; see also Comte, *The Essential Comte*, 20–21.

19. Pickering, *Auguste Comte*, 1:608.

20. Ibid., 1:151.

21. Karl Vogt, *Bilder aus dem Thierleben* (Frankfurt a.M.: Literarische Anstalt, 1852), 445–46; accessed on Google Books, December 12, 2012.

22. Annette Wittkau-Horgby, *Materialismus: Entstehung und Wirkung in den Wissenschaften des 19. Jahrhunderts* (Göttingen: Vandenhoek und Ruprecht, 1998), 90. On Vogt and Büchner, see also Frederick Gregory, *Scientific Materialism in Nineteenth Century Germany* (Dordrecht: D. Reidel, 1977); and Richard Weikart, *From Darwin to Hitler: Evolutionary Ethics, Eugenics, and Racism in Germany* (New York: Palgrave Macmillan, 2004).

23. Karl Vogt, *Untersuchungen über Thierstaaten* (Frankfurt: Literarische Anstalt, 1851), 21, 29–31.

24. Karl Vogt, *Vorlesungen über den Menschen, seine Stellung in der Schöpfung und in der Geschichte der Erde*, 2 vols. (Giessen: J. Ricker'sche Buchhandlung, 1863), 1:295.

25. Ibid., 1:214, 256.
26. Ludwig Büchner, *Kraft und Stoff. Empirisch-naturphilosophische Studien*, 3rd ed. (Frankfurt: Meidinger Sohn, 1856), 286–91.
27. Ibid., 296.
28. Ludwig Büchner, *Die Macht der Vererbung und ihr Einfluss auf den moralischen und geistigen Fortschritt der Menschheit* (Leipzig: Ernst Günthers Verlag, 1882), 39–59, 71.
29. Ludwig Büchner, "In der Urzeit," in Friedrich Hellwald, *Kulturgeschichte in ihrer natürlichen Entwickelung bis zur Gegenwart*, 4th ed. (Leipzig: P. Friesenhahn, 1896), 1:51.
30. Büchner, *Die Macht der Vererbung*, 100.
31. Bertrand Russell, "A Free Man's Worship," (published originally in 1903), in *Why I Am Not a Christian and Other Essays on Religion and Related Subjects*, ed. Paul Edwards (New York: Simon and Schuster, 1957), 107.
32. Bertrand Russell, "What I Believe" (published originally in 1925), in *Why I Am Not a Christian and Other Essays on Religion and Related Subjects*, ed. Paul Edwards (New York: Simon and Schuster, 1957), 56.
33. Ibid., 55.
34. Bertrand Russell, *Marriage and Morals* (London: George Allen and Unwin, 1929), 201–3, 206, 213.
35. Bertrand Russell, *Human Society in Ethics and Politics* (London: George Allen and Unwin, 1954), 40, 72, 80.
36. Ibid., 87.
37. Russell, "What I Believe," 62.
38. Katharine Tait, *My Father Bertrand Russell* (New York: Harcourt Brace Jovanovich, 1975), 62, 98, 184.
39. Ibid., 46–47, 177–78, 184, 186.
40. Bertrand Russell, *Has Man a Future?* (New York: Simon and Schuster, 1962), 14.
41. Russell to Constance Mellon (Colette O'Niel), October 23, 1916, in Bertrand Russell, *The Autobiography of Bertrand Russell, 1914–1944* (Boston: Atlantic Monthly Press, 1968), 96–97.
42. Russell, *The Autobiography of Bertrand Russell, 1914–1944*, 3.
43. Ibid., 36.

44. Francis Crick, *Of Molecules and Men* (Seattle: University of Washington Press, 1966), 92–93.

45. Francis Crick, *The Astonishing Hypothesis: The Scientific Search for the Soul* (New York: Charles Scribner's Sons, 1994), 3.

46. Quoted in Wesley Smith, *Culture of Death: The Assault on Medical Ethics in America* (San Francisco: Encounter Books, 2000), 55.

47. Lawrence Krauss, *A Universe from Nothing: Why There Is Something Rather than Nothing* (New York: Free Press, 2012), xii, 139, 142, 148, quote at 181.

48. Julian Baggini and Lawrence Krauss, "Philosophy v. Science: Which Can Answer the Big Questions of Life?" *The Observer*, September 8, 2012, at www.guardian.co.uk/science/2012/sep/09/science-philosophy-debate-julian-baggini-lawrence-krauss; accessed September 10, 2012.

49. Lawrence Krauss, quoted in Richard Panek, "Out There," *New York Times Magazine*, at www.nytimes.com/2007/03/11/magazine/11dark.t.html?r=1, accessed April 18, 2012.

50. Steven Weinberg, *The First Three Minutes: A Modern View of the Origins of the Universe* (New York: Basic Books, 1977), 154.

51. Ibid., 154–55.

52. Richard Lewontin, "Billions and Billions of Demons," *New York Times Books Reviews* (January 9, 1997). 28–31.

TWO: CREATED FROM ANIMALS

1. Charles Darwin, Notebook C, *Charles Darwin's Notebooks, 1836–1844: Geology, Transmutation of Species, Metaphysical Inquiries*, in Paul Barrett et al., eds. (Ithaca: Cornell University Press, 1987), 300. I have left his grammar uncorrected.

2. "PETA's Appeal for Jewish Community Support 'The Height of Chutzpah,'" Anti-Defamation League, October 14, 2003, http://www.adl.org/NR/exeres/654AAEAC-709A-4F4A-AADB-4C70BF65705C,0B1623CA-D5A4-465D-A369-DF6E8679CD9E,frameless.htm, accessed July 20, 2012.

3. Quoted in Wesley J. Smith, *A Rat Is a Pig Is a Dog Is a Boy: The Human Cost of the Animal Rights Movement* (New York: Encounter Books, 2010), 3.

4. See evidence of this in Richard Weikart, *Hitler's Ethic: The Nazi Pursuit of Evolutionary Progress* (New York: Palgrave Macmillan, 2009), 47.

5. Gerhard Weinberg, *The Foreign Policy of Hitler's Germany*, vol. 1: *Diplomatic Revolution in Europe, 1933–36* (Chicago: University of Chicago Press, 1970), 4.

6. "At London Zoo, Homo Sapiens Is Just Another Primate Species," *New York Times*, August 28, 2005, http://www.nytimes. com/2005/08/28/international/europe/28london.html, accessed July 12, 2012.

7. AP, "Humans Bare—Almost—All for Zoo Exhibit," *Sydney Morning Herald*, August 27, 2005, http://www.smh.com.au/news/world/humans-bare—almost—all-for-zoo-exhibit/2005/08/27/1124563057521.html, accessed July 12, 2012.

8. "London Zoo Exhibit: Humans," *USA Today*, August 26, 2005, http://www.usatoday.com/travel/news/2005-08-26-london-zoo_x.htm, accessed July12, 2012.

9. "Zoo in Copenhagen Exhibits New Primates (Fully Clothed)," *New York Times*, August 29, 1996, http://www.nytimes.com/1996/08/29/world/zoo-in-copenhagen-exhibits-new-primates-fully-clothed.html, accessed July 12, 2012.

10. Brad Crouch, "Zoo to Unveil Human Exhibit," *Advertiser* (Australia), November 25, 2006, www.news.com.au/adelaidenow/story/0,22606, 20820913-5011180,00.html, accessed March 14, 2007.

11. "The Humans," Adelaide Zoo website, 2007 human winners, http://www.humanzoo.com.au/thehumans.htm, accessed March 14, 2007.

12. Phillips Verner Bradford and Harvey Blume, *Ota: The Pygmy in the Zoo* (New York: St. Martin's Press, 1992), ch. 16, pp. 260–61.

13. Paola Cavalieri and Peter Singer, eds., *The Great Ape Project: Equality beyond Humanity* (New York: St. Martin's Press, 1993), 1–7.

14. I discuss these in greater detail in my book, *From Darwin to Hitler: Evolutionary Ethics, Eugenics, and Racism in Germany* (New York: Palgrave Macmillan, 2004).

15. Charles Darwin, *Charles Darwin's Notebooks, 1836–1844: Geology, Transmutation of Species, Metaphysical Inquiries*, Paul Barrett et al.,

eds. (Ithaca: Cornell University Press, 1987), 614, see also 532–33, 613. Punctuation as in original.

16. David Friedrich Strauss, *Der alte und der neue Glaube: Ein Bekenntnis* (Leipzig: S. Hirzel, 187), 202–7.

17. August Forel, *Out of My Life and Work*, trans. Bernard Miall (New York: Norton, 1937), 53, 256.

18. August Forel, *Die sexuelle Frage* (Munich: Ernst Reinhardt, 1905), 399–400.

19. August Forel, *Leben und Tod* (Munich: Ernst Reinhardt, 1908), 3.

20. August Forel, *Kulturbestrebungen der Gegenwart* (Munich: Ernst Reinhardt, 1910), 26–27.

21. Peter Singer, *Writings on an Ethical Life* (New York, 2000), 77–78, 220–21.

22. Peter Singer, *Practical Ethics* (Cambridge: Cambridge University Press, 1979), 331.

23. Peter Singer, interview with Johann Hari, "Peter Singer—On Killing Disabled Babies, Saving Animals, and the Dangers of Superstition," Johann Hari's website, July 1, 20014, www.johannhari.com/2004/07/01/peter-singer-on-killing-disabled-babies-saving-animals-and-the-dangers-of-superstition, accessed November 18, 2009.

24. James Rachels, *Created from Animals: The Moral Implications of Darwinism* (Oxford: Oxford University Press, 1990), 4–5, 79–80, and passim.

25. Richard Dawkins, "The Word Made Flesh," *Guardian*, December 27, 2001, www. world-of-dawkins.com/Dawkins/Work/Articles, accessed August 13, 2003; Dawkins also discusses these views in "Gaps in the Mind," in Paola Cavalieri and Peter Singer, eds., *The Great Ape Project: Equality beyond Humanity* (New York: St. Martin's Press, 1993), 80–87.

26. Wesley J. Smith, "Dawkins Claims Pig More 'Human' than Fetus," National Review Online, March 13, 2013.

27. "Richard Dawkins: 'Immoral' Not to Abort if Foetus has Down's Syndrome," www.theguardian.com/science/2014/aug/21/richard-dawkins-immoral-not-to-abort-a-downs-syndrome-foetus, accessed August 22, 2014.

28. "Richard Dawkins: How Would You Feel about a Half-Human Half-Chimp Hybrid?" Guardian Science Blog, January 2, 2009, www.guardian.co.uk/science/blog/2009/jan/02, accessed August 4, 2009.

29. Piet de Rooy, "In Search of Perfection: The Creation of a Missing Link," in *Ape, Man, Apeman: Changing Views since 1600*, ed. Raymond Corbey and Bert Theunissen (Leiden: Leiden University, 1995), 195–99.

30. Editorial, *Nature*, 447 (June 14, 2007), doi: 10.1038/447753a.

31. Ernst Haeckel, *Die Lebenswunder: Gemeinverständliche Studien über Biologische Philosophie* (Stuttgart: Alfred Kröner, 1904), 451–52.

32. Ernst Haeckel, *Natürliche Schöpfungsgeschichte*, 2nd edition (Berlin: Georg Reimer, 1870), 152–55; Haeckel, *Die Lebenswunder: Gemeinverständliche Studien über Biologische Philosophie* (Stuttgart: Alfred Kröner, 1904), 135–36.

33. Quoted in Paul F. Boller, Jr., *American Thought in Transition: The Impact of Evolutionary Naturalism, 1865–1900* (Chicago: Rand McNally, 1969), 59.

34. Karl Vogt, *Vorlesungen über den Menschen* (Giessen: J. Ricker'sche Buchhandlung, 1863), 1:214, 256; Andrew Zimmerman, *Anthropology and Antihumanism in Imperial Germany* (Chicago: University of Chicago Press, 2001), 75.

35. Wilhelm Schallmayer, *Vererbung und Auslese im Lebenslauf der Völker. Eine Staatswissenschaftliche Studie auf Grund der neueren Biologie* (Jena: Gustav Fischer, 1903), 371.

36. Ignaz Kaup, "Was kosten die minderwertigen Elemente dem Staat und der Gesellschaft?" *Archiv für Rassen- und Gesellschaftsbiologie* 10 (1913): 747. For more on Kaup, see Doris Byer, *Rassenhygiene und Wohlfahrtspflege: Zur Entstehung eines sozialdemokratischen Machtdispositivs in Österreich bis 1934* (Frankfurt: Campus, 1988).

37. Adolf Hitler, *Mein Kampf*, trans. Ludwig Lore (New York: Stackpole Sons, 1939), 282.

38. Johann Hari, Peter Singer Interview, www.johannhari.com/archive/article.php?id=410, accessed May 18, 2009.

39. Charles Darwin to Asa Gray, July 1860, in *The Life and Letters of Charles Darwin*, ed. Francis, Darwin, 2 vols. (New York: D. Appleton, 1919), 1:284–285.
40. Charles Darwin to Asa Gray, May 22, 1860, http://www. darwinproject.ac.uk/entry-2814, accessed July 20, 2012.
41. Charles Darwin, *Autobiography* (New York: Norton, 1969), 87.
42. Quoted in Alister E. McGrath, "The Ideological Uses of Evolutionary Biology in Recent Atheist Apologetics," in *Biology and Ideology from Descartes to Dawkins*, ed. Denis Alexander and Ronald Numbers (Chicago: University of Chicago Press, 2010), 338.
43. Karl Marx to Ferdinand Lassalle, January 16, 1861, in *Marx-Engels Werke* (Berlin, 1959ff.), 30:578.
44. Richard Dawkins, *The Blind Watchmaker: Why the Evidence of Evolution Reveals a Universe without Design* (New York: Norton, 1987), 5.
45. Richard Dawkins, "God's Utility Function," *Scientific American* 273 (Nov. 1995): 80–81.
46. Will Provine, "No Free Will," *Isis* 90, supplement (1999): S117–S123.
47. William Provine, "Evolution and the Foundation of Ethics," in *Science, Technology and Social Progress*, ed. Steven L. Goldman (Bethlehem, PA: Lehigh University Press, 1989), 261–62.
48. Stephen Jay Gould, *Rocks of Ages: Science and Religion in the Fullness of Life* (New York: Ballantine Books, 1999), 207. This closing sentence was the same as his sentence in the closing of *Wonderful Life* (quoted below).
49. Stephen Jay Gould, *Wonderful Life: The Burgess Shale and the Nature of History* (New York: W. W. Norton, 1989), 14, 44.
50. Ibid., 44, 51,14.
51. Ibid., 323.
52. *Charles Darwin's Notebooks, 1836–1844: Geology, Transmutation of Species, Metaphysical Inquiries*, eds. Paul Barrett et al., (Ithaca: Cornell University Press, 1987), 537.
53. Charles Darwin, *The Origin of Species* (London: Penguin, 1968), 230.
54. Charles Darwin, *The Descent of Man*, 2 vols. in 1 (Princeton: Princeton University Press, 1981), 1:162–63.
55. Ibid., 1:166, 106.

56. Ibid., 1:73.
57. Ibid., 1:97.
58. Ibid., 1:35.
59. Ibid., 1:84–85; see also 1:72.
60. Ibid., 1:93–94.
61. Ibid., 2:361.
62. Oliver Wendell Holmes, "Natural Law," (1918), in *The Mind and Faith of Justice Holmes: His Speeches, Essays, Letters, and Judicial Opinions*, ed. Max Lerner (New York: Modern Library, 1943), 397.
63. Oliver Wendell Holmes to Harold Laski, May 12, 1927, in *Holmes-Laski Letters: The Correspondence of Mr. Justice Holmes and Harold J. Laski, 1916–1935*, 2 vols., ed. Mark DeWolfe Howe (Cambridge, MA: Harvard University Press, 1953), 2:942.
64. Albert W. Alschuler, *Law without Values: The Life, Work, and Legacy of Justice Holmes* (Chicago: University of Chicago Press, 2000), 28.
65. Oliver Wendell Holmes, "The Soldier's Faith" (30 May 1895), in *The Collected Works of Justice Holmes: Complete Public Writings and Selected Judicial Opinions of Oliver Wendell Holmes*, ed. Sheldon M. Novick, 3 vols. (Chicago: University of Chicago Press, 1995), 3:487
66. Oliver Wendell Holmes to Frederick Pollock, February 1, 1920 and April 11, 1920, in *The Pollock-Holmes Letters: Correspondence of Sir Frederick Pollock and Mr [sic] Justice Holmes 1874–1932*, ed. Mark DeWolfe Howe, 2 vols. (Cambridge: Cambridge University Press, 1942), 2:36, 39; final quotation is from Albert W. Alschuler, *Law without Values: The Life, Work, and Legacy of Justice Holmes* (Chicago: University of Chicago Press, 2000), 27.
67. Oliver Wendell Holmes Jr., to Lewis Einstein, August 6, 1917, in *The Holmes-Einstein Letters: Correspondence of Mr. Justice Holmes and Lewis Einstein, 1903–1935*, ed. James Bishop Peabody (New York: St. Martin's Press, 1964), 145.
68. Oliver Wendell Holmes to Harold Laski, May 13, 1926, in *Holmes-Laski Letters: The Correspondence of Mr. Justice Holmes and Harold J. Laski, 1916–1935*, 2 vols., ed. Mark DeWolfe Howe (Cambridge, MA: Harvard University Press, 1953), 2:837.
69. Julian Huxley, *Evolutionary Ethics* (Oxford: Oxford University Press, 1943), 7, 32, 44, 51.

70. Julian Huxley, "The Humanist Frame," in *The Humanist Frame*, ed. Julian Huxley (New York: Harper and Brothers, 1961), 24.

71. Ernst Mayr, "Footnotes on the Philosophy of Biology," *Philosophy of Science* 36 (1969): 201.

72. Larry Taunton, "Richard Dawkins: The Atheist Evangelist," in *byFaith*, http://byfaithonline.com/richard-dawkins-the-atheist-evangelist, accessed August 22, 2014.

73. Michael Ruse, "Evolutionary Theory and Christian Ethics: Are They in Harmony?," *Zygon* 29 (1994): 23; also in Ruse, *The Darwinian Paradigm: Essays on Its History, Philosophy, and Religious Implications* (London: Routledge, 1989), 269.

74. Michael Ruse, *The Darwinian Paradigm: Essays on Its History, Philosophy, and Religious Implications* (London: Routledge, 1989), 266.

75. Will Provine, "No Free Will," *Isis* 90, supplement (1999): S117–S123.

76. William Provine, interview with Ben Stein, in *Expelled: No Intelligence Allowed* (DVD, 2008).

77. Tamler Sommers and Alex Rosenberg, "Darwin's Nihilistic Idea: Evolution and the Meaninglessness of Life," *Biology and Philosophy* 18 (2003): 655, 668.

78. William Lane Craig-Alex Rosenberg Debate, http://www.youtube.com/watch?feature=player_embedded&v=bhfkhq-CM84. For a critique of evolutionary explanations for morality, see Angus Ritchie, *From Morality to Metaphysics: The Theistic Implications of Our Ethical Commitments* (Oxford: Oxford University Press, 2012), ch. 2.

79. Adrian Desmond, *Huxley: From Devil's Disciple to Evolution's High Priest* (Reading, MA: Addison-Wesley, 1997), 271.

80. Charles Darwin, *The Origin of Species* (London: Penguin, 1968), 459.

81. I Corinthians 15:54.

82. Alfred Hoche, *Jahresringe: Innenansicht eines Menschenlebens* (Munich: J. F. Lehmann, 1935), 22.

83. Robby Kossmann, "Die Bedeutung des Einzellebens in der Darwinistischen Weltanschauung," *Nord und Süd* 12 (1880): 420–21. Emphasis is mine.

84. Jerry Coyne, "Mass Shootings Again Blamed on Evolution," http://whyevolutionistrue.wordpress.com/2012/07/21/mass-shootings-again-blamed-on-evolution/, accessed July 24, 2012.

85. Jerry Coyne, on "Conspiracy Road Trip," BBC, http://youtu.be/Oju_lpqa6Ug, accessed October 17, 2012.

86. Jerry Coyne, "Ross Douthat Is On Another Erroneous Rampage Against Secularism," *The New Republic*, http://www.newrepublic.com/article/116047/ross-douthat-wrong-about-secularism-and-ethics, accessed June 29, 2014.

87. Ibid.

88. Daniel C. Dennett, *Darwin's Dangerous Idea: Evolution and the Meanings of Life* (New York: Simon and Schuster, 1995), 513–14.

THREE: MY GENES MADE ME DO IT

1. Steven Pinker, "Why They Kill Their Newborns," *The New York Times Sunday Magazine*, February 11, 1997.

2. Ibid.

3. Ibid.

4. Ibid.

5. Steven Pinker, *The Blank Slate: The Modern Denial of Human Nature* (New York: Viking, 2002), x–xi.

6. Ibid., 224, 226.

7. Kim Wombles, "David Eagleman's Incognito: Not the Masters of Our Destinies, October 2011, http://www.science20.com/countering_tackling_woo/david_eaglemans_incognito_not_masters_our_destinies-83621, accessed July 20, 2012.

8. Richard Dawkins, "Let's All Stop Beating Basil's Car," www.edge.org/q2006/q06_9.html, accessed October 26, 2006.

9. Clarence Darrow, Closing Argument, *The State of Illinois v. Nathan Leopold & Richard Loeb*, August 22, 1924, http://law2.umkc.edu/faculty/projects/ftrials/leoploeb/darrowclosing.html, accessed July 12, 2012.

10. Jonathan I. Israel, *Radical Enlightenment: Philosophy and the Making of Modernity 1650–1750* (Oxford: Oxford University Press, 2001), 162, 218–20, 235.

11. Quoted in Louis Dupré, *The Enlightenment and the Intellectual Foundations of Modern Culture* (New Haven, CN: Yale University Press, 2004), 119; see also Jonathan Israel, *Enlightenment Contested: Philosophy, Modernity, and the Emancipation of Man 1670–1752* (Oxford: Oxford University Press, 2006), 695; and Ann Thomson, *Bodies of Thought: Science, Religion, and the Soul in the Early Enlightenment* (Oxford: Oxford University Press, 2008), 212.

12. Julien Offray de La Mettrie, *Man a Machine* (La Salle, IL: Open Court, 1912), 109, 119.

13. Ibid., 96.

14. Jonathan Israel, *Enlightenment Contested: Philosophy, Modernity, and the Emancipation of Man 1670–1752* (Oxford: Oxford University Press, 2006), 812.

15. Mary Pickering, *Auguste Comte: An Intellectual Biography* (Cambridge: Cambridge University Press, 1993), 1:303–305.

16. Richard T. Gray, *About Face: German Physiognomic Thought from Lavater to Auschwitz* (Detroit: Wayne State University Press, 2004).

17. Quoted in Robert Zubrin, *Merchants of Despair: Radical Environmentalists, Criminal Pseudo-Scientists, and the Fatal Cult of Antihumanism* (New York: New Atlantis Books, 2012), 68.

18. Nicholas Wright Gillham, *A Life of Sir Francis Galton: From African Exploration to the Birth of Eugenics* (Oxford: Oxford University Press, 2001), 328, 197.

19. Diane B. Paul, *Controlling Human Heredity, 1865 to the Present* (Atlantic Highlands, NJ: Humanities Press, 1995), 34.

20. Gillham, *A Life of Sir Francis Galton*, 216–17.

21. Maria Sophia Quine, review of *Building the New Man*, in *Journal of Modern History* 85 (2013): 455.

22. Charles Darwin, Notebook M, in *Charles Darwin's Notebooks, 1836–1844: Geology, Transmutation of Species, Metaphysical Inquiries*, eds. Paul Barrett et al. (Ithaca: Cornell University Press, 1987), 549–50.

23. Charles Darwin, *The Descent of Man, and Selection in Relation to Sex*, 2 vols in 1 (Princeton: Princeton University Press, 1981), 1:97.

24. George L. Mosse, *Toward the Final Solution: A History of European Racism* (New York: Howard Fertig, 1985), 52–54.

25. Richard Weikart, *Hitler's Ethic: The Nazi Pursuit of Evolutionary Progress* (New York: Palgrave Macmillan, 2009), ch. 4.
26. Ibid.
27. Carl Degler, *In Search of Human Nature: The Decline and Revival of Darwinism in American Social Thought* New York: Oxford University Press, 1991).
28. Konrad Lorenz, "Nochmals: Systematik und Entwicklungsgedanke im Unterricht," *Der Biologe: Monatsschrift des Deutschen Biologen-Verbandes, des Sachgebietes Biologie des N.S.L.B.* 9 (1940): 27.
29. Konrad Lorenz, *On Aggression*, trans. Marjorie Kerr Wilson (New York: Harcourt, Brace and World, 1966), 220–22, 226–27.
30. Ibid., 299.
31. Lorenz, "Nochmals: Systematik und Entwicklungsgedanke im Unterricht," 32.
32. Edward O. Wilson, *Sociobiology: The New Synthesis* (Cambridge: Belknap Press of Harvard University Press, 1975), 4.
33. E. O. Wilson and Michael Ruse, "The Evolution of Ethics," *New Scientist* 108 (17 October 1985): 50–52.
34. Wilson, *Sociobiology*, 575.
35. Ibid., 3.
36. Edward O. Wilson, *On Human Nature* (Cambridge, MA: Harvard University Press, 1978), 167.
37. Edward O. Wilson, *Naturalist* (Washington, DC: Island Press, 1994), xi.
38. Edward O. Wilson, *Consilience: The Unity of Knowledge* (New York: Alfred A. Knopf, 1998), 248.
39. Ibid., 261.
40. Ibid., ch. 6, quote at 11; see also E. O. Wilson, *The Social Conquest of the Earth* (New York: Liveright Publishing, 2012), 287–88.
41. E. O. Wilson, "Foreword," in *Evolution: The First Four Billion Years*, ed. Michael Ruse and Joseph Travis (Cambridge, MA: Harvard University Press, 2009), vii–viii. Wilson elaborates on these questions further in *The Social Conquest of the Earth* (New York: Liveright Publishing, 2012).
42. E. O. Wilson, *The Meaning of Human Existence* (NY: Liveright, 2014), 173.

43.   Ibid., 174.

44.   Ibid., chs. 3, 12–13.

45.   Richard Dawkins, *The Selfish Gene* (New York: Oxford University Press, 1976), ix, 64.

46.   Ibid., 151.

47.   Ibid., 132–40.

48.   Ibid., 2–3, 215.

49.   Richard Dawkins, *A Devil's Chaplain: Reflections on Hope, Lies, Science, and Love* (Boston: Mariner Books, 2004), 11–12.

50.   Richard Dawkins, *The Selfish Gene* (New York: Oxford University Press, 1976), 3.

51.   Charlotte Hunt-Grubbe, "The elementary DNA of Dr. Watson," *The Sunday Times* (October 14, 2007).

52.   "DNA: Pandora's Box," PBS (with James Watson).

53.   James Watson, "Children from the Laboratory," *AMA Prism* (May 1973), 2.

54.   Randy Thornhill and Craig Palmer, *A Natural History of Rape: Biological Bases of Sexual Coercion* (Cambridge, MA: MIT Press, 2000), 2, 59–60, 84.

55.   Justin Brierley, interview with Richard Dawkins, http://www. premierradio.org.uk/listen/ondemand?mediaid=%7Bffad6f7d-9f77-4045-9416-7d92377f84c6%7D, accessed August 20, 2012.

56.   David Sloan Wilson, *Darwin's Cathedral: Evolution, Religion, and the Nature of Society* (Chicago: University of Chicago Press, 2002).

57.   Kevin MacDonald, *Separation and Its Discontents: Toward an Evolutionary Theory of Anti-Semitism* (Westport, CT: Praeger, 1998), viii.

58.   Robert Wright, "Our Cheating Hearts," *Time* 144 (August 15, 1994): 44–52.

59.   Sarah Blaffer Hrdy and Glenn Hausfater, "Comparative and Evolutionary Perspectives on Infanticide: Introduction and Overview," in *Infanticide: Comparative and Evolutionary Perspectives*, eds. Glenn Hausfater and Sarah Blaffer Hrdy (New York: Aldine Publishing Company, 1984), xiii–xxxv.

60.   Martin Daly and Margo Wilson, "A Sociobiological Analysis of Human Infanticide," in *Infanticide: Comparative and Evolutionary*

Perspectives, eds. Glenn Hausfater and Sarah Blaffer Hrdy (New York: Aldine Publishing Company, 1984), 502.

61. Sarah Blaffer Hrdy, *Mother Nature: A History of Mothers, Infants, and Natural Selection* (New York: Pantheon Books, 1999), 316–17.
62. Marc Hauser, *Moral Minds: How Nature Designed Our Universal Sense of Right and Wrong* (New York: HarperCollins, 2006), 361.
63. Ibid., xvii.
64. Ibid., xix, quote at 425.

FOUR: MY UPBRINGING MADE ME DO IT

1. Clarence Darrow, Closing Argument, *The State of Illinois v. Nathan Leopold & Richard Loeb*, August 22, 1924, http://law2.umkc.edu/faculty/projects/ftrials/leoploeb/darrowclosing.html, accessed July 12, 2012.
2. Ibid.
3. M. Helvétius, *A Treatise on Man, His Intellectual Faculties and His Education* trans. W. Hooper (London: B. Law and G. Robinson, 1777), 1:279; M. Helvétius, *A Treatise on Man, His Intellectual Faculties and His Education* trans. W. Hooper (n.p. [probably London]: Albion Press, 1810), 2:11, 409.
4. Isaiah Berlin, *Freedom and Its Betrayals: Six Enemies of Human Liberty* (Princeton: Princeton University Press, 2002), 22–23.
5. M. Helvétius, *A Treatise on Man, His Intellectual Faculties and His Education* trans. W. Hooper (n.p. [probably London]: Albion Press, 1810), 2:410–11.
6. Robert Owen, *The Life of Robert Owen Written by Himself* (London, 1857; rprt. New York: Augustus M. Kelley Publishers, 1967), 1:76.
7. Robert Owen, *The Book of the New Moral World, Containing the Rational System of Society, Founded on Demonstrable Facts, Developing the Constitution and Laws of Human Nature and of Society* (London: Effingham Wilson, 1836), 20.
8. Owen, *The Life of Robert Owen Written by Himself*, 1:xli.
9. Robert Owen, *A New View of Society and Other Writings* (London: J. M. Dent and Sons, 1927), 45.
10. Ibid., 72.
11. Owen, *The Life of Robert Owen Written by Himself*, 1:59–60.

12. J. F. C. Harrison, *Quest for the New Moral World: Robert Owen and the Owenites in Britain and America* (New York: Charles Scribner's Sons, 1969), 163–65.

13. Owen, *The Life of Robert Owen Written by Himself,* 1:79.

14. Robert Owen, *The Book of the New Moral World, Containing the Rational System of Society, Founded on Demonstrable Facts, Developing the Constitution and Laws of Human Nature and of Society* (London: Effingham Wilson, 1836), 24.

15. Robert Owen, *A New View of Society and Other Writings* (London: J. M. Dent and Sons, 1927), 40–41.

16. Robert Owen, *Marriages of the Priesthood of the Old Immoral World,* in A. L. Morton, *The Life and Ideas of Robert Owen* (London: Lawrence and Wishart, 1962), 161–68.

17. Owen, *The Life of Robert Owen Written by Himself,* 1:16.

18. Owen, *A New View of Society and Other Writings,* 22.

19. Owen, *The Life of Robert Owen Written by Himself,* 1:36.

20. Stéphane Courtois et al., *The Black Book of Communism: Crimes, Terror, Repression,* trans. Jonthan Murphy et al (Cambridge, MA: Harvard University Press, 1999), xviii, 4, 9–10.

21. Karl Marx and Friedrich Engels, *The Communist Manifesto* (New York: International Publishers, 1948), 9, 10, 21.

22. Karl Marx, *Kapital,* in *Marx-Engels Gesamtausgabe* (Berlin, 1975ff.,), II/5:13–14.

23. Karl Marx, Preface to *A Contribution to the Critique of Political Economy,* in *The Marx-Engels Reader,* ed. Robert C. Tucker, 2nd ed. (New York: Norton, 1978), 4.

24. Karl Marx, *Poverty of Philosophy,* http://www.marxists.org/archive/marx/works/subject/hist-mat/pov-phil/ch02.htm, accessed July 19, 2013.

25. Karl Marx, "Theses on Feuerbach," in *The Marx-Engels Reader,* ed. Robert C. Tucker, 2nd ed. (New York: Norton, 1978), 144.

26. Ibid., 145.

27. Marx and Engels, *The Communist Manifesto,* 31.

28. Ibid., 30.

29. Eugene Kamenka, *Marxism and Ethics* (London: MacMillan, 1969), ch. 5.

30. Alexander Solzhenitsyn, *One Day in the Life of Ivan Denisovich*, trans. Ralph Parker (New York: Signet Books, 1963), 105.

31. Quoted in Joseph Stalin, *Leninism*, trans. Eden and Cedar Paul (New York: International Publishers, 1928), 113.

32. Lenin, "Fright at the Fall of the Old and the Fight for the New" (1918), in *The Lenin Anthology*, ed. Robert C. Tucker (New York: Norton, 1975), 424–25.

33. Richard Pipes, ed., *The Unknown Lenin: From the Secret Archive*, trans. Catherine A. Fitzpatrick (New Haven: Yale University Press, 1996), 1, 8, 11.

34. Robert Gellately, *Lenin, Stalin, and Hitler: The Age of Social Catastrophe* (New York: Vintage, 2008), 71–72.

35. Eugene Kamenka, *The Ethical Foundations of Marxism* (London: Routledge and Kegan Paul, 1972), 180.

36. Joseph Stalin, *Dialectical and Historical Materialism* (New York: International Publishers, 1940), 19–20.

37. Robert Service, *Stalin: A Biography* (Cambridge, MA: Belknap Press of Harvard University Press, 2004), 341–42.

38. Stalin, *Dialectical and Historical Materialism*, 14.

39. Norman Naimark, *Stalin's Genocides* (Princeton UP, 2010), 32, 58–59, 111, 131.

40. John B. Watson, *Behaviorism* (New York: Norton, 1970), ix, 3, 6, 19, 94, 269–70.

41. Ibid., 104, 183.

42. Kerry W. Buckley, *Mechanical Man: John Broadus Watson and the Beginnings of Behaviorism* (New York: Guilford Press, 1989), 181.

43. John B. Watson, *Psychological Care of Infant and Child* (New York: Norton, 1928), 5–6, 12–13.

44. Ibid., 44, 71, 78, 85.

45. Watson, *Psychological Care of Infant and Child*, 81–84.

46. Ibid., 43–44.

47. John B. Watson, *Behaviorism* (New York: Norton, 1970), 185.

48. Quotes in Kerry W. Buckley, *Mechanical Man: John Broadus Watson and the Beginnings of Behaviorism* (New York: Guilford Press, 1989), 162–65.

49. Ibid., 179–80.

50. Ibid., 169.

51. Katharine Tait, *My Father Bertrand Russell* (New York: Harcourt Brace Jovanovich, 1975), 58–63.

52. Daniel W. Bjork, *B. F. Skinner: A Life* (New York: Basic Books, 1993), 46, 226.

53. Ibid., 26, 115, 229.

54. B. F. Skinner, *Beyond Freedom and Dignity* (New York: Alfred Knopf, 1972), 3–5, 19, 211.

55. Ibid., 101.

56. Ibid., 200–1.

57. B. F. Skinner, *Walden Two* (New York: Macmillan, 1948), 257.

58. Ibid., 296–97.

59. Ibid., 273.

60. Ibid., 115, 235.

61. Bjork, *B. F. Skinner*, 152.

62. Ibid., 25, 219.

63. Rita Marker, *Deadly Compassion: The Death of Ann Humphry and the Truth about Euthanasia* (New York: William Morrow and Company, 1993), 47, 50–51.

FIVE: THE LOVE OF PLEASURE

1. II Timothy 3:1–4.

2. Didier Eribon, *Michel Foucault*, trans. Betsy Wing (Cambridge, MA: Harvard University Press, 1991), 31; James Miller, *The Passion of Michel Foucault* (New York: Simon and Schuster, 1993), 26–27, 45, 55.

3. Stephen Greenblatt, *The Swerve: How the Renaissance Began* (London: Bodley Head, 2011), 202, 262–63.

4. Roy Porter, *The Creation of the Modern World: The Untold Story of the British Enlightenment* (New York: W. W. Norton, 2000), 258, 260.

5. Faramerz Dabhoiwala, *The Origins of Sex: A History of the First Sexual Revolution* (Oxford: Oxford University Press, 2012), 116; see also Jonathan I. Israel, *Radical Enlightenment: Philosophy and the Making of Modernity 1650–1750* (Oxford: Oxford University Press, 2001), 4–5, 92–93.

6.   Julien Offray de La Mettrie, *The System of Epicurus*, in *Machine Man and Other Writings*, ed. Ann Thomson (Cambridge: Cambridge University Press, 1996), 111.

7.   Julien Offray de La Mettrie, *Anti-Seneca or the Sovereign Good*, in *Machine Man and Other Writings*, ed. Ann Thomson (Cambridge: Cambridge University Press, 1996), 119.

8.   Lester G. Crocker, *Nature and Culture: Ethical Thought in the French Enlightenment* (Baltimore: Johns Hopkins Press, 1963), 240; see also Ann Thomson, *Materialism and Society in the Mid-Eighteenth Century: La Mettrie's* Discours Préliminaire (Geneva: Librairie Droz, 1981), 48–50; Kathleen Wellman, *La Mettrie: Medicine, Philosophy, and Enlightenment* (Durham, NC: Duke University Press, 1992), 217–19.

9.   Julien Offray de La Mettrie, *Preliminary Discourse* [this was written as introduction to his collected philosophical works], in *Machine Man and Other Writings*, ed. Ann Thomson (Cambridge: Cambridge University Press, 1996), 157–58.

10.   La Mettrie, *Anti-Seneca or the Sovereign Good*, 121, 132.

11.   La Mettrie, *Preliminary Discourse*, 157–58.

12.   Julien Offray de La Mettrie, *Man a Machine* (La Salle, IL: Open Court, 1912), 148.

13.   Ibid., 121.

14.   Ibid.

15.   La Mettrie, *Anti-Seneca or the Sovereign Good*, 120.

16.   Aram Vartanian, *La Mettrie's l'Homme Machine: A Study in the Origins of an Idea* (Princeton: Princeton University Press, 1960), 3, 32–33.

17.   Quoted in Crocker, *Nature and Culture*, 359.

18.   Jonathan Israel, *Enlightenment Contested: Philosophy, Modernity, and the Emancipation of Man 1670–1752* (Oxford: Oxford University Press, 2006), 803.

19.   Ibid., 810; see also Kathleen Wellman, *La Mettrie: Medicine, Philosophy, and Enlightenment* (Durham, NC: Duke University Press, 1992), 272–77.

20.   Crocker, *Nature and Culture*, 353.

21. Lester G. Crocker, *An Age of Crisis: Man and World in Eighteenth Century French Thought* (Baltimore: Johns Hopkins Press, 1959), 10–11, 213.
22. Crocker, *Nature and Culture*, 405.
23. Crocker, *An Age of Crisis*, 99.
24. Crocker, *Nature and Culture*, 402.
25. Crocker, *An Age of Crisis*, 212–13.
26. M. Helvétius, *A Treatise on Man, His Intellectual Faculties and His Education* trans. W. Hooper (London: B. Law and G. Robinson, 1777), 1:142–43.
27. D. W. Smith, *Helvétius: A Study in Persecution* (Oxford, UK: Clarendon Press, 1965), 14, 116, 209.
28. Helvétius, *A Treatise on Man*, 1:58–59.
29. Ibid., 1:143–44.
30. Crocker, *Nature and Culture*, 359.
31. D. W. Smith, *Helvétius: A Study in Persecution* (Oxford, UK: Clarendon Press, 1965), 12.
32. Helvétius, *A Treatise on Man*, 1:282, 302–3, 319.
33. M. Helvétius, *A Treatise on Man, His Intellectual Faculties and His Education* trans. W. Hooper, vol. 2 (n.p. [probably London]: Albion Press, 1810), 2:433.
34. Ibid., 2:198, 205, 303, 307–8.
35. M. Helvétius, *A Treatise on Man, His Intellectual Faculties and His Education* trans. W. Hooper (London: B. Law and G. Robinson, 1777), 1: 303.
36. Arthur M. Wilson, *Diderot* (New York: Oxford University Press, 1972), 236.
37. Denis Diderot, "Supplement to Bougainville's 'Voyage,'" in *Rameau's Nephew and Other Works*, trans. Jacques Barzun and Ralph H. Bowen (Garden City, NY: Doubleday Anchor Books, 1956), 187–239; Israel, *Enlightenment Contested*, 584–86.
38. Wilson, *Diderot*, 202, 205, 207.
39. Ibid., 672–73.
40. John Dinwiddy, *Bentham* (Oxford: Oxford University Press, 1989), 18.

41. Jeremy Bentham, *An Introduction to the Principles of Morals and Legislation*, ed. J. H. Burns and H. L. A. Hart (London: University of London, The Athlone Press, 1970), 11.
42. Ibid., 100.
43. Ibid., 38.
44. Dinwiddy, *Bentham*, 114.
45. Isaiah Berlin, *Freedom and Its Betrayals: Six Enemies of Human Liberty* (Princeton: Princeton University Press, 2002), 25.
46. Dinwiddy, *Bentham*, 112.
47. Ibid.
48. Faramerz Dabhoiwala, *The Origins of Sex: A History of the First Sexual Revolution* (Oxford: Oxford University Press, 2012), 134–37.
49. Ibid., 135.
50. John Stuart Mill, *Autobiography* (1873), www.utilitarianism.com/millauto/index.html; accessed August 2003, ch. 5.
51. Ibid.
52. John Stuart Mill, *Utilitarianism*, in *The Essential Works of John Stuart Mill*, ed. Max Lerner (New York: Bantam Books, 1961), 194.
53. Ibid., 227.
54. Ibid., 195.
55. Ibid., 204.
56. Mill, *Autobiography,* accessed August 2003.
57. Jonathan Beecher and Richard Bienvenu, "Introduction," in Charles Fourier, *The Utopian Vision of Charles Fourier,* trans. and ed. Jonathan Beecher and Richard Bienvenu (Boston: Beacon Press, 1971), 64.
58. Charles Fourier, *The Utopian Vision of Charles Fourier,* trans. and ed. Jonathan Beecher and Richard Bienvenu (Boston: Beacon Press, 1971), 211–12.
59. Jonathan Beecher, *Charles Fourier: The Visionary and His World* (Berkeley: University of California Press, 1986), 66.
60. Fourier, *The Utopian Vision of Charles Fourier,* 215–17.
61. Ibid., 329.
62. Beecher, *Charles Fourier,* ch. 15; quote at 303.
63. Sigmund Freud, *Civilization and Its Discontents,* trans. James Strachey (New York: W. W. Norton, 1989), 25.

64. Sigmund Freud, *Beyond the Pleasure Principle* (New York: Liveright Publishing, 1961), 56.

65. Freud, *Civilization and Its Discontents*, 34.

66. Ibid., 57.

67. Ibid., 66–67.

68. Douglas Kellner, *Herbert Marcuse and the Crisis of Marxism* (Berkeley: University of California Press, 1984), 1, 155.

69. Ibid., ch. 6.

70. Herbert Marcuse, *Eros and Civilization: A Philosophical Inquiry into Freud* (Boston: Beacon Press, 1955), 200–1; other commentators, such as Alasdair MacIntyre have complained about the fuzziness of Marcuse's proposal involving "resexualization" of the body; see Douglas Kellner, *Herbert Marcuse and the Crisis of Marxism* (Berkeley: University of California Press, 1984), 182.

71. Marcuse, *Eros and Civilization*, 235–37.

72. Peter Singer, *Practical Ethics* (Cambridge: Cambridge University Press, 1979), 80–81.

73. Ibid., 81.

74. Ibid., 216–17.

75. Peter Singer, *How Are We to Live?: Ethics in an Age of Self-Interest* (Oxford: Oxford University Press, 1997), 275.

76. Ibid., 204–5.

77. Ibid., 258.

78. Ibid., 280.

79. Ibid., 223–26.

80. Singer, *Practical Ethics*, 50.

81. Ibid., 133–34, 139.

82. Ibid., 155.

83. C. Everett Koop, "The Slide to Auschwitz," *Human Life Review* 39, 2 (Spring 2013): 99 (this essay was originally published in 1977).

SIX: SUPERMAN'S CONTEMPT FOR HUMANITY

1. Friedrich Nietzsche, *Also sprach Zarathustra*, in *Werke in Drei Bänden*, ed. Karl Schlechta, vol. 2, part 1 (Munich: Carl Hanser, 1966), 333–36.

2. Clarence Darrow, Closing Argument, *The State of Illinois v. Nathan Leopold & Richard Loeb*, http://law2.umkc.edu/faculty/projects/ftrials/leoploeb/darrowclosing.html, accessed July 12, 2012.

3. George Nasmyth, *Social Progress and the Darwinian Theory: A Study of Force as a Factor in Human Relations* (New York: Putnam's Sons, 1916), 13; Benjamin Kidd, *The Science of Power* (New York: G. P. Putnam's Sons, 1918), 61; see also N. Martin, "Nietzsche as Hate-Figure in Britain's Great War: 'The Execrable Neech,'" in *The First World War as a Clash of Cultures*, ed. F. Bridgham (Rochester, NY: 2006), 147–66.

4. Quoted in Max Whyte, "The Uses and Abuses of Nietzsche in the Third Reich: Alfred Baeumler's 'Heroic Realism,'" *Journal of Contemporary History* 43 (2008): 175.

5. Steven E. Aschheim, *The Nietzsche Legacy in Germany, 1890–1990* (Berkeley: University of California Press, 1992), 133–34.

6. Denis Mack Smith, *Mussolini: A Biography* (New York: Vintage, 1983), 11–12.

7. Quoted in Richard Wolin, *The Seduction of Unreason: The Intellectual Romance with Fascism from Nietzsche to Postmodernism* (Princeton: Princeton University Press, 2004), 27.

8. Max Whyte, "The Uses and Abuses of Nietzsche in the Third Reich: Alfred Baeumler's 'Heroic Realism,'" *Journal of Contemporary History* 43 (2008): 171–94, provides a good survey of the current debate.

9. Friedrich Nietzsche, *Thus Spake Zarathustra*, in *The Portable Nietzsche*, ed. and trans. Walter Kaufmann (New York: Penguin, 1976), 125.

10. Ibid., 124.

11. Rüdiger Safranski, *Nietzsche: A Philosophical Biography*, trans. Shelley Frisch (New York: Norton, 2002), 262.

12. Friedrich Nietzsche, *David Strauss: Der Bekenner und der Schriftsteller*, § 7, in *Unzeitgemässe Betrachtungen*, in *Werke in Drei Bänden*, ed. Karl Schlechta (Munich: Carl Hanser, 1966), 1:167–69.

13. Friedrich Nietzsche, *Beyond Good and Evil*, trans. Walter Kaufmann (New York: Vintage, 1966), § 257, p. 201.

14. Ibid., § 258, p. 202.

15. Ibid., § 260, p. 204.

16. Ibid., § 259, p. 203.

17. Friedrich Nietzsche, *The Genealogy of Morals: An Attack*, in *The Birth of Tragedy and The Genealogy of Morals*, trans. Francis Golffing (Garden City, NY: Doubleday Anchor, 1956), Essay 2, § 11, p. 207.

18. Ibid.

19. Friedrich Nietzsche, *Antichrist*, in *Werke in Drei Bänden*, ed. Karl Schlechta (Munich: Carl Hanser, 1966), § 7, vol. 2, p. 1,168.

20. Nietzsche, *The Genealogy of Morals*, Essay 2, § 12, p. 210.

21. Nietzsche, *Will to Power*, part 872, quoted in Jean Gayon, "Nietzsche and Darwin," in *Biology and the Foundation of Ethics*, ed. Jane Maienschein and Michael Ruse (Cambridge: Cambridge University Press, 1999), 183.

22. Friedrich Nietzsche, *Ecce Homo*, "Die Geburt der Tragödie," § 4, in *Werke in Drei Bänden*, ed. Karl Schlechta (Munich: Carl Hanser, 1966), 2:1111.

23. Quoted in Rüdiger Safranski, *Nietzsche: A Philosophical Biography*, trans. Shelley Frisch (New York: Norton, 2002), 268.

24. Nietzsche, *Also sprach Zarathustra*, in *Werke in Drei Bänden*, ed. Karl Schlechta (Munich: Carl Hanser, 1966), Part 1, "Vom freien Tod," vol. 2, pp. 333–36.

25. Friedrich Nietzsche, *Twilight of the Idols*, in *The Portable Nietzsche*, ed. and trans. Walter Kaufmann (New York: Penguin, 1976), § 36, pp. 536–37.

26. Friedrich Nietzsche, *Die fröhliche Wissenschaft*, in *Werke in Drei Bänden*, ed. Karl Schlechta (Munich: Carl Hanser, 1966), § 73, vol. 2, pp. 84–85.

27. Michael Lackey, *The Modernist God State: A Literary Study of the Nazis' Christian Reich* (New York: Continuum, 2012), 65.

28. Simon May, *Nietzsche's Ethics and His War on 'Morality'* (New York: Oxford University, The Clarendon Press, 1999), 132.

29. Karl Jaspers, "Letter to the Freiburg University Denazification Committee (December 22, 1945)," in *The Heidegger Controversy: A Critical Reader*, ed. Richard Wolin (Cambridge, MA: MIT Press, 1993), 148–49.

30. Jeffrey Andrew Barash, "Martin Heidegger in the Perspective of the Twentieth Century: Reflections on the Heidegger Gesamtausgabe," *Journal of Modern History* 64 (1992): 69.

31. Hugo Ott, *Martin Heidegger: Unterwegs zu seiner Biographie* (Frankfurt: Campus Verlag, 1988), 264.

32. Yvonne Sherratt, *Hitler's Philosophers* (New Haven: Yale University Press, 2013), 124.

33. Martin Heidegger, "German Students," November 3, 1933, in *The Heidegger Controversy: A Critical Reader*, ed. Richard Wolin (Cambridge, MA: MIT Press, 1993), 47.

34. John Caputo, "Heidegger's Scandal: Thinking and the Essence of the Victim," in *The Heidegger Case: On Philosophy and Politics*, ed. Tom Rockmore and Joseph Margolis (Philadelphia: Temple University Press, 1992), 265.

35. For example, see Hugo Ott, *Martin Heidegger: Unterwegs zu seiner Biographie* (Frankfurt: Campus Verlag, 1988), and Tom Rockmore, *On Heidegger's Nazism and Philosophy* (Berkeley: University of California Press, 1992).

36. Tom Rockmore, *On Heidegger's Nazism and Philosophy* (Berkeley: University of California Press, 1992), 237–38.

37. Ott, *Martin Heidegger*, 267.

38. Richard Weikart, *Hitler's Ethic: The Nazi Pursuit of Evolutionary Progress* (New York: Palgrave Macmillan, 2009), 114–17.

39. Ott, *Martin Heidegger*, 255–58.

40. Richard Wolin, "Fascism and Hermeneutics: Gadamer and the Ambiguities of 'Inner Emigration,'" in *Nazi Germany and the Humanities*, eds. Wolfgang Bialas and Anson Rabinbach (Oxford: Oneworld, 2007), 103.

41. Elisabeth de Fontenay, "In Its Essence the Same Thing," in *Martin Heidegger and the Holocaust*, eds. Alan Milchman and Alan Rosenberg (Atlantic Highlands, NJ: Humanities Press, 1996), 236.

42. Robert John Sheffler Manning , "The Cries of Other and Heidegger's Ear: Remarks on the Agriculture Remark," in *Martin Heidegger and the Holocaust*, eds. Alan Milchman and Alan Rosenberg (Atlantic Highlands, NJ: Humanities Press, 1996), 30; for another view of Heidegger's agriculture remark, see John Caputo, "Heidegger's

Scandal: Thinking and the Essence of the Victim," in *The Heidegger Case: On Philosophy and Politics*, ed. Tom Rockmore and Joseph Margolis (Philadelphia: Temple University Press, 1992), 265–81; and Tom Rockmore, *On Heidegger's Nazism and Philosophy* (Berkeley: University of California Press, 1992), 241–42.

43. Jean-Paul Sartre, "On Genocide," 1967, http://www.brusselstribunal. org/GenocideSartre.htm, accessed May 29, 2014.
44. Tony Judt, *Past Imperfect: French Intellectuals, 1944–1956* (Berkeley: University of California Press, 1992), 125–28.
45. Jean-Paul Sartre, *Life/Situations: Essays Written and Spoken*, trans. Paul Auster and Lydia Davis (New York: Pantheon Books, 1977), 86–87.
46. Ibid., 60–62.
47. Jean-Paul Sartre, *Existentialism and Human Emotions* (New York: Wisdom Library, 1957), 51.
48. Jean-Paul Sartre, *Talking with Sartre: Conversations and Debates*, ed. and trans. John Gerassi (New Haven: Yale University Press, 2009), 81–82.
49. Ibid., 82.
50. Jean-Paul Sartre, *Existentialism and Human Emotions* (New York: Wisdom Library, 1957), 23.
51. Jean-Paul Sartre, "Existentialism Is a Humanism," in *Existentialism from Dostoevsky to Sartre*, ed. Walter Kaufmann (New York: Meridian Books, 1989), 353–66.
52. Ibid., 349.
53. Sartre, *Talking with Sartre*, ed. and trans. Gerassi, 16–17.
54. Jean-Paul Sartre, "Existentialism Is a Humanism," in *Existentialism from Dostoevsky to Sartre*, ed. Walter Kaufmann (New York: Meridian Books, 1989), 360.
55. Sartre, *Life/Situations*, trans. Auster and Davis, 25.
56. Ibid., 45–46.
57. Sartre, *Talking with Sartre*, ed. and trans. Gerassi, 131.
58. Sartre, "Existentialism Is a Humanism," 353.
59. Sartre, *Existentialism and Human Emotions*, 48; for more on Sartre's ethics, see Juliette Simont, "Sartrean Ethics," in *The Cambridge*

Companion to Sartre, ed. Christina Howells (Cambridge: Cambridge University Press, 1992), 178–210.

60. Sartre, *Existentialism and Human Emotions*, 31.
61. Peter Singer, *How Are We to Live?: Ethics in an Age of Self-Interest* (Oxford: Oxford University Press, 1997), 222.
62. Sartre, *Talking with Sartre*, ed. and trans. Gerassi, 97.
63. Quoted in Juliette Simont, "Sartrean Ethics," in *The Cambridge Companion to Sartre*, ed. Christina Howells (Cambridge: Cambridge University Press, 1992), 195.
64. Sartre, *Talking with Sartre*, ed. and trans. Gerassi, 121.
65. Tony Judt, *Past Imperfect: French Intellectuals, 1944–1956* (Berkeley: University of California Press, 1992), 81.
66. Sartre, *Talking with Sartre*, ed. and trans. Gerassi, 99.
67. Sartre, *Life/Situations*, trans. Auster and Davis, 27.
68. Sartre, *Talking with Sartre*, ed. and trans. Gerassi, 14–15.
69. Ibid., 17–18.
70. James Miller, *The Passion of Michel Foucault* (New York: Simon and Schuster, 1993), 28.
71. Ibid., 78–79.
72. Michel Foucault, "Dream, Imagination, and Existence," *Review of Existential Psychology and Psychiatry* 19, 1 (1986): 69.
73. Quoted in Miller, *The Passion of Michel Foucault*, 351.
74. Ibid., 306, 349–50.
75. Quoted in Ibid., 34.
76. Ibid., 20.
77. Michel Foucault, *Politics, Philosophy, Culture: Interviews and Other Writings, 1977–1984*, trans. Alan Sheridan et al., ed. Lawrence D. Dritzman (New York: Routledge, 1988), 12.
78. Ibid., 176.
79. Michel Foucault, *The Birth of Biopolitics: Lectures at the Collège de France, 1978–79*, ed. Michel Senellart, trans. Graham Burchell (New York: Palgrave Macmillan, 2008), 3.
80. Michel Foucault, *Foucault Live (Interviews, 1961–1984)*, ed. Sylvère Lotringer, trans. Lysa Hochroth and John Johnston (New York: Semotext[e]), 1996), 301.
81. Miller, *The Passion of Michel Foucault*, 203.

82.	Noam Chomsky and Michel Foucault, *The Chomsky-Foucault Debate: On Human Nature* (New York: The New Press, 2006), 39–40.
83.	Ibid., 47–52.
84.	Michel Foucault, *Power/Knowledge: Selected Interviews and Other Writings, 1972–1977*, ed. Colin Gordon (New York: Pantheon Books, 1980), 1–2, 8–9, 22, 27.
85.	Michel Foucault, "Confronting Governments: Human Rights," in Noam Chomsky and Michel Foucault, *The Chomsky-Foucault Debate: On Human Nature* (New York: The New Press, 2006), 211–12.
86.	Didier Eribon, *Michel Foucault*, trans. Betsy Wing (Cambridge, MA: Harvard University Press, 1991), 298–99.
87.	James W. Bernauer and Michael Mahon, "The Ethics of Michel Foucault," in *The Cambridge Companion to Foucault*, ed. Gary Gutting (Cambridge: Cambridge University Press, 1994), 142, 155.
88.	Gary Gutting, "Introduction: Michel Foucault: A User's Manual," in *The Cambridge Companion to Foucault*, ed. Gary Gutting (Cambridge: Cambridge University Press, 1994), 21.
89.	James Miller, *The Passion of Michel Foucault* (New York: Simon and Schuster, 1993), 39, 63; Didier Eribon, *Michel Foucault*, trans. Betsy Wing (Cambridge, MA: Harvard University Press, 1991), 4–5.
90.	Miller, *The Passion of Michel Foucault*, 245.
91.	Michel Foucault, *Politics, Philosophy, Culture: Interviews and Other Writings, 1977–1984*, trans. Alan Sheridan et al, ed. Lawrence D. Dritzman (New York: Routledge, 1988), 12–13.
92.	Miller, *The Passion of Michel Foucault*, 173.
93.	Quoted in Didier Eribon, *Michel Foucault*, trans. Betsy Wing (Cambridge, MA: Harvard University Press, 1991), 157.
94.	Michel Foucault, *The Order of Things: An Archaeology of the Human Sciences* (London: Routledge, 2002), 419–22.
95.	Miller, *The Passion of Michel Foucault*, 8–9.
96.	Ibid., 384.

SEVEN: A MATTER OF LIFE AND DEATH

1.   "Belgian Helped to Die after Three Sex Change Operations," BBC News, October 2, 2013, http://www.bbc.co.uk/news/world-europe-24373107, accessed November 14, 2013.
2.   Matt. 24:12.
3.   Michael Cook, "Another Speed Bump for Belgian Euthanasia," *BioEdge: Bioethics News from around the World* (February 8, 2013), http://www.bioedge.org/index.php/bioethics/bioethics_article/10388, accessed June 2, 2014.
4.   Michael Cook, "Belgian Intensive Care Doctors Back Involuntary Euthanasia," *BioEdge: Bioethics News from around the World* (February 8, 2013), *www.bioedge.org/index.php/bioethics/bioethics_article/10922; accessed June 2, 2014.*
5.   Alberto Giubilini and Francesca Minerva, "After-Birth Abortion: Why Should the Baby Live?," *Journal of Medical Ethics* (2012), http://jme.bmj.com/content/early/2012/03/01/medethics-2011-100411.full, accessed May 3, 2014.
6.   I Cor. 3:16–17; 6:19–20.
7.   For an overview of the Christian view on the sanctity (or sacredness) of human life, see David P. Gushee, *The Sacredness of Human Life: Why an Ancient Biblical Vision Is Key to the World's Future* (Grand Rapids, MI: William B. Eerdmanns, 2013); for a history of the Christian attitude toward assisted suicide, see Edward J. Larson and Darrel W. Amundsen, *A Different Death: Euthanasia and the Christian Tradition* (Downers Grove, IL: Intervarsity Press, 1998).
8.   Michael MacDonald and Terence R. Murphy, *Sleepless Souls: Suicide in Early Modern England* (Oxford: Clarendon Press, 1990), 2–5.
9.   Lester G. Crocker, "The Discussion of Suicide in the Eighteenth Century," *Journal of the History of Ideas* 13, 1 (1952): 70.
10.   Alberto Radicati di Passerano, *A Philosophical Dissertation upon Death* (London: W. Mears, 1732), 5–6, 10–14, 56–65, 86–93; Jonathan I. Israel, *Radical Enlightenment: Philosophy and the Making of Modernity 1650–1750* (Oxford: Oxford University Press, 2001), 68–69.
11.   Michael MacDonald and Terence R. Murphy, *Sleepless Souls: Suicide in Early Modern England* (Oxford: Clarendon Press, 1990), 156–57.

12. Ibid., 6, 149, 170; S. E. Sprott, *The English Debate on Suicide from Donne to Hume* (La Salle, IL: Open Court, 1961), 71–78, 85, 96–97; Lester G. Crocker, *An Age of Crisis: Man and World in Eighteenth Century French Thought* (Baltimore: Johns Hopkins Press, 1959), 13–14, 37; Lester G. Crocker, "The Discussion of Suicide in the Eighteenth Century," *Journal of the History of Ideas* 13, 1 (1952): 47–72.

13. Jennifer Michael Hecht, *Stay: A History of Suicide and the Philosophies against It* (New Haven: Yale University Press, 2013), 112–13; see also Georges Minois, *History of Suicide: Voluntary Death in Western Culture*, trans. Lydia G. Cochrane (Baltimore: Johns Hopkins University Press, 1999), 223–24.

14. David Hume, *Enquiry Concerning Human Understanding*, in *Enquiries Concerning Human Understanding and Concerning the Principles of Morals*, ed. L. A. Selby-Bigge, 2nd ed. (Oxford: At the Clarendon Press, 1902), 165.

15. S. E. Sprott, *The English Debate on Suicide from Donne to Hume* (La Salle, IL: Open Court, 1961), 128.

16. Georges Minois, *History of Suicide: Voluntary Death in Western Culture*, trans. Lydia G. Cochrane (Baltimore: Johns Hopkins University Press, 1999), 253.

17. David Hume, "On Suicide," in *Life, Death and Meaning: Key Philosophical Readings on the Big Questions*, ed. David Benatar (Lanham, MD: Rowman and Littlefield Publishers, 2004), 291–92.

18. Ibid., 292.

19. Lester G. Crocker, "The Discussion of Suicide in the Eighteenth Century," *Journal of the History of Ideas* 13, 1 (1952): 63, also makes this point.

20. David Hume, "On Suicide," in *Life, Death and Meaning: Key Philosophical Readings on the Big Questions*, ed. David Benatar (Lanham, MD: Rowman and Littlefield Publishers, 2004), 292, 294–95.

21. "Humanist Manifesto II," (1973), http://www.americanhumanist. org/Humanism/Humanist_Manifesto_II, accessed December 2013.

22. Jennifer Michael Hecht, *Stay: A History of Suicide and the Philosophies against It* (New Haven: Yale University Press, 2013), 5.

23. Ibid., 226.

24. David Hume, "On Suicide," in *Life, Death and Meaning: Key Philosophical Readings on the Big Questions*, ed. David Benatar (Lanham, MD: Rowman and Littlefield Publishers, 2004), 295.

25. Jennifer Michael Hecht, *Stay: A History of Suicide and the Philosophies against It* (New Haven: Yale University Press, 2013), 5.

26. Ibid., 5–6.

27. Ernst Haeckel, *Natürliche Schöpfungsgeschichte*, 2nd ed. (Berlin: Georg Reimer, 1870), 152–55; quote at 155.

28. Ernst Haeckel, *Die Lebenswunder: Gemeinverständliche Studien über Biologische Philosophie* (Stuttgart: Alfred Kröner Verlag,, 1904), 135–36; see also Haeckel, *Ewigkeit. Weltkriegsgedanken über Leben und Tod, Religion und Entwicklungslehre* (Berlin: George Reimer, 1917), 33–34. For further discussion of Haeckel's position on euthanasia, see Richard Weikart, *From Darwin to Hitler: Evolutionary Ethics, Eugenics, and Racism in Germany* (New York: Palgrave Macmillan, 2004), 146–48.

29. N. D. A. Kemp, '*Merciful Release*': *The History of the British Euthanasia Movement* (Manchester: Manchester University Press, 2002), 11–21, quotes at 20.

30. Ibid., 35–36.

31. F. H. Bradley, "Some Remarks on Punishment," *International Journal of Ethics* 4 (1894): 269–84; quotes at 276, 278.

32. Ian Dowbiggin, *A Merciful End: The Euthanasia Movement in Modern America* (Oxford, 2003), 1, 10–12, 20–21.

33. Ibid., 2, 8.

34. N. D. A. Kemp, '*Merciful Release*': *The History of the British Euthanasia Movement* (Manchester: Manchester University Press, 2002), 3, quote at 19.

35. Hans-Walter Schmuhl, *Rassenhygiene, Nationalsozialismus, Euthanasie: Von der Verhütung zur Vernichtung 'lebensunwerten Lebens' 1890–1945* (Göttingen: Vandenhoek und Ruprecht, 1987), 18–19, quote at 106.

36. Udo Benzenhöfer, *Der gute Tod? Euthanasie und Sterbehilfe in Geschichte und Gegenwart* (Munich: C. H. Beck, 1999), ch. 4; on the connections between Darwinism and euthanasia, see also Weikart, *From Darwin to Hitler*, ch. 8.

37. Martin S. Pernick, *The Black Stork: Eugenics and the Death of "Defective" Babies in American Medicine and Motion Pictures since 1915* (New York: Oxford University Press, 1996), 3–6, 85–87.

38. Ibid., 95–98.

39. Ibid., 11, 96.

40. N. D. A. Kemp, '*Merciful Release*': *The History of the British Euthanasia Movement* (Manchester: Manchester University Press, 2002), 88, 109.

41. Ian Dowbiggin, *A Merciful End: The Euthanasia Movement in Modern America* (Oxford, 2003), 74.

42. Karl Binding and Alfred Hoche, *Die Freigabe der Vernichtung lebensunwerten Lebens: Ihr Mass und Ihre Form* (Leipzig: Felix Meiner, 1920). For more on Hoche, see Richard Weikart, *From Darwin to Hitler: Evolutionary Ethics, Eugenics, and Racism in Germany* (New York Palgrave Macmillan, 2004), 155–56.

43. Adolf Hitler, "Appell an die deutsche Kraft" (August 4, 1929), in *Hitler: Reden, Schriften, Anordnungen: Februar 1925 bis Januar 1933*, 5 vols. in 12 parts (Munich: Institut für Zeitgeschichte, 1992–98), 3: 348–49.

44. For more on Hitler's position on euthanasia, see Richard Weikart, *Hitler's Ethic: The Nazi Pursuit of Evolutionary Progress* (New York: Palgrave Macmillan, 2009), 179–87.

45. Ulf Schmidt, *Karl Brandt* (London: Hambledon Continuum, 2007).

46. For more on the Nazi euthanasia program, see Michael Burleigh, *Death and Deliverance: Euthanasia in Germany, 1900–1945* (Cambridge: Cambridge University Press, 1994) and Henry Friedlander, *The Origins of Nazi Genocide: From Euthanasia to the Final Solution* (Chapel Hill: University of North Carolina Press, 1995).

47. Albert R. Jonsen, *The Birth of Bioethics* (New York: Oxford University Press, 1998), 42–45, 264.

48. Joseph Fletcher, *Memoir of an Ex-Radical*, ed. Kenneth Vaux (Louisville: Westminster/John Knox, 1993), 58–60, 74, 76–77, quotes at 82, 84.

49. Joseph Fletcher, *Morals and Medicine* (London: Victor Gollancz Limited, 1955), 9.

50. Ibid., 190–93.

51. Ibid., 172, 191, 205, 218–22.
52. Joseph Fletcher, *Humanhood: Essays in Biomedical Ethics* (Buffalo: Prometheus Books, 1979), 12–16.
53. Ibid., 10–11, 135.
54. For a more robust critique of personhood theory, see Francis J. Beckwith, *Defending Life: A Moral and Legal Case against Abortion Choice* (Cambridge: Cambridge University Press, 2007), ch. 6.
55. Joseph Fletcher, *Humanhood: Essays in Biomedical Ethics* (Buffalo: Prometheus Books, 1979), 143–44.
56. Ibid., 146, 155.
57. Peter Singer, *Practical Ethics* (Cambridge: Cambridge University Press, 1979), 76, 122–23, 125.
58. Ibid., 155.
59. Ibid., 134.
60. Johann Hari, Peter Singer Interview, www.johannhari.com/archive/article.php?id=410, accessed May 18, 2009.
61. Rita Marker, *Deadly Compassion: The Death of Ann Humphry and the Truth about Euthanasia* (New York: William Morrow and Company, 1993), back cover, 17–19.
62. Derek Humphry and Mary Clement, *Freedom to Die: People, Politics, and the Right-to-Die Movement* (New York: St. Martin's Press, 1998), 8.
63. Derek Humphry and Ann Wickett, *The Right to Die: Understanding Euthanasia* (New York: Harper and Row, 1986), 293–94.
64. Ibid., 10.
65. Derek Humphry and Mary Clement, *Freedom to Die: People, Politics, and the Right-to-Die Movement* (New York: St. Martin's Press, 1998), 313.
66. I Timothy 6:10.
67. Derek Humphry and Mary Clement, *Freedom to Die: People, Politics, and the Right-to-Die Movement* (New York: St. Martin's Press, 1998), 313.
68. Neal Nicol and Harry Wylie, *Between the Dying and the Dead: Dr. Jack Kevorkian's Life and the Battle to Legalize Euthanasia* (Madison: Terrace Books, University of Wisconsin Press, 2006), 7, 8, 37, 66–67.
69. Ibid., 21, 147, 187,

70. Udo Benzenhöfer, *Der gute Tod? Euthanasie und Sterbehilfe in Geschichte und Gegenwart* (Munich: C. H. Beck, 1999), 176–82; Robert B. Baker and Laurence B. McCullough, "Medical Ethics through the Life Cycle in Europe and the Americas," in *The Cambridge World History of Medical Ethics*, ed. Robert B. Baker and Laurence B. McCullough (Cambridge: Cambridge University Press, 2009), 159–60.

71. Xavier Symons, "British Woman 'Weary of Modern Life' Euthanized in Switzerland," *BioEdge: Bioethics News from around the World* (April 23, 2014), http://www.bioedge.org/index.php/bioethics/bioethics_article/10929, accessed June 2, 2014.

72. Wesley Smith, "What Happened to Switzerland" (May 2, 2014), http://www.firstthings.com/web-exclusives/2014/05/what-happened-to-switzerland, accessed May 3, 2014.

73. James C. Mohr, *Abortion in America: The Origins and Evolution of National Policy, 1800–1900* (New York: Oxford University Press, 1978).

74. Ernst Haeckel, *Die Lebenswunder: Gemeinverständliche Studien über Biologische Philosophie* (Stuttgart: Alfred Kröner Verlag,, 1904), 375.

75. Helene Stöcker, "Strafrechtreform und Abtreibung," *Die neue Generation.* 4 (1908): 399–410, quote on 401.

76. Lily Braun, *Memoiren einer Sozialistin*, vol. 2: *Kampfjahre* (Munich: Albert Langen, 1911), 635. For more on Braun's ideology, see Alfred Meyer, *The Feminism and Socialism of Lily Braun* (Bloomington: Indiana University Press, 1985).

77. Moira Davison Reynolds, *Women Advocates of Reproductive Rights: Eleven Who Led the Struggle in the United States and Great Britain* (Jefferson, NC: McFarland and Company, 1994), 37.

78. Colin Francome, *Abortion Freedom: A Worldwide Movement* (London: George Allen and Unwin, 1984), 62–63.

79. Atina Grossmann, *Reforming Sex: The German Movement for Birth Control and Abortion Reform, 1920–1950* (New York: Oxford University Press, 1995), ch. 4.

80. James F. Keenan points out in "The Concept of Sanctity of Life and Its Use in Contemporary Bioethical Discussion," in *Sanctity of Life*

and Human Dignity, ed. Kurt Bayertz (Dordrecht: Kluwer Academic Publishers, 1996), 2, that Williams is attacking a straw man.

81.   Glanville Williams, *The Sanctity of Life and the Criminal Law* (New York: Alfred Knopf, 1970), ix–x.

82.   Ibid., 17–22, quote on 17.

83.   Ibid., 217, 226, 313.

84.   Judith Jarvis Thomson, "A Defense of Abortion," *Philosophy and Public Affairs* 1,1 (1971): 47–66.

85.   For a more extended critique of Thomson's argument, see Francis J. Beckwith, *Defending Life: A Moral and Legal Case against Abortion Choice* (Cambridge: Cambridge University Press, 2007), ch. 7.

86.   Mallory Millett, "Marxist Feminism's Ruined Lives," *Front Page*, www.frontpagemag.com/2014/mallorymillett/marxist-feminisms-ruined-lives, accessed September 8, 2014.

87.   *Roe v. Wade*, 1973.

88.   Joseph W. Dellapenna, *Dispelling the Myths of Abortion History* (Durham, NC: Carolina Academic Press, 2006), 13–15, and passim.

EIGHT: THE FUTURE OF HUMANITY

1.   Mary Shelley, *Frankenstein, or The Modern Prometheus* (New York: Alfred A. Knopf, 1992), 230.

2.   Ibid., 46, 50, 71,171.

3.   Ibid., 96, 98.

4.   Susan Tyler Hitchcock, *Frankenstein: A Cultural History* (New York: W. W. Norton, 2007), 7.

5.   Don Locke, *A Fantasy of Reason: The Life and Thought of William Godwin* (London: Routledge and Kegan Paul, 1980), 1–8.

6.   William Godwin, *Enquiry Concerning Political Justice*, ed. and abridged by K. Codell Carter (Oxford: At the Clarendon Press, 1971), 184–85.

7.   Ibid., 71, 300–2.

8.   Ibid., 78.

9.   Ibid., 70–71.

10.   William Godwin, "Thought Occasioned by the Perusal of Dr. Parr's Spital Sermon, Preached at Christ Church, April 15, 1800," in William

Godwin, *Enquiry Concerning Political Justice*, ed. and abridged by K. Codell Carter (Oxford: At the Clarendon Press, 1971), 328–30.

11. Ibid., 329–30.

12. William Godwin, *Enquiry Concerning Political Justice*, ed. and abridged by K. Codell Carter (Oxford: At the Clarendon Press, 1971), 74, 89.

13. H. G. Wells, *The Definitive Time Machine: A Critical Edition*, ed. Harry M. Geduld (Bloomington: Indiana University Press, 1987).

14. H. G. Wells, *Experiment in Autobiography: Discoveries and Conclusions of a Very Ordinary Brain (since 1866)* (New York: Macmillan, 1934), 562.

15. H. G. Wells, *A Modern Utopia*, intro. by Mark R. Hillegas (Lincoln: University of Nebraska Press, 1967), 135–44.

16. H. G. Wells, *Men like Gods, and The Dream*, in *The Works of H. G. Wells*, vol. 28 (New York: Charles Scribner's Sons, 1927), 68–69, 260.

17. H. G. Wells, "Introduction" to *Pivot of Civilization* by Margaret Sanger, at Project Gutenberg, http://www.gutenberg.org/files/1689/1689-h/1689-h.htm, accessed May 20, 2014.

18. H. G. Wells, *Men like Gods, and The Dream*, in *The Works of H. G. Wells*, vol. 28 (New York: Charles Scribner's Sons, 1927), 80, 228, 288–89.

19. Ibid., 107.

20. Mark R. Hillegas, *The Future as Nightmare: H. G. Wells and the Anti-Utopians* (New York: Oxford University Press, 1967), 3–6.

21. Aldous Huxley, *Brave New World* (London: Chatto and Windus, 1977), 31, 80, 121.

22. Ibid., 75–77.

23. Ibid., 146, 186, 197.

24. Aldous Huxley, *Ends and Means: An Inquiry into the Nature of Ideals and into the Methods Employed for Their Realization* (New York: Harper and Brothers, 1937), 312.

25. Ibid., 316.

26. Ibid., 313–14, 317.

27. Ibid., 309–11.

28. C. S. Lewis, *That Hideous Strength: A Modern Fairy-Tale for Grownups* (New York: Scribner, 1974), 39–40.

29. Ibid., 194, 255–56.

30. C. S. Lewis, *The Abolition of Man* (New York: Macmillan, 1965), 13–15.

31. Ibid., 41, 84.

32. Jennifer Burns, *Goddess of the Market: Ayn Rand and the American Right* (Oxford: Oxford University Press, 2009), 9, 13, 16.

33. Ibid., 24–25.

34. Ayn Rand, *Atlas Shrugged* (New York: Random House, 1957), 1061.

35. Ayn Rand, *The Fountainhead* (New York: Plume, 2005), 15.

36. Ibid., 29.

37. Ibid., 83–84, 103–4, 762–70.

38. Ayn Rand, *The Virtue of Selfishness: A New Concept of Egoism* (New York: New American Library, 1964), 22–23.

39. Rand, *The Fountainhead*, 765.

40. Burns, *Goddess of the Market*, 263, 275.

41. Rand, *The Fountainhead*, 244–45.

42. Ayn Rand, *Anthem* (Caldwell, Idaho: Caxton, 1961), 96.

43. Rand, *The Virtue of Selfishness*, 49–53, quote at 49.

44. Rand, *Atlas Shrugged*, 1,028.

45. Nick Bostrom, "The History of Transhumanism," www.nickbostrom.com, accessed December 2013.

46. Many of the articles and books Savulescu has published have been co-authored with other scholars, especially Ingmar Persson, but for the sake of convenience I will use Savulescu's name to describe the views put forward in his co-authored works.

47. Julian Savulescu, "It's Our Duty to Have Designer Babies," *Reader's Digest*, http://www.readersdigest.co.uk/magazine/readers-digest-main/the-maverick-its-our-duty-to-have-designer-babies, accessed August 22, 2012.

48. Julian Savulescu, "Unfit for Life: Genetically Enhance Humanity or Face Extinction," keynote address at *Festival of Dangerous Ideas*, Sydney, Australia, 2009, www.themonthly.com.au/genetically-enhance-humanity-or-face-extinction-julian-savulescu-2065, accessed September 26, 2012.

49. Ibid.

50. Ingmar Persson and Julian Savulescu, *Unfit for the Future: The Need for Moral Enhancement* (Oxford: Oxford University Press, 2012), 118–19.

51. Julian Savulescu and Anders Sandberg, "Engineering Love," *New Scientist* 214 (May 12, 2012): 28–29.

52. Julian Savulescu and Guy Kahane, "The Moral Obligation to Create Children with the Best Chance of the Best Life," *Bioethics* 23 (2009): 279.

53. Russell Powell, Guy Kahane, and Julian Savulescu, "Evolution, Genetic Engineering, and Human Enhancement," *Philosophy and Technology* 25 (2012): 444.

54. Julian Savulescu and Anders Sandberg, "Engineering Love," *New Scientist* 214 (May 12, 2012): 28–29.

55. Julian Savulescu and Ingmar Persson, "Moral Enhancement, Freedom, and the God Machine," *The Monist* 95, 3 (2012): 399–421.

56. I. Persson and J. Savulescu, "The Perils of Cognitive Enhancement and the Urgent Imperative to Enhance the Moral Character of Humanity," *Journal of Applied Philosophy* 25, 3 (2008): 162–177.

57. Ingmar Persson and Julian Savulescu, *Unfit for the Future: The Need for Moral Enhancement* (Oxford: Oxford University Press, 2012), ch. 8.

58. Ingmar Persson and Julian Savulescu, "Getting Moral Enhancement Right: The Desirability of Moral Bioenhancement," *Bioethics* 27 (2013): 127.

59. Julian Savulescu and Guy Kahane, "The Moral Obligation to Create Children with the Best Chance of the Best Life," *Bioethics* 23 (2009): 276–77.

60. Julian Savulescu, "It's Our Duty to Have Designer Babies," *Reader's Digest*, http://www.readersdigest.co.uk/magazine/readers-digest-main/the-maverick-its-our-duty-to-have-designer-babies, accessed August 22, 2012.

CONCLUSION

1. Anders Sandberg, "Ethics of Brain Emulations," *Journal of Experimental and Theoretical Artificial Intelligence* (2014), http://www.tandfonline.com/doi/full/10.1080/0952813X.2014.895113.

2. Quoted in Derek Humphry and Ann Wickett, *The Right to Die*: *Understanding Euthanasia* (New York: Harper and Row, 1986), 165.
3. Sue Blackmore, "Survival of the Selfish," http://www.theguardian. com/commentisfree/2006/mar/28/billionsaregoingtodiebut, accessed June 2, 2014; for more examples of this kind of environmental antihumanism, see Wesley Smith, *War on Humans* (Seattle: Discovery Institute Press, 2014); and Robert Zubrin, *Merchants of Despair*: *Radical Environmentalists, Criminal Pseudo-Scientists, and the Fatal Cult of Antihumanism* (New York: New Atlantis Books, 2012).
4. Blackmore denied any purpose in the universe in an interview with "Third Way," http://www.thirdwaymagazine.co.uk/editions/ november-10/high-profile/do-we-copy.aspx; accessed June 4, 2014.
5. Jean Baudrillard, *The Spirit of Terrorism and Requiem for the Twin Towers*, trans. Chris Turner (London: Verso, 2002), 5, 12, 41, and passim.
6. Kurt Bayertz, "Introduction: Sanctity of Life and Human Dignity," in *Sanctity of Life and Human Dignity*, ed. Kurt Bayertz (Dordrecht: Kluwer Academic Publishers, 1996), xi.
7. II Peter 2:1–2.
8. For an excellent statement of the case for Christianity, see Douglas Groothuis, *Christian Apologetics*: *A Comprehensive Case for Biblical Faith* (Downers Grove, IL: IVP Academic, 2011), or William Lane Craig, *Reasonable Faith*: *Christian Truth and Apologetics*, 3rd ed. (Wheaton, IL: Crossway Books, 2008). For a discussion of the reliability of the New Testament, see F. F. Bruce, *The New Testament Documents*: *Are They Reliable?*, 6th ed. (Grand Rapids, MI: William B. Eerdmans, 1981); or Craig Blomberg, *Can We Still Believe the Bible?* (Grand Rapids, MI: Brazos Press, 2014). There are many other excellent works in Christian apologetics, far too many to enumerate here.
9. John 10:10.

Index

A

Abolition of Man, The (Lewis), 150, 264–65

abortion, xiii, 5, 10, 14–15, 58, 66, 115, 119, 121, 148, 157, 169, 216, 221, 235–37, 242–51, 253, 279, 282
  "after-birth abortion," 216, 225, 281
  selective abortions, 66, 279

Adelaide Zoo, 51–52

Adkins, Janet, 240

adultery, 97, 118, 121–22, 169, 194

Africans, 52, 100, 115

agnosticism, 24, 97, 157, 239

AIDS, 205–6

altruism, 30–33, 86–87, 94, 97, 111, 115, 267, 269, 272, 276, 278–79, 285

American Civil Rights Movement, 15, 105, 153

American Eugenics Society, 102–3

American Revolution, 17

Americans with Disabilities Act, 14, 66

Animal Farm (Orwell), 53

Animal Liberation Brigade, 6

Animal Liberation Front, 6

animal rights, 6–7, 58, 60

Anthem (Rand), 269–70